The European Parliament

A

The European Parliament

Structure, Procedure & Practice

Sir Barnett Cocks

London
Her Majesty's Stationery Office
1973

SBN 11 700190 2*

PREFACE

This is a work of reference designed to help Members of the United Kingdom Parliament to acquaint themselves with the structure, rules and practice of the European Parliament. The White Paper published by the Government in July 1971 described the role of the European Parliament as being largely advisory. Yet experience of other international assemblies, such as that of the Council of Europe, suggests that an institution which lays emphasis on the development of its own procedure can by that means increase its power and authority to a great and generally unforeseen extent.

What has been set down for the first time in this book shows that already the framework for a large expansion in the authority of the European Parliament has been quietly prepared over the years. The adherence in 1973 of the British Members – whether they are individually for or against the European concept – will contribute a degree of maturity to the European Parliament which will be eagerly welcomed by its present Members. When I was invited in the spring of this year to prepare this book I approached my friend and colleague, the Secretary-General of the European Parliament, M. Hans Nord. He generously gave me every facility to meet and confer with the most senior and experienced members of the Parliament's Secretariat. I would like to acknowledge how much I owe to them all in accuracy and informed guidance. In particular I must thank M. Georges Van den Eede and M. Th. Ruest, two officers of the Parliament who gave continuous assistance to myself and my colleagues. My understanding of the Commission has also been assisted by the help and wisdom of M. J.-J. Schwed, one of its officers. I am indebted to the Librarian of the House of Commons, Mr. D. C. L. Holland, to Mr. S. Z. Young, and to Mr Robert Rogers for their ready co-operation. Finally I must thank the Controller of Her Majesty's Stationery Office, Mr. C. H. Baylis, CB, for the speedy and efficient way his staff have produced the book.

Because I have had only a short time in which to devise and construct the work for publication before our Members take their places in the European Parliament in January 1973, the bulk of the writing has been done by two colleagues in my Department at the House of Commons, Mr. Douglas Millar and Mr. William Proctor. In recognition of their untiring help, which was provided in addition to their routine work in our Overseas Office, I am appointing them to edit jointly the future and improved editions which I am modestly confident will be required.

BARNETT COCKS
October 1972

CONTENTS

Part I

Structure of the
European Parliament

Chapter I

Origin and formation of the European Parliament

1 Introduction

Early in May each year the European flag of twelve gold stars on an azure field may be seen flying over palaces and public buildings from Sweden and Iceland in the north to Turkey and Malta in the south. Those countries send representatives to a European assembly which sits in the House of Europe at Strasbourg but none are members of the European Parliament, although that body also holds sittings in the same debating chamber. One purpose of this book is to distinguish between the European Parliament and the several other European assemblies which are outside the Community, and to describe the European Parliament's particular responsibilities and its relation with the other institutions which comprise the European Communities.

The earliest European parliamentary assembly in the modern era may be traced to the unofficial international congress known as 'The Congress of Europe' which met at The Hague in May 1948 under the presidency of Winston Churchill who was at that time Leader of the Opposition in the British House of Commons. The purpose of this assembly was to further the cause of European unity. It led to the setting up of the official Council of Europe with its own Consultative Assembly which first met in August 1949.

THE SCHUMAN PLAN, 1950

In a speech made on 9 May 1950, M. Robert Schuman, the then French Foreign Minister, outlined on behalf of the French Government a scheme for pooling Europe's coal and steel resources, sometimes known as the Schuman Plan. At the next Session of the Council of Europe's Consultative Assembly M. Robert Schuman was invited to address the Assembly on his proposals. Subsequently the Consultative Assembly recommended to the Committee of Ministers 'that a renewed effort should be made by all the Governments concerned to find a basis for agreement which will enable all the principal coal and steel producing countries of Europe to participate fully in the scheme'. Only six Governments were prepared to adhere to this scheme, which within a few months was embodied in a treaty setting up the first of three European communities.

EUROPEAN COAL AND STEEL COMMUNITY (ECSC), 1951

The Treaty establishing the European Coal and Steel Community – the earliest of the six-power Communities – was signed in Paris on 1 April 1951. The six member states who agreed to form the Community were Belgium, France, the Federal Republic of Germany, Italy, Luxembourg and the Netherlands. By the Treaty, which was finally ratified in July 1952, these six member states agreed to form a common pool of their coal and steel resources and a common market for those products. In 1954 the High Authority concluded an Agreement of Association with the United Kingdom on the basis of which further development of commercial relations took place.

The purposes of the European Coal and Steel Community were achieved by the work of its four institutions – the Council of Ministers, the High Authority, the Court of Justice and the Common Assembly.

EUROPEAN ECONOMIC COMMUNITY (EEC) AND THE
TREATY OF ROME, 1957

The Treaty establishing the European Economic Community[1] was signed in Rome on 25 March 1957 on behalf of the six states who were already members of the European Coal and Steel Community, namely, Belgium, France, the Federal Republic of Germany, Italy, Luxembourg and the Netherlands. By the time that the treaty entered into force on 1 January 1958 a considerable amount of preparatory work had been done by an interim committee set up by the governments of member states when they signed the Treaty.

One of the aims of the Community, as set out in the preamble to the Treaty, was to lay the foundations of an ever closer union in Europe by eliminating the barriers between the countries to economic and social progress. It was recognised that concerted action was necessary to guarantee the removal of obstacles to the introduction of a common market and progressively harmonious economic policies between member states.

The Treaty established institutions similar to those of the European Coal and Steel Community to fulfil these aims. The institutional framework comprises an Assembly, a Council of Ministers, a Commission (the executive authority) and a Court of Justice.

EUROPEAN ATOMIC ENERGY COMMUNITY (EURATOM), 1957

The Treaty for the European Atomic Energy Community (Euratom) was signed in Rome on 25 March 1957 on behalf of the same six states who had just signed the companion treaty for the European Economic Community, namely Belgium, France, the Federal Republic of Germany, Italy, Luxembourg and the Netherlands. The Treaty also entered into force on 1 January 1958, creating a community structured on similar lines to the EEC, the Assembly and the Court of Justice being common to both communities.

[1]See Appendix A, E E C Treaty, as amended.

The object of the Community is to raise the standard of living in member states and develop commercial exchanges with other countries by creating conditions necessary for the rapid establishment and growth of nuclear industries. This object is achieved by investment and the encouragement of joint enterprises; by the supply of ores and nuclear fuels; by the ownership of special fissionable materials; by the creation of a common market for such specialised materials and equipment; by research, international co-operation and the exchange of information; by establishing safety standards for the protection of public health; and by a security control to ensure that specialised materials are used for the proper purpose. Euratom has no functions relating to the use of atomic energy for military purposes; it is exclusively concerned with the development of atomic energy for peaceful purposes.

2 Enlargement of the Communities

Several attempts have been made, since the foundation of the communities and before the successful negotiations which began in June 1970, to extend the membership of the Communities both by adding to the full members and by establishing association agreements with other states. Greece signed an agreement of Association on 9 July 1961 and Turkey a similar agreement on 12 September 1963.

In August 1961 three member states of the Council of Europe, namely Denmark, Ireland, the United Kingdom, and a little later Norway, applied for full membership of the European Communities. In November 1961 three other countries – Austria, Switzerland and Sweden – applied for associate membership; and Spain made a similar application in February 1962. Prolonged negotiations to expand the membership of the Communities were abandoned early in 1963; and the prospects of association of other states except Greece and Turkey were also ended for some years. Subsequently subjects of common economic interest were discussed by the Governments of the six member states of the European Communities and of the United Kingdom at periodic meetings of the Council of Western European Union, to which all seven countries belong.

In May 1967 a second application for membership of the Communities was made by the United Kingdom, Denmark and Ireland and in July 1967 by Norway. In the same month Sweden requested the President of the Council of the Communities to open negotiations to allow Sweden to take part, in a manner compatible with that country's policy of neutrality, in the enlargement of the Community. In September 1967 the requests for accession were examined by the Communities' Commission which expressed the opinion that negotiations should be opened with the states concerned in order to consider whether it was possible to satisfy the conditions necessary to ensure the cohesion and vitality indispensable to an enlarged Community.

B

In December 1967 the Council of Ministers failed to agree on whether to endorse the opinion submitted to them by the Commission. The requests for accession remained on the Council's agenda until 1971, when the applications of the United Kingdom, Denmark, Ireland and Norway were finally approved by the Ministers. The initiative in opening negotiations had been taken at The Hague Conference of Heads of State of Member Governments in December 1969. Following from this, negotiations had begun in June 1970 and were completed at the beginning of 1972. The four applicants signed the Treaty of Accession accepting the conditions of the Treaty of Rome on 22 January 1972. Provision for full membership, after ratification of the Treaty by their national parliaments, was arranged to date from 1 January 1973.[4] Instruments of ratification were deposited during 1972 by the governments of Denmark, Ireland and the United Kingdom. Following the unfavourable outcome of an advisory referendum held in September 1972, the Treaty of Accession was not ratified by the Norwegian Storting and in consequence Norway did not join the Communities on 1 January 1973.

3 The European Parliamentary Assembly, 1958

The European Parliamentary Assembly was one of the three institutions[1] common to the three Communities. It first met in Strasbourg in the House of Europe on 19 March 1958, a few weeks after the final sittings (24 to 28 February) of the Common Assembly of ECSC, which it superseded.[2] The European Parliamentary Assembly adopted its own title at this first sitting, marking the fact that it now enjoyed more effective powers. Those powers emphasise the new concept in international affairs that the executive organs of the Communities are no longer the sole or paramount authority on international questions. The Assembly's powers are established by Articles 137 to 144 of the Treaty of Rome, 1957, establishing the European Economic Community. The Assembly's purpose, as described in Article 137, is to 'exercise the advisory and supervisory powers' conferred on it by the Treaty. The Assembly resolved on 30 March 1962 to change its name to the European Parliament.

The intended role of the Assembly was further defined in the First Annual Report of the European Economic Community in 1958:

'The Assembly, composed of representatives of the various peoples, exercised democratic control over the activities of the Community. It has the right to pass a vote of censure on the Commission. This control, however,

---

[1]The others were the Court of Justice and the Economic and Social Committee. See the Convention on certain institutions common to the European Communities of 25 March 1957.
[2]In accordance with Articles 1 and 2 of the Convention relating to certain institutions common to the European Communities, annexed to the Treaty of Rome, 1957, setting up the European Economic Community.

is not negative in character, but rather a spur, an inspiration and a help for the activities of the institutions and it brings the public opinion of the Community to the support of all steps or endeavours made in the service of Europe.'

The Assembly is directed by Article 138 (3) of the EEC Treaty to draw up proposals for direct universal suffrage with a uniform system of election for all member states. During its session in May 1960, it adopted a draft Convention for this purpose. Under this Convention the new directly elected Assembly would comprise 426 representatives – 108 each for France, the Federal Republic of Germany and Italy, 42 each for Belgium and the Netherlands, and 18 for Luxembourg. During a transitional period which would be defined by the first elected Assembly, one-third of the membership would continue to be designated by national Parliaments. The draft Convention must obtain the unanimous approval of the six Foreign Ministers and also be ratified by the national Parliaments before it can become effective. Although the European Parliament has continually reminded the Ministers of this issue, they have not yet pronounced on it. At the end of 1969, the Parliament threatened to take the Council of Ministers to the European Court over its failure to act on this matter. At the same time general interest in the proposals was aroused and the proposals are again being studied.

The Parliament was directed to hold an annual session beginning on the third Tuesday in October or, at the request of a majority of its members, or of the Councils or Commissions, it may hold extraordinary sessions. The date of the opening of the annual session was almost immediately changed by the Parliament to the month of March. In practice up to eleven part-sessions a year are now held.

The European Parliament appoints its own President and officers and adopts its own rules of procedure. Members of the Commission may attend its meetings to answer questions or be heard at their own request on behalf of the Commission. Members of the Council are heard by the Parliament under conditions laid down in the Council's rules of procedure. The Parliament takes decisions by an absolute majority of the votes cast.

The Parliament is directed to discuss in public the annual general report submitted to it by the Commission; and if a motion of censure on the Commission is tabled, a vote is taken not less than three days later. If the motion of censure is supported by a two-thirds majority of the votes cast and a majority of members of the Parliament, the members of the Commission must collectively resign their office. The control over the executive which the Parliament is given is considerable but not complete, since there is no absolute sanction over the Ministers who form the Council; yet the Treaties give the Parliament enough power to render the work of the Commission very difficult without its co-operation.

Chapter II

The institutions of the Communities

Since 1967 the principal institutions in addition to the Parliament have been common to all three Communities. There is the Council of Ministers which is the only Community institution in which member states are directly represented; the Commission, which is charged with ensuring that the Treaties are carried out, and is responsible ultimately to the Parliament; and the Court of Justice which is empowered to settle disputes over the interpretation of the Treaties. There is also another body established by Article 193 of the EEC Treaty, the Economic and Social Committee. Although it is purely advisory, it has a much wider role than any of the other Committees which have subsequently been appointed to advise the Commission on aspects of European policies.

1 Unification of the Communities

The three European Communities are legally separate and are still governed by their different founding Treaties. But their unity is demonstrated in many ways, above all by their common institutions. Since January 1958 when the European Economic Community and Euratom came into being, the European Parliament (which superseded the Common Assembly of ECSC) and the European Court of Justice have been common institutions. On 8 April 1965 a further step towards unification was taken when the six member states signed a Treaty providing for the setting up of a single Council of Ministers to replace the three existing Councils of Ministers and for a single Commission to replace the Commissions of EEC and Euratom and the High Authority of ECSC. By October 1966, the Treaty, usually known as the Merger Treaty, was ratified by the six member states, but it did not come into force until 1 July 1967 when the six Governments finally reached agreement on the composition of the new Commission. On 6 July 1967 the Commission under its first President, Mr. Jean Rey (Belgium), took up its duties. On the same date the terms of office of the members of the Commissions of EEC and Euratom and of the High Authority of ECSC came to an end. It is intended that this development should be completed by a fusion of the Treaties themselves to form a single Community. But at present the common institutions deal with the affairs of each Community in accordance with the provisions of the appropriate treaty.

The setting up of a single Council of Ministers was of symbolic rather than practical importance because the same Ministers had always been able to sit in the three Councils, and under the Merger Treaty each member state was still able to send to the Council the most appropriate Minister to deal with the matters to be discussed. The merger of the three Commissions posed graver problems which took time to solve. One was the location of the seat of the new Commission. The Commissions of EEC and Euratom had been located in Brussels, and the High Authority of ECSC in Luxembourg. It was finally decided that certain departments of the former High Authority should move to Brussels, thus allowing the merger of the three executives, but that the Court of Justice and Secretariat of the Parliament, already in Luxembourg, were to be joined there by the European Investment Bank, together with departments dealing with such subjects as statistics and publications. It was also agreed that the Council of Ministers should meet in Luxembourg in three months of each year. Another problem was the size of the new Commission. The Commission of EEC and the High Authority of ECSC each had nine members and the Commission of Euratom five. In the event the Merger Treaty provided for a single executive of nine members; however for a transitional period of three years, the executive consisted of fourteen members (three each for France, the Federal Republic of Germany and Italy, two each for Belgium and the Netherlands, and one for Luxembourg). The membership of the Commission of the enlarged Communities is now thirteen (two each for France, the Federal Republic of Germany, Italy and the United Kingdom, and one each for Belgium, Denmark, Ireland, Luxembourg, and the Netherlands).[1]

2 The Council of Ministers of the European Communities

The Council of Ministers is made up of representatives of the governments of member states, each government sending one of its Ministers. The Council's membership may thus vary according to the matter under consideration although foreign ministers generally take part in all major Community decisions. The Council, which meets several times in each month, holds its sessions in Brussels except in the months of April, June and October when it meets in Luxembourg in accordance with a decision annexed to the Merger Treaty of 1965 which established a single Council and Commission of the Communities. The chairmanship of the Council passes in rotation among the representatives of each government for six-month periods.

The Council has its own secretariat and permanent staff based in Brussels. It is also assisted in its work by the Committee of Permanent Representatives (or Ambassadors). The Committee prepares and co-ordinates the work of the Council by dividing items of business on the Council's agenda into an 'A' list and a 'B' list. Items on the 'A' list

[1]The Act of Accession of 1972 also provided for one Commissioner from Norway.

require only formal Ministerial approval while matters on the 'B' list await further consideration by the Ministers. At a lower level, technical questions are prepared for the Permanent Representatives by committees of national civil servants, also meeting in Brussels. Such committees are established for each of the main sections of Community activity. The Commission is also represented in all stages of the Council's work. The full Council met on forty-one occasions in both 1969 and 1970 and on fifty-three occasions in 1971.

Since the Council takes the final decision on almost all fundamental Community problems, it is important to establish how such decisions are reached. Decisions of the Council are taken unanimously, by simple majority, or by qualified (or weighted) majority. Since the end of the transitional period of the Community of the Six, a qualified majority is generally required. In a weighted vote under the original terms of Article 14 of the Act of Accession annexed to the Treaty of Accession, the United Kingdom, France, Germany and Italy had ten votes, Belgium and the Netherlands five votes, Denmark, Ireland and Norway three votes and Luxembourg two votes; forty-three of the sixty-one votes represented a qualified majority.[1] Proposals of the Commission can be adopted or rejected by qualified majority but amended only by unanimous votes. Proposals considered by the Council not emanating from the Commission may require in addition to a qualified majority the support of six states.[1] This latter provision is made to protect the interests of the smaller states when proposals have not come from the Commission.

Certain major decisions which are laid down in the EEC Treaty such as the extension of the role of the European Social Fund are subject to unanimous decision; an abstention does not vitiate this requirement. Minor decisions may be taken by simple majority of Ministers present.

These rules must be considered, however, in the context of the Luxembourg agreement of January 1966 which amounted to an agreement to disagree among the member governments on the interpretation of the decision making process within the Council. The Communiqué issued after the agreement noted that where

> 'very important interests of one or more partners are at stake, the members of the Council will endeavour within a reasonable time to reach solutions which can be adopted by all members',

and that the French Delegation considered that 'discussion should continue until unanimous agreement is reached'. It was further noted that there was a divergence of views on what should be done when members failed to reach final agreement.

In the negotiations for enlargement and in Command Paper No. 4715

---

[1]These figures will require adjustment by the Council of Ministers, in accordance with Article 2 of the Treaty of Accession, to take account of the Norwegian decision not to join the European Communities.

paras. 29 and 30, the British Government has accepted the French view. It has become increasingly accepted that the vital interests of a member state shall not be overriden. In practice compromise decisions have always been reached by unanimous agreement without a vote being taken.

During 1971 the Council, in addition to dealing with purely procedural matters and with budgets and financial regulations, adopted 302 regulations, 26 directives and 45 decisions. In 1970 the Council had adopted 249 regulations, 25 directives, 71 decisions, and the important second medium-term programme.

3 The Commission of the European Communities

The Commission is the executive organ of the three European Communities. The executive power of the Commission is in effect shared with the Council of Ministers in that the Commission's functions are to provide the general staff of the Communities and to supervise and organise the working of the Treaties, subject to the general directions of the Council of Ministers. There are thirteen members of the Commission (two each for France, the Federal Republic of Germany, Italy and the United Kingdom, and one each for Belgium, Denmark, Ireland, Luxembourg, and the Netherlands) and they are chosen by member governments 'on the grounds of their general competence and whose independence can be fully relied upon'.[1] Commissioners are forbidden to seek or take instructions from any government or other body and member states undertake not to seek to influence them. Only nationals of the member states may be members of the Commission and not more than two members may be of the same nationality. A member is appointed for four years and his term is renewable. The practice so far has been that members have been chosen from amongst politicians, senior diplomats or civil servants. The President and five Vice-Presidents are chosen from among the Commissioners for two-year renewable terms.

The Commission is required to publish an annual report on the activities of the Communities not less than a month before the Session of the European Parliament in March of each year, which then debates the Commission's report. In recent years it has also become the practice of the Commission to submit to the Parliament a programme of Community activity for the coming year. The Commission as a whole, though not Commissioners individually, may be dismissed from office as a result of a motion of censure passed by the Parliament and supported by a two-thirds majority of votes cast. The principle of parliamentary control is thus upheld.

Each member of the Commission is responsible for one or more of

[1]The Rt. Hon. Sir Christopher Soames and the Rt. Hon. George Thomson were nominated by the British Government as members of the Commission in October 1972.

the main Community activities among which are legal affairs, economic and financial policy, external relations, industrial affairs, research and technology, agriculture, development aid, competition, energy, social affairs, transport and regional policy. The administration is divided into departments known as Directorates-General, each headed by one or more Directors-General. Each Director-General is responsible to the Commission as a whole, but works in close collaboration with the Commissioner in charge of his field of activities. The Director-General and the Commissioner with whom he works have normally been of different nationalities. The preparatory work on any proposal is done by the Directorate-General and then presented to the Commission. In addition to his staff in the Directorates-General, each Commissioner has his own personal staff (or *cabinet*). The principle that staff should be appointed to maintain national balance extends to all senior levels of the Commission. Officials of the Commission may be permanent career officers or may return to their national government service after a certain period.

The Commission meets regularly once a week for a whole day. All major questions, such as proposals for legislation to be submitted to the Council, are dealt with by the Commission as a whole. The rules of procedure of the Commission provide for a quorum of seven. There is collective responsibility for all decisions which, if a vote is necessary, are taken by a simple majority vote. Many matters of an uncontentious nature are expedited by written procedure and do not require a formal decision by the Commission, but such matters are entered in the minutes of proceedings of the Commission which have to be ratified by the Commission at a plenary meeting.

During 1971 the Commission took decisions on 2,591 regulations, 287 decisions, two directives, nineteen opinions, and five recommendations.

4 The process of Community legislation

The various stages through which Community legislation passes depend on the type of legislation involved and the procedure for its adoption. In accordance with Article 189 of the EEC Treaty, the Council and the Commission may make regulations, issue directives, take decisions, make recommendations or deliver opinions. Regulations, directives and decisions of the Council and of the Commission must give reasons and refer to the proposals or opinions on which they are based.

(a) Types of legislation

(i) *Regulations* have general application and are directly applicable in all member states. They are published in the Official Journal of the Communities, Legislation (L) series, and come into force on the date specified in them or on the twentieth day following their publication.

(ii) *Directives*,[1] which are binding as to their result upon the member states to whom they are addressed, allow national authorities to choose the form and method of implementation. This may be effected by legislation in national parliaments or by statutory instrument, as provided in Section 2 (2) and Schedule 2 of the European Communities Act 1972. Time limits are generally set for the implementation of directives. The value-added tax was introduced in the member states of the Communities by directive within a fixed period.

(iii) *Decisions* are binding in their entirety upon those to whom they are directed (i.e. upon governments, firms, etc.). They are enforceable in national courts.

(iv) *Recommendations and opinions* have no binding force but merely state Community views.

(b) *The process of legislation*

The Treaties provide that most acts of the Communities originate, at least in formal terms, in the Commission which has a general duty to ensure that the Treaties are applied. This duty in fact amounts to the right of initiative, and thus in formulating proposals the Commission exerts considerable influence on the terms in which Community issues are considered. Community legislation does not allow a uniform pattern since many different requirements are laid down in the Treaties for the passage of legislation on different aspects of the Communities' work. The sequence of events is, in general terms, as follows:

(i) The Commission formulates proposals for the Council of Ministers after wide consultations with national officials, experts and representatives of interest groups.

(ii) The proposal of the Commission is transmitted to the Council of Ministers. At this stage members of the Council may (or must under German law) refer the proposals to their national parliaments.

(iii) At the time when legislative proposals are sent by the Commission to the Council, the Commission also sends a copy to the Parliament for information. On the basis of this, the committees of the Parliament can begin a preliminary unofficial study of the proposals in preparation for the formal consultation by the Council which follows (see also Chapter XIII on Decisions of the Parliament).

(iv) The Council may, and in some cases must, then consult either or both the European Parliament and the Economic and Social Committee before adopting the legislation. At this point, the legislative proposal is, if referred to the Parliament, published as a draft in the Official Journal, Communications (C) series.

(v) A Committee of the Parliament reports on the matter and the proposal and the report are debated in plenary session. Following the debate, an opinion is adopted often proposing amendments to

[1]Known as Recommendations under Article 14 of the ECSC Treaty 1951.

the legislation. The Report and opinion are published in the Official Journal (C) series while the Official Report of the debates is published *in extenso* in each Community language in a separate annex to the Official Journal.

(vi) The Opinion of the Economic and Social Committee, based on the work of one of its specialised sections, is published in the Official Journal (C) series.[1]

(vii) The consideration given by the Council to legislative proposals varies according to their seriousness and political sensitivity. The Council may consider proposals in three stages – in a committee of national experts convened by the Council Secretariat, in the Committee of Permanent Representatives, and in the Council itself.

(viii) When the Council finally adopts a piece of legislation, it is published in the Official Journal (L) series. The Council is bound by Article 190 of the EEC Treaty and by practice confirmed by M. Harmel on behalf of the Council of Ministers in 1970 to give reasons for its treatment of proposals made in respect of draft legislation by the Parliament.

The process outlined above excludes from account the legislation made directly by the Commission. Such legislation is almost entirely of a technical and routine nature to implement earlier Council regulations. In most serious cases, the Commission carries out more extensive consultations with government representatives through a structure of Management Committees and there is provision in certain instances for the Council to overturn Commission actions within a specified period where the Management Committee's opinion is adverse.

The Commission makes many regulations in the course of each year. Regulations are frequently made to adjust the agricultural levy from week to week or month to month as market prices change and as earlier instruments lapse. Commission instruments made pursuant to the common agricultural policy are considered by the Agricultural Management Committee which is composed of officials of member governments and is presided over by a representative of the Commission.

5 The Court of Justice (E C S C, E E C and Euratom)

The European Court of Justice is a basic element in the constitutional framework of the Communities. It is empowered to judge finally on the legality of Community actions and on the interpretation of the Treaties, and is bound by Article 164 of the EEC Treaty to 'ensure that, in the interpretation and application of the Treaty, the law is observed'. The Court has a similar function in respect of Euratom and also has taken over the duty of the former court of the European Coal and Steel Community. It was thus, with the Parliament, one of the original common institutions of the Communities.

[1]See page 16.

The Court, which sits in Luxembourg, is composed of eleven judges and three advocates-general nominated by the member governments.[1] All are appointed for six-year renewable terms, the terms of one and two advocates-general and five and six judges expiring alternately every three years. The Court elects its own President. It sits in two parts, known as Chambers, except where the Treaties provide for a plenary session of at least seven of the judges.

The position of the advocate-general is without an equivalent in British terms: one of the advocates-general must make an independent and impartial assessment of the issues in each case before judgment is passed. This assessment, which is given in addition to the statements of counsel for the parties, is read in public and afterwards published, but it in no way binds the Court in its decision. Rulings of the Court are binding on all parties, including the governments, and are not subject to appeal.

The Court has several functions. It acts as an international court to hear a case by one member state contending that another has failed to fulfil its obligations under the Treaty; as a constitutional court to ensure that the institutions of the Communities act only in accordance with the provisions of the Treaties; and as a tribunal to decide claims by any individual or body corporate against a decision affecting them or which is of direct and specific concern to them. The Court also acts as an administrative tribunal to decide any case between the Community and its employees. Finally the Court may take preliminary decisions concerning the interpretation of the Treaties, acts of the institutions and the Statutes of any bodies set up by an act of the Council. The wide competence of the Court of Justice reflects its important function of securing the rule of law in the activities of the Communities and checking the legality of the operations of the Council and the Commission.

National Courts are responsible for the application of Community law in the first instance. National Courts may, and courts from which there is no appeal must, seek a ruling from the European Court on general questions of validity or interpretation of Community law before they apply it to a particular case. It is the responsibility of the national court to decide on such action.

There are few limitations on the access to the Court on the part of member governments and the Commission. Individuals and companies, however, may only bring cases to the court in respect of the decisions of the Council or the Commission of the Communities. This right is further qualified by the requirement that the case must relate to a decision affecting the individual or company bringing the action or to a decision which is of direct concern to that individual or company.

In 1963, the European Court described the relationship of the Com-

[1]These figures may require adjustment by the Council of Ministers, in accordance with Article 2 of the Treaty of Accession, to take account of the Norwegian decision not to join the European Communities.

munity to the member states in the following terms: 'the Community constitutes a new legal order in international law, in whose favour the states have limited, albeit in delimited areas, their sovereign rights, and the subjects of which are not only member states, but also their nationals'.

As Community law has grown, so the Court's work has increased. During the period from 1953 to 1967, five hundred and twenty cases came before the Court and three hundred and eighty judgments were delivered. In 1968, it was seized of thirty-three new cases: in 1969 seventy-seven more were brought, in 1970 eighty and in 1971 ninety-six new cases. In that year the Court gave judgment on seventy-eight cases, eleven cases ended when the parties withdrew and eighty-two were still outstanding at 31 December 1971. An analysis of the cases dealt with by the Court each year is appended to the Annual General Report of the Communities.

An example of a judgment of the Court which has influenced the institutional development of the Communities was that of 17 December 1970 (*Einfuhr und Vorratsstelle für Getreide v Köster*, case 25–70). The Commission had, for many years, been granted the power to make regulations to implement general regulations made by the Council. The Management Committee procedure, used mainly in connection with the agricultural policy, had become increasingly more important in this process (see p. 14). In the above judgment, the Court found that the procedure did not derogate from the procedures laid down by the EEC Treaty, since the final provision of Article 155 permitted the Commission to 'exercise the powers conferred upon it by the Council for the implementation of the rules laid down by the latter'. Since the delegation of powers is at the discretion of the Council, it may also require the Commission to exercise those powers in accordance with certain procedures, e.g. after consulting Management Committees. The structural balance of the Communities was therefore not affected. At the same time the Court also accepted the legality of the Council itself adopting instruments to implement basic regulations by procedures other than those laid down in Article 43 of the EEC Treaty.

6 The Economic and Social Committee (E E C and Euratom)

The Economic and Social Committee is a purely consultative body of 144 experts, comprising twenty-four each from France, the Federal Republic of Germany, Italy and the United Kingdom, twelve from Belgium and the Netherlands, nine from Denmark and Ireland and six from Luxembourg. Under Article 194 of the EEC Treaty and Article 166 of the Euratom Treaty there were 101 members. The representation of the founder members has remained constant except that Luxembourg representation has since been increased from five to six members. The members are appointed by the Council for four year renewable terms after consultation with the Commission from a list provided by member states.

The intention of the Treaty is to allow representation to professional employers, trade unions and similar interests, whose advice must be sought by the Council and Commission of the European Communities in certain cases defined in the founding Treaties, as for example the establishment of the common agricultural policy. In general terms one-third of the Members are chosen to represent employers' organisations, one-third the trades unions and one-third to defend the general interest. Nonetheless the members once appointed are bound to act in a personal capacity and cannot accept outside instruction.

The Economic and Social Committee has eight specialised sections for the principal fields covered by the Treaties including one to deal with matters relating to Euratom. No specialised section may be consulted independently of the Committee but the opinion of a section together with that of the Committee and its minutes of proceedings are forwarded to the Council and the Commission when consultations take place. The opinion of the Committee is published in the Official Journal (C) series. The view of the Committee has increasingly been sought by the Council on matters not prescribed in the Treaties.[1]

In 1971 the Committee held eight sessions, gave sixty opinions and took note of four reports. Among the important matters on which opinions were given in 1970 were the reform of the European Social Fund, regional development, energy problems and the financing of the common agricultural policy; and in 1971 the Committee rendered opinions on agricultural reform, the level of compulsory petroleum stocks, on proposed directives for the co-ordination of company law, and on the European Fund for interest subsidies to promote regional development.

[1]For examples of consultations not prescribed by the Treaty see Official Journal No. C146, 11 December 1970 pp. 20 and 26.

Chapter III

The powers of the European Parliament

Under Article 137 of the EEC Treaty, the role and powers of the Parliament were defined as to 'exercise the advisory and supervisory powers which are conferred upon it by this Treaty'. In addition, several Articles of the ECSC Treaty of 1951 and the EEC and Euratom Treaties of 1957 envisage the Parliament undertaking a specific role in relation to the Commission.

1 Parliamentary control over the Commission

The Commission and Parliament have established a close working relationship which has grown out of their common European approach to Community issues. This contrasts with the more national approach adopted by the Council on which member states try to defend their special interests. As a result contacts between the Commission and the Parliament have been initiated from both sides: the Commission has tried to enlist the support of the Parliament in its efforts to increase the pace of European integration.

MOTION OF CENSURE

Despite the common aims shared by the two bodies the Parliament has still an ultimate sanction against the Commission. The Parliament can remove the Commission as a body in accordance with the procedure laid down in Article 144 of the EEC Treaty, Article 24 of the ECSC Treaty and Article 114 of the Euratom Treaty. Any member of the Parliament may table a motion of censure on the activities of the Commission. Such a motion cannot be voted on until at least three days after it has been tabled and then only by open ballot. If the motion is carried by a two-thirds majority of the Members of the Parliament, the members of the Commission must collectively resign their office.

This power, which is embodied in Rule 21 of the Parliament's Rules of Procedure,[1] has not yet been used and seldom threatened. No such motion of censure has in fact ever been tabled. This may be, in part, due to the fact that the Parliament has no say in the appointment of Members of the Commission; moreover there is nothing to prevent the outgoing Commissioners being reappointed. The common approach

[1]See Appendix B, Rules of Procedure of the European Parliament.

of the Commission and Parliament to Community problems has also prevented conflicts from running too deeply. The weapon is further weakened by the inability of the Parliament to remove or censure individual Commissioners. In essence, therefore, the motion of censure is a final sanction, the existence of which could lend authority to any criticism made by the Parliament of the Commission, but which has seemed too drastic to use.

THE ANNUAL GENERAL REPORT

Under the terms of the Treaties,[1] the Commission must publish annually, not later than one month before the opening of the Session of the Parliament, a general report on the activities of the Communities which the Parliament is bound to discuss in open session. It has been claimed that the report constitutes 'an essential condition for the effective control of the executive's activity'.[2] Initially the Parliament considered the Report together with reports from each of its committees; but since 1962, one major Parliamentary report has been prepared, on the basis of working documents by the committees, by a single rapporteur. The report of the general rapporteur assumes less significance than in the early years. In 1972 it was prepared within two months and considered at the short May session.

Since 1970, the President of the Commission has also presented to the Parliament an annual programme of the Communities' future activity which the Parliament had pressed to be presented at the beginning of each year. This new procedure enables the Parliament to comment on the framing of Community policies at an early stage and reinforces the ability of the Parliament to challenge Community policies. A debate on the programme of future activity takes place in the part-session at which it has been presented, usually in February.

QUESTIONS

Members of the Parliament have the right to be informed of the progress of the work of the Commission through the medium of parliamentary questions. Under the terms of Article 140 of the EEC Treaty, amplified in Rules 45 to 47 of the Parliament's Rules of Procedure, the Commission must reply to questions within a specified period. Questions may be for written answer, oral answer without debate or oral answer with debate. Answers are published in the Official Journal. The use of questions other than those for written answer has so far been limited.

COMMITTEES

The reports of committees serve as the basis of most debates in the

[1]Article 156 of the EEC Treaty 1957, Article 17 of the ECSC Treaty 1951 and Article 125 of the Euratom Treaty 1957, as amended by the Merger Treaty of 1965.
[2]See the Derringer Report, Document 74, Session 1962–63.

Parliament. Any member may table a motion for a resolution on a matter falling within the sphere of Community activities, and that motion is referred to the appropriate committee. Similarly when the Council of Ministers asks the Parliament to give an opinion on a matter, it is also referred to the appropriate committee for report. Committees also prepare the reports on legislative proposals when the Parliament is consulted.

A system of twelve committees exists to meet these demands. Each committee generally meets at least once a month, between the part-sessions of the Parliament, and the appropriate Commissioner usually appears before it to give an account of the decisions taken by the Commission, decisions referred to the Council, and the position adopted by the Commission in relation to the Council. It is possible therefore for the committees to be informed and to influence Community thinking, the more so since committee meetings are in camera and therefore confidential matters are frequently discussed.

The Parliament has an important role as the only European check on the activities of the Commission. It fulfils this role, partly through its right to be informed and to comment on Community policy, and partly by the specific right, conferred by the Treaties, to be consulted on certain legislative proposals of the Commission.

2 Parliamentary scrutiny of legislation

In accordance with Article 155 of the EEC Treaty, it is laid down that the Commission

'shall ... have its own power of decision and participate in the shaping of measures taken by the Council and by the Assembly[1] in the manner provided for in the Treaty'.

The Commission is also empowered by Article 149 of the EEC Treaty to withdraw the proposals which it has made to the Council and submit them in revised form (provided that the Council has not yet taken a decision) especially where the Assembly[1] has been consulted on that proposal.

These are the only general references in the Treaties to the role of the Parliament in the legislative process.[2] Almost all important legislative acts are made by the Council on the proposal of the Commission. In many specific cases, laid down in the founding Treaties, before the Council comes to a decision, it must consult the Parliament.

In the ECSC Treaty of 1951, the Common Assembly was only to be consulted on proposals for the amendment of the Treaty. Relations between the High Authority and the Common Assembly therefore developed not from a belief in the right of the Assembly to a place in the

---

[1]The European Parliament adopted its present title on 30 March 1962.
[2]The stages of Community legislation are described in pages 12 to 14.

legislative process but from the single right of the Assembly, under Article 24 of the Treaty, to discuss the annual report of the High Authority and to dismiss the members of the High Authority by means of a motion of censure on the report.[1] In the Rome Treaties, however, the position of the Parliament was altered to provide it with a right of consultation on many of the more important legislative proposals of the Commission. There were eighteen references to parliamentary consultation in the EEC Treaty[2] and eleven in the Euratom Treaty.[3] In practice the Parliament has been consulted in more cases than those laid down in the Treaties.

When the Parliament receives notice of a proposed piece of legislation and the draft of the legislation is published in the Official Journal (Communications) series, the draft is referred by the President of the Parliament to the appropriate committee. The committee presents to the Parliament a report on the draft legislation containing a draft opinion on which a vote can be taken. The opinion of the Parliament is then sent to the Presidents of the Council and Commission.

The influence which the opinion of the Parliament has on the Council's deliberations on an item of legislation varies from case to case. At the very least Article 190 of the EEC Treaty provides that the regulations, directives and decisions of the Council and of the Commission shall be fully reasoned and shall refer to any proposals or opinions which have been received. The response of the Council and of the Commission to Parliament's opinions and proposals has not been consistent. At times Parliament's advice has been followed; at other times it has been ignored. Nevertheless, the receipt of an opinion of the Parliament by the Council and Commission leads to a reappraisal of measures proposed even if the original draft legislation is left intact at the end of the process.

3 Parliamentary control over the Community Budget

Under the terms of the Treaties establishing the Communities, the draft budget is prepared by the Commission from the estimates drawn up by each institution. The Commission has then to submit the draft budget to the Council which after consultation with the Commission agrees the terms of the draft. The budget is then placed before the Assembly.

The role of the Parliament in the budgetary process was somewhat restricted until 1970. Before that time, the draft budget had to be laid before the Parliament by 31 October each year, and in accordance with Article 203 (3) of the EEC Treaty,[4] the Parliament had the right to

[1]The procedure relating to motions of censure is discussed in Chapter XIII, page 107.
[2]Articles 7, 14, 43, 54, 56, 57, 63, 75, 87, 100, 126, 127, 201, 203, 228, 235, 236 and 238.
[3]Articles 31, 76, 85, 90, 96, 98, 173, 177, 203, 204 and 206.
[4]And Article 177 (3) of the Euratom Treaty 1957.

C

propose modifications to the draft budget but had only one month to do
so. Notwithstanding the proposals of the Parliament, the Council
could finally adopt the budget acting by a qualified majority.[1]

Following the meeting of Heads of State of Member Governments
at The Hague in December 1969, a new procedure for dealing with the
Community budget was agreed and was incorporated in a Treaty
signed at Luxembourg on 22 April 1970 and in a decision of the Council
of 21 April 1970. During a transitional period lasting from 1971 to
1974, the Community will progressively acquire its own resources
instead of, as hitherto, receiving its income from financial contributions
from member states.

Since 1 January 1971 the total revenue from agricultural levies has
formed part of the budget of the Community. From the same date it
was decided that revenue from customs duties should also progressively
form part of the budget. Ten per cent of both the agricultural levies and
the external tariff are reserved to the member states to cover the cost of
collection. These provisions were subject to certain safeguards so that
no member would have its share of the contributions to the Community budget greatly increased until 1978, when any restrictions will
be removed. From 1 January 1975, the Budget will be financed entirely
from Community resources. In addition to the sources of revenue
already established, the revenue may be supplemented by a value added
tax not exceeding 1 per cent levied on an assessment basis determined in
a uniform manner from member states according to Community rules.

In the preamble to the Treaty of Luxembourg it was considered that
the replacement of financial contributions of member states by the
Communities' own resources required a strengthening of the budgetary
power of the Parliament. It was therefore decided to associate the
Parliament more closely in the supervision of the implementation of
the budget of the Communities. In order to give sufficient time for the
additional processes through which the budget had to pass, the date
on which the budget had to be laid before Parliament was advanced to
5 October.

The powers conferred on the Parliament by the Treaty of Luxembourg[2]
differ between the transitional period and the period commencing on
1 January 1975 when the Community is expected to be financially
independent. Until the end of 1974 the Parliament has forty-five days
annually in which to propose modifications to the draft budget. The
scope for amendment is limited to the administrative expenditure of the
Communities amounting to at most 5 per cent of the budget. The
remainder of the budget is spent in direct consequence of Community
legislation and as such may not be challenged. If the Parliament gives
its approval to the budget, or if no modification has been proposed, the

[1]See page 10.
[2]See Articles 203 and 203a of the EEC Treaty, Article 78 and 78a of the ECSC Treaty and
Articles 177 and 177a of the Euratom Treaty.

budget is deemed to be finally adopted. If the Parliament has proposed modifications the draft budget is forwarded to the Council.

The Council must then, after consulting the Commission and where appropriate the other institutions concerned, take action on the modifications proposed by the Parliament. Provided that no increase in expenditure is proposed and provided that the Council does not object by a qualified majority,[1] the modifications of the Parliament are deemed to be adopted. If, however, an increase of expenditure is proposed, the proposal must be supported by a qualified majority in the Council. The Council has also given an undertaking that the Parliament's control over its own budget will not be challenged.

The Council of Ministers and the Parliament made further arrangements for co-operation in the drafting, examination and approval of the budget during discussions in the autumn of 1971. These arrangements, which supplement the provisions of the Luxembourg Treaty of 1970, are explained in Chapter XIII. Despite the new procedures, the report of the President of the Parliament, Herr Walter Behrendt, on the activities of the Parliament in 1971 expressed continued disquiet about the arrangements for consultation between the Parliament and the Council.[2]

FROM THE BEGINNING OF 1975

After the full implementation of the provisions of the Luxembourg Treaty, the Parliament will have qualified control over the administrative expenditure of the Communities. Within limits prescribed by the Treaty, the Parliament will be able to increase the administrative budget, including its own, a power possessed by few national Parliaments in Europe.

The Parliament will continue to receive the draft budget from the Council and to have forty-five days within which to propose alterations in the budget.

Under the revised terms of Article 203 of the EEC Treaty[3] the Parliament will be able to amend those parts of the draft budget relating to the administration of the Communities, and to propose modifications to those parts of the draft relating to expenditure necessarily resulting from the Treaties and Acts adopted in accordance therewith.

If the Parliament has adopted amendments or proposed modifications, the draft budget together with the amendments and proposed modifications must be forwarded to the Council. After discussing the draft budget with the Commission the Council may, by qualified majority, modify any of the amendments and pronounce on the proposed modifications. The Council has to take action on amendments within fifteen

[1]See page 10.
[2]Annex to the Bulletin of the European Parliament No. 49/71, 14 January 1972.
[3]And Article 78 of the ECSC Treaty and Article 177 of the Euratom Treaty.

days; otherwise they are deemed to be adopted. On the other hand, unless the proposed modifications are accepted by the Council within the same period, the proposals lapse.

If the Council does not accept the amendments made and modifications proposed by the Parliament, the draft budget is returned. The Parliament can then, also within a fifteen-day period, restore the amendments by a majority of its members and three-fifths of the votes cast and adopt the budget accordingly. If within the period the Parliament fails to act, the budget as amended by the Council is deemed to be adopted.

When the procedure described above has been completed the President of the Assembly shall declare that the budget has been finally adopted.

The proposals which the Parliament might make for increasing the administrative budget are limited by the 'maximum rate of increase' determined by the Commission on criteria set out in revised Article 203 (8) of the EEC Treaty.[1] If the actual rate of increase in expenditure in the draft budget established by the Council is over half of the maximum rate, the Assembly can use its right of amendment to further increase the amount of expenditure to a limit not exceeding half of the maximum rate. Additionally in exceptional cases, a new 'maximum rate' can be established by agreement between the Council and the Parliament.

4 Relations with the Council of Ministers

There is no provision in the treaties establishing the Communities and their institutions for parliamentary control of the Council of Ministers. Under Article 140 of the EEC Treaty, is is provided that

'the Council shall be heard by the Assembly[2] in accordance with the conditions laid down by the Council in its Rules of Procedure'.

Rule 19 of the Council's Rules of Procedure provides that it can delegate its President or any other Member to be its representative at sessions of the Parliament. The Council may also communicate its views to the Parliament in writing. It is only on that slight foundation that relations between the Parliament and Council have developed.

As a result of the lack of any formal arrangements, the relations between the two institutions have developed gradually and are now based on the customary practices which have grown up. A Resolution adopted by the Parliament after the first colloquy between the Councils, the Commission and the Parliament in 1959 evoked a response in the Councils. At their session of March and April, 1960, the President in

---

[1]And Article 78 of the ECSC Treaty 1951 and Article 177 of the Euratom Treaty 1957.
[2]The Assembly changed its name to the European Parliament on 30 March 1962.

office of the Council announced that the Councils would make more frequent use of consultations with the Parliament. In addition to accepting the holding of further colloquies the Council agreed that in future it would forward replies to Parliamentary Questions on matters already explored in the Councils. Finally, the President initiated a new practice by submitting to the Parliament a brief statement on the work of the Councils.

The practice relating to Questions has now become established. In accordance with Rules 45 (1) and 46 (1) of the Parliament's Rules of Procedure Members are able to table written or oral questions to the Council in a similar manner to those addressed to the Commission.

Since 1960, it has also become the practice that the President of the Council each year makes an oral report to Parliament on the activities of the Council. Other Council Members may also make statements from time to time.

A further development of the Parliament's relations with the Council has taken place in connection with the arrangements for discussions on political unification on the basis of the report of the Davignon Committee. According to the General Report of the Communities for 1971,

'In application of the agreement reached by the six Governments in October 1970, the President of the Council had submitted the annual progress report on political unification. In addition, the Political Affairs Committee had held two meetings with Foreign Ministers of Member States to discuss the problems of political union, and, finally, during the November session a joint meeting of the Parliament, the Council and the Commission had been held to discuss the role of the enlarged Community in developing international relations and strengthening peace. Consequently, the Parliament had had several opportunities of expressing its views to the Council about European political co-operation. However, the Parliament thought that "the Community continues to suffer from the lack of a political agreement between its Governments".'

It is intended that the twice yearly meetings of the Foreign Ministers with the Political Affairs Committee and the annual report to the Parliament on the progress of political union should become regular features of the parliamentary calendar.

5 Colloquies between the Parliament and the Council of Ministers

Apart from the arrangements described above, an annual exchange of views or 'colloquy' has occupied an important place in the relations between the Parliament and the Council.

Following the precedent of a colloquy held in November 1957 between the Council and Common Assembly of the ECSC, the Councils, the Executives and the Parliament held a colloquy in November 1959 at the request of the Parliament. Three subjects were discussed, the debates being opened by statements from the Presidents in office of the Councils. The subjects were:

- Relations between the Parliament and the Councils,
- Co-ordination of the external policy of the member states towards non-member countries, especially the countries in course of development,
- Problems concerning the association of the Overseas Countries and Territories with the Community.

At the end of the colloquy, the Parliament adopted a resolution on its relations with the Councils.[1] Among other things it suggested that 'the Councils do everything possible to increase and improve their collaboration with the Parliament, in particular by taking an active part in debates, by furnishing precise replies to Parliamentary questions and by making available more information on their activities'. Finally, the Parliament requested the Councils 'to extend the consultation procedure to all important problems even where the Treaty lays down no obligation to consult'.

The Council approved the requests of the Parliament at its session of March and April 1960. The President in office of the Council proposed that a second colloquy be arranged for the second half of 1960. Thus the principle of an annual exchange of views was established.

Many important subjects fundamental to the development of the Communities have been debated at the annual colloquies. Among subjects discussed have been: 'the foreign policies of member states as they effect the EEC' and 'the merger of the three Executives' (1960) and 'Economic Union and the outlook for monetary union in the Community' (1970). Contributions have been made in each of the debates by Foreign and other Ministers from the Governments of member states.

The colloquy now assumes a comparatively less important place in the relations between the Parliament and the Council than in the early days of the Communities. Since then, the Parliament has developed contacts with the Council through questions and the participation of members of the Council in debates.

[1]See 3rd Report of the EEC 21 March 1959 to 15 May 1960.

Chapter IV

The role of national parliaments in Community affairs

1 Introduction

Under the terms of the Treaties of Rome and Paris, the European Parliament was given the major role in exercising parliamentary control over the other Community institutions. None the less the Treaties have reserved certain fundamental matters for the decision of national Parliaments. Moreover, the drawing of the members of the Parliament from among the members of national parliaments has further complicated this position. Thus the role of national parliaments in the Communities and the relations between the national and international assemblies have become increasingly significant.

The continuing and growing power of the Council of Ministers has also provided an impetus for national participation in Community decisions. The representative of each government on the Council is answerable to his national parliament for his actions and national parliaments have been able to discuss Community matters according to their customary procedures. Although certain minor changes in the procedures of national parliaments have been made to meet this need, in general the parliaments have adapted existing procedures of debates, questions, interpellations, and committee studies to deal with Community issues. It is only in the Belgian House of Representatives and the Italian Senate that committees which were set up to examine specifically European questions have continued to operate.

2 The European Parliament's relations with national parliaments

Since little progress has been made towards the goal set in Article 138 (3) of the EEC Treaty of elections to the Parliament by direct universal suffrage, the membership of the European Parliament is still designated from among the members of the parliaments of member states. Thus there is a body of members of parliament in each country who are members of the European Parliament. As a result of this, even without any deliberate attempt on the part of those members to canvass Community issues, a certain level of awareness of each question is achieved.

There has been little encouragement by the European Parliament for the intervention of its members in the national assemblies. Unlike the

Consultative Assembly of the Council of Europe and the Assembly of Western European Union, which have established committees to assist their members to pursue the interests of these organisations in the national parliaments, the European Parliament has no such institutionalised arrangement.

There are substantial reasons based on the institutional provisions of the Treaties establishing the Communities for the separation of the European Parliament and the national parliaments. The powers of the Parliament were formulated to fit it for its task of parliamentary control of the European Commission. Since the Commission has executive functions on a European level, the Parliament is the only parliamentary body able to act directly on its proposals. For this reason, the Parliament has not developed the same links with parliaments in member states, as have organisations in which sole executive power is invested in a committee or Council of Ministers.

The European Parliament has not, however, completely neglected the national parliaments. In January 1963, a special conference was held in Rome at which the presidents (or speakers) and secretaries-general of the national parliaments were present. In the chair at the conference was the late Signor Martino, the then President of the European Parliament. The conference had been initiated to discuss the harmonisation of the parliamentary calendars of the European and national Parliaments and the promotion of the views of the Parliament in the member states. However, the final resolution of the conference exhorted the European Parliament to refrain from fixing the dates of its plenary meetings until the national parliaments had been consulted. On the other main topic, the resolution placed emphasis on the importance of the national parliaments' role in relation to the Communities.

Another initiative of the Parliament in the early 1960s was the informal nomination of a member of each national delegation to act as a 'liaison officer' with his national parliament to promote the Parliament's views in the national bodies. Furthermore these Members were to meet from time to time to exchange views and to co-ordinate their promotional efforts on behalf of the Parliament. However, the practice did not become established and soon lapsed.

One informal way in which the Parliament has maintained links with the institutions of member states has been to hold meetings of committees of the Parliament from time to time in the capitals of member states, often in the buildings of national parliaments.

3 Obligations of national parliaments in Community affairs

The founding Treaties of the Communities place certain responsibilities upon the national parliaments of member states. While the Treaties do not allow the national institutions a role in the making of Community law, certain matters which require the extension of the Treaties, or the implementation of Community decisions on a national level, necessitate national action.

AMENDMENT OR APPLICATION OF THE TREATIES

When the Communities propose to take measures which amount to the extension or amendment of the founding Treaties, it is necessary for the amendments to be ratified by all the member states in accordance with their respective constitutional requirements. Such amendments are generally made by the ratification of a separate treaty. In the United Kingdom the practice with regard to treaty ratification is governed by the 'Ponsonby rule' (see Erskine May's *Parliamentary Practice*, Eighteenth Edition, p. 251). When a treaty requires ratification, the Government does not usually proceed with ratification until a period of twenty-one days has elapsed from the date on which the text of such a treaty was laid before Parliament by Her Majesty's command. This practice is subject to modification, if necessary, when urgent or other important considerations apply.

Several different matters are required by the Treaties to be dealt with by separate treaty:

(i) *Enlargement of the Communities:* Under Article 237 of the EEC Treaty and Article 205 of the Euratom Treaty, any European state may apply to become a member of the Communities. An agreement to admit new states can only come into effect after ratification by member states 'in accordance with their respective constitutional requirements'. It was under these Articles and under the procedures laid down therein that the United Kingdom, Denmark and Ireland acceded to the Communities.

(ii) *Amendment of the Treaties of Rome, 1957 and Paris, 1951:* Article 236 of the EEC Treaty, Article 96 of the ECSC Treaty and Article 204 of the Euratom Treaty allow that any member state, or the Commission, may submit proposals to amend the Treaties which to be adopted require ratification by member states. The agreement of 1965 to establish a single Council and a single Commission of the European Communities which amended all three Treaties was effected by the ratification of the Merger Treaty. The Treaty was the subject of considerable discussion in national parliaments before it entered into effect.

(iii) *Changes in the Structure of the Communities:* Certain changes in Community structure were set down in the founding Treaties to be applied at a later stage in the development of the Communities. Direct elections by universal suffrage to the European Parliament, provided for in Article 138 (3) of the EEC Treaty, have still not been introduced. But if such a step is taken, it must be accomplished by the Council submitting a unanimous recommendation to member states for approval and implementation. A similar procedure is necessary with regard to the implementation of Article 201 of the EEC Treaty for the creation of the Communities' own resources. A step in this direction has been taken by the ratification of the Treaty of Luxembourg of April 1970 (see pp. 21–24 on Parliamentary control of the Budget).

(iv) *The conclusion of trade and association agreements:* The Communities are empowered to make certain international trade or association agreements which, if sufficiently important, require ratification by the member states. These agreements, based on Articles 113 and 238 of the EEC Treaty and Article 206 of the Euratom Treaty, are adopted by both the European and national institutions. Examples of agreements which have been approved in this way are the Convention of Association with Greece in 1961, with Turkey in 1963 and with the Association of African States and Madagascar in 1969.

IMPLEMENTATION OF COMMUNITY LEGISLATION

(i) *Regulations*

The principal instrument of Community legislation is the Regulation which may be made by the Council or, in the case of less important matters, by the Commission. Regulations take direct effect in member countries after they have been formally adopted and have been published in the Official Journal. Once Regulations have been made, there is no possibility of parliamentary action in member states to modify them. In certain circumstances, for example where penalties are needed to enforce a Regulation, national governments may be required to support Regulations with their own subordinate legislation. In the United Kingdom, this could be achieved under the terms of Section 2 of the European Communities Act 1972.

(ii) *Directives*

One aspect of Community law-making requires the direct involvement of national institutions. Directives (or Recommendations, as they are called in the ECSC Treaty) are made by the Council; they are binding as to the result achieved upon each member state to which they are addressed but allow national authorities to choose the form and methods of implementation. Directives have been used as the principal means of harmonisation of the law within the Communities. They are issued by the Council with a time limit set for their implementation. There has been only one important example of member states failing to comply with a Directive within the stipulated period. The introduction of the value-added tax was delayed beyond the time limit in both Belgium and Italy in part for national policy reasons. The Communities had to agree to authorise the postponement of the introduction of the VAT for a further period.

The practice of implementation of Directives varies between member states. In the United Kingdom, in accordance with the terms of Section 2 of the European Communities Act, effect can be given to a Directive by administrative action where no legislative sanction is required; by Statutory Instrument made under an Act amended by the Schedules to that Act; or by the passage of a new Act of Parliament.

Although Directives differ substantially from Regulations in form and give the member states a degree of discretion in their implementation, the role of member states is none the less somewhat limited. Community Directives are frequently so precise and comprehensive that the national parliament has little to do other than to discuss the means of enactment, whether by act or by Statutory Instrument.

Part II

The external relations of the Communities

Chapter V

The association agreements of the Communities

1 General

In the Preamble to the Treaty establishing the European Economic Community, 1957, the member states of the EEC declare themselves 'determined to lay the foundations of an ever closer union among the peoples of Europe,' resolve 'common action to eliminate the barriers which divide Europe,' and 'call upon the other peoples of Europe who share their ideas to join in their efforts.' Since then every country in non-Communist Europe apart from Finland and Iceland has applied either for membership or some form of association. Article 3 (k) of the Treaty of Rome has as a final objective of the Treaty 'the association of the overseas countries and territories in order to increase trade and to promote jointly economic and social development'. Association agreements have been concluded with Greece, Turkey, Morocco, Tunisia, and Malta; long negotiation with Austria has so far failed to produce a result. The Communities have a trade agreement with Yugoslavia and special agreements, short of association, with Israel, Spain, the Lebanon, and Iran. Outside Europe and the Mediterranean countries, an association agreement has been concluded with the Associated African States and Madagascar (AASM) and with three Commonwealth countries in East Africa – Kenya, Uganda and Tanzania. In Part Four of the Treaty of Rome the member states agreed 'to associate with the Community the non-European countries and territories which have special relations with Belgium, France, Italy and the Netherlands'.[1] This arrangement was extended in Article 24 of the Act of Accession annexed to the Treaty of Accession of 1972 to include the non-European countries and territories which have special relations

[1]French West Africa: Senegal, French Sudan, French Guinea, Ivory Coast, Dahomey, Mauretania, Niger and Upper Volta;
French Equatorial Africa: Middle Congo, Ubangi-Shari, Chad and Gabon;
Saint Pierre and Miquelon, the Comoro Archipelago, Madagascar and dependencies, French Somaliland, New Caledonia and dependencies, French Settlements in Oceania, Southern and Antarctic Territories;
The Autonomous Republic of Togoland;
The Trust Territory of the Cameroons under French administration;
The Belgian Congo and Ruanda-Urundi;
The Trust Territory of Somaliland under Italian administration;
Netherlands New Guinea.

with the United Kingdom.[1] Declarations annexed to the Treaty of Rome announced the readiness of the member states to negotiate association agreements with Morocco, Tunisia, Libya, Italian Somaliland, Surinam and the Netherlands Antilles.

The Treaty of Rome deals with external relations in Articles 110–116, 131–136 and 227–238, and in several of the Protocols and Declarations. Of necessity, Community 'foreign policy' has been mainly economic in character. Article 228 of the EEC Treaty refers to the conclusion of 'agreements'; this term could mean extension of Community membership, agreements of association, purely commercial agreements and agreements with international organisations. Article 228 states that 'such agreements shall be negotiated by the Commission' and 'shall be concluded by the Council', although it makes no provision for early consultation between the Council and the Commission. In Articles 111, 113 and 114 on commercial agreements, the scheme is clearer: the Commission recommends the opening of negotiations and the Council authorises the Commission to begin negotiating and appoints a committee to assist it. No mention is made of the Parliament. Article 238, dealing with association agreements negotiated as such from the beginning, states that the Council shall conclude agreements, but by unanimous decision, and, significantly, 'after consulting the Assembly'.[2] In practice, some agreements have been signed before submission to the Parliament, on the theoretical grounds that a text can be published only if it is signed. But in the case of the Association Agreement with Malta, the Parliament was informed of the text before final signature and was able to have included in the Agreement provision for a joint parliamentary committee.

[1]Anglo-French Condominium of the New Hebrides;
The Bahamas;
Bermuda;
British Antarctic Territory;
British Honduras;
British Indian Ocean Territory;
British Solomon Islands;
British Virgin Islands;
Brunei;
Associated States in the Caribbean: Antigua, Dominica, Grenada, St Lucia, St Vincent, St Kitts-Nevis-Anguilla;
Cayman Islands;
Central and Southern Line Islands;
Falkland Islands and Dependencies;
Gilbert and Ellice Islands;
Montserrat;
Pitcairn;
St Helena and Dependencies;
The Seychelles;
Turks and Caicos Islands.
Article 24 of the Act of Accession also extended the arrangement to include the Norwegian possessions in the Antarctic.
[2]The European Parliament adopted its present title on 30 March 1962.

An agreement of association involves 'reciprocal rights and obligations, common action and special procedures'.[1] The Treaty of Rome does not specify requirements and qualifications for participation in this sort of relationship rather than in a commercial agreement or full membership, and the Communities' concept of association has developed gradually. Shortly after the collapse of the negotiations with OEEC[2] in November 1958, the Commission produced a First Memorandum, dealing with the problems of economic association.[3] Most of the Six found its general approach too negative, and set up a special committee to study the problems of economic association. The First Memorandum noted that 'association . . . allows of all solutions: those which adopt only certain features of the Treaty of Rome, and those which take over that instrument in its entirety.' There were two particular difficulties: whether an associated country should be in any way involved in Community decision-making, and whether there should be a formalised process for the conclusion and conduct of all association agreements. The First Memorandum stated that 'any European countries anxious to go further in economic integration' could bring into play Articles 237 and 238 of the Treaty of Rome, and while the Commission felt that any new member should accept the Treaty as it stood, it laid down no formal requirements for association, as the agreement with Greece[4] seems to show.

The Parliament has played a considerable part in the attempts to define 'association' and its role in the external affairs of the Community. In January 1962 M. Birkelbach prepared a report on behalf of the Political Affairs Committee on political and institutional aspects of accession or association with the EEC. This document was the first attempt to set out policy in this field. It held that full membership should be reserved for those democratic states politically and militarily aligned with the West. Agreements of association might be made with economically less sophisticated countries, but there would be no question of the permanent association of a country which could be a full member of the Community. The report approved of most-favoured-nation treatment being accorded to non-member countries but disapproved of preferential arrangements. While considering the idea that association ought to be limited to European countries unable to become full members, the report recommended that overseas countries having long-standing links with a member state of the Community should also be candidates qualified for association.

In the Parliamentary debate of January 1962 on this subject, the main points of the report were stressed, the difficulty of defining 'association' was noted, and it was felt that the only candidates for association

---

[1]Article 238 of the EEC Treaty.
[2]See page 48.
[3]February 1959.
[4]The Athens Agreement of July 1961.

D

would be European states and those states geographically linked with
Europe. The agreement with the Associated African States and
Madagascar was thought to be a necessary exception. Special agreements for economic co-operation should, it was thought, be used where
candidates were not qualified for association; association itself would
involve customs union at the very least. Where, for political reasons,
European countries could not contemplate association as a first step
towards membership, then consideration should be given to the
possibility of a trade agreement under Article 113. A proposal was
made for the setting up of a Joint Association Council consisting of
representatives of the European Parliament and of the Parliament of
the State concerned.

The European Parliament has taken part in Joint Committees on the
Association with Greece,[1] on the Agreement with the Associated
African States and Madagascar, and on the Association with Turkey. The
members of the Parliament serving on these committees are also mem-
bers of the relevant internal committees of the European Parliament.
The Political Affairs Committee and the Committee on External Trade
Relations are also concerned with aspects of association and trade
agreements.

When the Dehousse Report from the Political Affairs Committee
appeared in May 1967, its two main points were that qualifications for
association ought to be less demanding, and that consideration should
be given to the possibility of preferential arrangements without membership or association. The change shows how far the Communities' views
on association had been modified by the intervening five years.

The Communities' early association agreements suffered from the
strictures of the General Agreement on Tariffs and Trade (GATT),[2] and
GATT has since been used as an international forum for criticism of the
association agreements in particular and of the Communities' external
relations in general.

The following sections describe the association agreements already
concluded.

2 The Association with Greece

Shortly after the talks aimed at establishing a Free Trade Area throughout the Organisation for European Economic Co-operation[3] had
collapsed in November 1958, negotiations for the setting up of the
European Free Trade Area (EFTA)[4] began. Greece, which was not a
party to these negotiations, made a formal application for association
in a note of 8 June 1959 under the terms of Article 238 of the EEC

[1]See page 39.
[2]See page 51.
[3]See page 48.
[4]See page 53.

Treaty. Negotiations began in March 1960 and the agreement was initialled on 30 March 1961 and signed in Athens on 9 July 1961. The Athens Agreement came into force on 1 November 1962, and was the first bilateral agreement between the EEC and a third country. Some provisions of the Agreement went beyond contemporary Community competence and thus member states as well as the Council were signatories to it.

The Parliament studied the Agreement in September 1961, and passed two resolutions. The first strongly criticised the Council of Ministers' signing of the Agreement before consulting the Parliament, and hoped that such a situation would not occur again. The second resolution noted the importance of the Agreement for the Community's external policy, and the fact that under its terms later accession was possible. The setting up of an Association Council[1] was approved, and the institution of a Joint Parliamentary Committee for the Association was proposed. This was composed of 14 Greek and 14 Community members[2], and considered three annual reports on the activities of the Association Council. There was some general parliamentary criticism of the Council's procedures, especially in the issuing of mandates and directives and the setting up of an expert committee to give technical assistance.

Under the terms of the Agreement, Greek goods were to have free entry into the Community by 1968, and there was to be full reciprocity by 1984. New Greek industries could be protected by tariffs of as much as 25 per cent, but over only 10 per cent of her imports. Very little agricultural produce was dealt with in the provisions of the Agreement, pending 'the formation of common policies'. Certain products, such as citrus fruits and nuts, were to have their tariffs progressively reduced over twelve years. An immediate 50 per cent reduction was made in the tariff on tobacco, which accounted for 35 per cent of all Greece's exports. Protocol 19 provided for financial assistance (125 million units of account[3] annually for five years).

On 21 April 1967, the military coup d'état took place. On 11 May the Parliament passed a resolution noting that the provisions for Greek accession could not be implemented unless 'democratic structures, political freedom and freedom for trade unions are restored in Greece.' It felt that the absence of elected institutions in Greece made the functioning of the Joint Parliamentary Committee impossible, and that this meant that the Association Agreement could not operate properly. The observations on full membership contained in the Birkelbach

---

[1] This consisted of representatives of the member states, the Council, the Commission and Greece.
[2] The members of the European Parliament on the committee are also members of the Parliament's own internal committee on the Association with Greece.
[3] One unit of account (u.a.) is equivalent to one U.S. dollar.

Report of 1962 (see page 37) and afterwards frequently restated made an undemocratic Greece an unacceptable partner. Financial assistance was withdrawn. The 'timetable' action for customs union has been proceeded with automatically, but as the Fifth General Report on the Activities of the Communities (1971) says, in view of the situation in Greece, 'the Community has been obliged to continue to limit the application of the Athens Agreement to current affairs'.

When the Agreement was signed, Greece obtained extremely favourable terms. This was partly a result of the Communities' desire to conclude an agreement with a third country, and thus to demonstrate that they had a common external policy.

3 The Association with Turkey

Turkey applied for association with the EEC under Article 238 of the EEC Treaty on 31 July 1959. Negotiations began in the following December and the signing of an Association Agreement took place in Ankara on 12 September 1963. The Agreement came into force on 1 December 1964: the member states of the EEC as well as the Commission were signatories.

Once again consultation with the Parliament did not take place until after the agreement had been signed. The Council's action in signing before consultation was deplored in a resolution passed on 28 November 1963, and the Parliament expressed its desire to have discussions with the Council to ensure effective consultation in future.

The good terms on which Greece had become associated with the EEC gave rise to some difficulty over an agreement with Turkey. For example, Greek and Community interests would have been threatened by the removal of tariffs on tobacco and raisins. Tariff quotas would have given a guarantee to the Community, but would not be large enough to satisfy Turkey unless Greece agreed to a lowering of her quota, which was unlikely. If the tariff quotas had been preferential for Turkey alone, then the Communities would have had to ask GATT for a special derogation under the terms of Article 25. Thus a customs union was necessary in order to comply with the requirements of GATT[1] and incompatibility with the terms of the Treaty of Athens was avoided by the agreement being one of association.

Under the Agreement of Ankara, Turkey received preferential reduced-tariff arrangements for her four main exports (tobacco, raisins, nuts and figs) for an initial period of five years. She also received financial aid. In 1970 two protocols were signed, one specifying the means and timing of the transitional phase and the second giving financial aid of 195 million units of account. An interim agreement, designed to run until both protocols became effective, came into force on

[1]See page 51.

1 September 1971. When the protocols are implemented, internal Community tieatment will be given to all imports originating in Turkey. Special provision is made for petroleum products and some textiles. Other tariff reductions are to take place over 12 or 22 years according to the product concerned. Turkey has 22 years to adapt her agricultural policy in readiness for the implementation of 'those common agricultural policy measures whose application is indispensable for the establishment of the free movement of products between the Community and Turkey.'[1]

In the second part of the resolution passed on 28 November, 1963, the Parliament noted that the Association Agreement made provision for Turkey's subsequent full membership, and pointed out that a Joint Parliamentary Committee on the lines of that on the Greek Association was necessary for the smooth running of the Association with Turkey. Such a Joint Committee was set up by a resolution of 14 May 1965; it had 15 European Parliament members and 15 Turkish members. The main concern of the committee has been the annual reports of the Association Council on its activities. The European Parliament's committee members also meet independently as an internal committee of the Parliament.

It is significant that in the resolution of 28 November 1963, the Parliament also noted that the 'form and content of the Association Agreement were justified by the special situation of the Turkish economy,' and as a result should not be thought of as a model for any subsequent agreement. The Turkish Agreement was concluded at a time when the strictures of GATT dictated both the type and the extent of the Community's external agreements.

4 The Agreement with the Associated African States and Madagascar (A A S M)

ORIGINS

At the time of signature of the Treaty of Rome, long-standing links existed between some of the signatories and various overseas territories. These close ties could not be ignored, and yet full membership of a European economic community was impossible. It was with these countries and territories in mind that Part Four[2] of the EEC Treaty was framed. The Preamble to the Treaty of Rome declares the Contracting Parties' intention 'to confirm the solidarity which binds Europe and the overseas countries' and their desire 'to ensure the development of [these countries'] prosperity, in accordance with the principles of the Charter of the United Nations'.

[1]Fourth General Report, 1970, p. 277.
[2]Articles 131–136.

Annexed to the EEC Treaty is an 'Implementing Convention on the Association of the Overseas Countries and Territories with the Community'. Together with Part Four of the Treaty, this makes provision for the gradual setting up of a free trade area and the giving of financial aid, paid into a Development Fund, to promote 'social and economic development'. Over the next five years, the member states of the Communities paid 581·25 million units of account (eurodollars) into the Fund. The provisions of Part Four applied to the countries and territories listed in Annex IV of the Treaty of Rome,[1] and also to the French overseas departments and Algeria.

In the early days of this association, the European Parliament set up a Committee of Associations which met for the first time in March 1958. Three delegations made visits to parts of Africa and submitted reports to the Parliament.

The form of association based on the Treaty could not survive the gaining of independence by the associated countries and territories,[2] and negotiations began for a new type of association.

THE YAOUNDÉ CONVENTIONS

The negotiations between the European Commission and the Associated African States and Madagascar (AASM) resulted in the signature of a Convention of Association in Yaoundé, Cameroon, on 20 July 1963. The Convention came into force on 1 July 1964. The member states of the Community took part in this Convention in their own right as well as being represented by the Commission. In effect the Convention established eighteen separate free trade areas, since there were no trade agreements within the AASM. All the members of the AASM were bound to give equal treatment to the member states of the Community, and were not permitted to give better treatment to any non-member country unless this was under customs union or free trade area arrangements. The Convention was to remain in force for five years.

[1]French West Africa: Senegal, French Sudan, French Guinea, Ivory Coast, Dahomey, Mauretania, Niger and Upper Volta;
French Equatorial Africa: Middle Congo, Ubangi-Shari, Chad and Gabon;
Saint Pierre and Miquelon, the Comoro Archipelago, Madagascar and dependencies, French Somaliland, New Caledonia and dependencies, French Settlements in Oceania, Southern and Antarctic Territories;
The Autonomous Republic of Togoland;
The Trust Territory of the Cameroons under French administration;
The Belgian Congo and Ruanda-Urundi;
The Trust Territory of Somaliland under Italian administration;
Netherlands New Guinea.

[2]Guinea in 1958;
Cameroon, Togo, Senegal, Mali, Madagascar, Italian Somaliland, Belgian Congo, Dahomey, Niger, Upper Volta, Ivory Coast, Chad, Central African Republic, Congo-Brazzaville, Gabon, Mauretania in 1960.
Ruanda and Burundi in 1962.
Guinea left the association when she left the French Community, but all the other countries remained associated.

The Convention provided for gradual elimination of customs duties on AASM products imported into the Community. Tariff restriction on ten tropical products were to be removed immediately. A second Development Fund of 730 million units of account (eurodollars) was set up. African development was safeguarded by the provision that new quantitative restrictions could be made, and an Association Council, a Parliamentary Conference and a Court of Arbitration were set up. The Association Council is assisted by an Association Committee. Annexed to the Convention is a Declaration of Intent which states the Community's readiness to conclude similar agreements with countries in a comparable position. The agreement with Nigeria in 1966 is an example of such an attempt.

The Second Yaoundé Convention of Association was signed in 1969 and came into force on 1 January 1971. A transitional period of 18 months separated the expiry of the First Convention and the beginning of the Second. The Second Convention made less provision for reciprocal trade concessions, but set up a third Development Fund, increasing the total amount to 918 million units of account.

At the request of the AASM, the Association Council of the EEC and AASM held a special meeting on 30 November 1971. At this meeting the Association Council discussed the probable association policy of the enlarged Community, the arrangements for the period between the new members joining the Community and the expiry of the Second Convention, and the conditions which the enlarged Community would offer to developing Commonwealth Countries.

The Association's Parliamentary Conference consists of a maximum of 108 members. The Parliaments of the AASM appoint three members from each associated state, and the European Parliament appoints an equal number of representatives from amongst its own members. The President and nine Vice-Presidents are elected annually by the Conference. Five members of the Bureau are European and five are African or Madagascan. The Conference meets annually, alternately in Europe and Africa, and considers the Association Council's report on the year's activities. Preparations for the Conference are made by a Joint Committee, which consists of one representative from each Associated State and an equal number of representatives from the European Parliament. The Conference appoints these representatives from among its members, and elects the chairman and vice-chairman of the Joint Committee. When the chairman is European, the vice-chairman must be chosen from the representatives of the AASM, and *vice versa*. A similar procedure is followed in the case of the President of the Conference. The Joint Committee meets twice each year, by turns in Europe and Africa. There are eighteen members of the European Parliament who are members of the Joint Committee; these members also function as an internal committee of the Parliament on the Association.

5 The Arusha Agreement

The first Arusha Agreement of Association was made between the
EEC and three East African countries: Kenya, Uganda and Tanzania.
It was signed in 1968 but expired before it could be ratified. The Second
Agreement was signed just after the signature of the Second Yaoundé
Convention in 1969, and came into force on 1 January 1971. The
industrial products of the three East African countries were allowed
free entry into the Community, and special arrangements were made for
agricultural products. Where customs duties remained, they were largely
replaced by fiscal entry charges. Under the terms of the Agreement,
Kenya, Uganda and Tanzania had the freedom to participate in separate
geographical customs unions or free trade areas. In the event of
the enlargement of the Community, the Arusha agreement requires the
Community to keep its partners informed of developments. Since the
Agreement was to expire in 1975, re-negotiation with an enlarged
Community could be deferred until then.

When the Agreement came into force, the preparatory Interim
Committee gave way to the Association Council and its Association
Committee.

6 The Association with Morocco and Tunisia

The Agreements of Association between the Community and Morocco
and Tunisia have their origin in the Third Declaration of Intent annexed
to the EEC Treaty of 1957. Both agreements came into force on 1 September 1969, when nearly all Moroccan and Tunisian products received
internal Community treatment. Special arrangements were made for
some types of agricultural produce; for example, an 80 per cent tariff
preference on citrus fruits was introduced. In the Agreements of
Association, both Morocco and Tunisia undertook not to discriminate
between the member states of the EEC. The insertion of such an undertaking into the Agreements was probably prompted by the fact that
both countries were former French colonies. The Agreements signed
in 1969 made no provision for the enlargement of the Community. The
original Agreements laid down that 'negotiations for new Agreements
should begin in the autumn of 1972 and be concluded by the spring of
1973'.[1] By the end of 1971, the Commission and the Moroccan and
Tunisian Governments were jointly examining the probable effects on
the Agreements of the enlargement of the Community.

7 The Association with Malta

An Agreement of Association between the EEC and Malta was negotiated in April, June and July 1970. The Agreement was signed in

[1] 5th General Report, p. 312.

Valetta on 5 December 1970, and came into force on 1 April 1971. Terms for the first stage of the establishment of a customs union were included in the Agreement, which provided for negotiations on the terms of the second stage (1976–81) to start in October 1974. Malta was the fifth Mediterranean country[1] to become associated with the EEC. Preferential relations with the United Kingdom were continued and the Fifth General Report[2] on the Activities of the Communities noted that the 'problems posed by the enlargement of the Community' had thereby 'been partially resolved in advance'.

During the first stage of the Agreement, Malta was gradually to reduce duties on nearly all imports from the Community by up to 35 per cent. Community customs duties on imports of Maltese industrial products were reduced by 70 per cent when the Agreement came into force. The Agreement also included provision for a joint committee of parliamentarians, but no such committee has yet been established.

[1]After Greece, Turkey, Morocco and Tunisia.
[2]p. 313.

Chapter VI

The relations of the Communities with international organisations

1 General

Formalised provision for the Communities' relations with international organisations is contained in Articles 229, 230 and 231 of the EEC Treaty of 1957. These Articles state that:

'It shall be for the Commission to ensure the maintenance of all appropriate relations with the organs of the United Nations, of its specialised agencies[1] and of the General Agreement on Tariffs and Trade. The Commission shall also maintain such relations as are appropriate with all international organisations.

'The Community shall establish all appropriate forms of co-operation with the Council of Europe[2].

'The Community shall establish close co-operation with the Organisation for European Economic Co-operation[3], the details to be determined by common accord.'

Identical provisions are made in Articles 199, 200, and 201 of the Euratom Treaty of 1957. The ECSC Treaty of 1951 is less wide-ranging in its provisions but Articles 93 and 94 mention relations with the United Nations, the OEEC and the Council of Europe. Annexed to the Treaty is a six-Article Protocol on relations with the Council of Europe, mainly concerned with the exchange of information.

Annexed to the EEC Treaty is a 'Joint Declaration on Co-operation with the States Members of International Organisations', dealing with individual as well as collective relations. The Declaration stated that the member governments were ready 'to conclude, as soon as these Treaties enter into force, agreements with other countries, particularly within the framework of the international organisations to which they belong, in order to attain these objectives of common interest [i.e. economic and social progress] and to ensure the harmonious development of trade in general'.

The Communities' external relations have been largely commercial, but as can be seen from the terms of the Treaties, a wider role is foreseen.

[1]See Chapter VII on the relations of the Communities with the United Nations and its Specialised Agencies.
[2]For relations with the Council of Europe, see pages 62 to 67.
[3]OEEC became the Organisation for Economic Co-operation and Development (OECD) on 30 September 1961.

Article 299 of the EEC Treaty names the Commission as the negotiating body on behalf of the Communities, while Articles 230 and 231 make no specification. The position is clarified in Article 211, which establishes the Commission as the Community's legal representative, and in Article 228, where it is laid down that agreements between the Community and other states or international organisations shall be negotiated by the Commission. However, 'subject to the powers vested in the Commission in this field, such agreements shall be concluded by the Council, after consulting the Assembly when required by this Treaty'.[1]

2 Community authority over external relations

Article 228 of the EEC Treaty provides that 'The Council, the Commission or a Member State may obtain beforehand the opinion of the Court of Justice as to whether an agreement envisaged is compatible with the provisions of this Treaty.'

The Court of Justice has played an active part in the determination of the scope of Community power over external relations, and of the degree of independent action which member states are permitted. Of particular significance in this context is the judgement delivered in March 1971, specifically concerned with the agreement on international road transport personnel.[2] The importance of the judgement lies in its extension to external relations of 'the system of the EEC Treaty as well as its specific provisions'.

Article 113 of the EEC Treaty provides for the implementation of the common commercial policy whereby the Council must authorise the Commission to negotiate agreements with 'third countries' and appoint a special committee to assist the Commission. Article 238 of the EEC Treaty[3] says 'The Community may conclude with a third State, a union of States or an international organisation agreements establishing an association involving reciprocal rights and obligations, common action and special procedures'. Article 210 of the EEC Treaty gives legal identity to the Community.

In interpretation of these three Articles, the judgement notes that 'only the Community is in a position to take over and fulfil, in respect of the entire field of application of the Community legal order, obligations undertaken vis-à-vis non-member States'. Thus, no member state may enter into any agreement which might involve obligations impinging on the common rules of the Community. While this judgement was

---

[1]Article 228 of the EEC Treaty.
[2]CJEC, 31 March 1971 (Commission *v.* Council, case 22–70) Recueil 1971, p. 263.
[3]The extent of Community authority over external relations is dealt with in Chapter X of Title II of the Euratom Treaty (Articles 103–105) and in Article 72 of the ECSC Treaty.

specifically concerned with the EEC, similar rules may be adduced for the Communities as a whole.[1]

If member states of the Communities participate in the work of international organisations, they must first ascertain whether their relations fall within the competence of one of the Communities. Because of the wide scope of the Communities, this is frequently the case. Member states cannot bind the Communities by what they do, although the reverse is not so. The negotiating power of member states is thus limited for practical purposes within the spheres of interest of the Communities, and participation by the Communities as a whole becomes necessary.

The EEC is represented by the Commission in international negotiations but in some circumstances, for example where there is only partial Community responsibility for the subject concerned, this may not suffice. Participation by member states in a national capacity is then necessary; this is normally achieved by a mixed delegation consisting of representatives of the Commission and of the Governments of member states.

Economic aspects of negotiations by a member state in which the Community is not otherwise concerned are regulated by Article 116 of the EEC Treaty which lays down that member states 'shall . . . proceed within the framework of international organisations of an economic character only by common action'.

Although the legal identity of the Community is the basis of its dealings, this identity is not always fully recognised. For example, the United Nations' policy of accepting only individual states as members has caused difficulty over Community representation.[2] The Fifth General Report remarks, 'The provisional arrangements adopted to date, whereby the Community has the status of an observer, cannot be regarded as wholly in accord with the EEC Treaty'.

The main areas of international co-operation undertaken by the Communities are described below.

3 The Organisation for Economic Co-operation and Development (OECD)

ORIGINS

This organisation, founded as the Organisation for European Economic Co-operation (OEEC), was set up by the Convention for European Economic Co-operation of 16 April 1948. Its origin lay in the condition laid down by the then US Secretary of State, General Marshall, that self-help by the receiving countries must accompany the distribution of

---

[1]CJEC, 14 December 1971 (Commission *v.* French Republic, case 7–71); interpretation of Chapter VI of Title II of the Euratom Treaty.
[2]See Chapter VII.

dollar aid. All the member states of the Communities were included in OEEC, together with several other European countries. Canada and the United States were associate members. Under the terms of the Convention the European member states agreed to draw up joint general programmes for their economic activities, to develop trade and to aim at a multilateral system of payments.

By the end of 1959 it was apparent that with the improved economic situation in Europe the primary objectives of OEEC had been achieved. Accordingly in January 1960 the twenty members and associate members of OEEC set up a group of four experts to make proposals for an improved organisation for economic co-operation.

The experts' report, *A Remodelled Economic Organisation*, was published in 1960, and discussed the proposed aims and tasks of the future economic organisation, for which the title of Organisation for Economic Co-operation and Development (OECD) was proposed.

The Convention for the Organisation for Economic Co-operation and Development was signed on 14 December 1960 and came into force on 30 September 1961. All the member states of the European Communities are members of OECD as are Australia, Austria, Canada, Finland, Greece, Iceland, Japan, Portugal, Spain, Sweden, Switzerland, Turkey and the United States. Yugoslavia has a special status entitling it to take part in certain activities of OECD.

AIMS AND STRUCTURE

OECD has three major aims: first, to promote the highest standard of economic growth and employment that can be sustained and a rising standard of living in member countries, while maintaining financial stability and so contributing to the development of the world economy; second, to contribute to the sound economic expansion of both member and non-member nations; and third, to further world trade of a multilateral, non-discriminating kind in accordance with international obligations.

The supreme body in OECD is the Council whose decisions on matters of general policy and administration are final. Composed of one representative of each member country, the Council meets from time to time at the level of Ministers and regularly at the level of Permanent Representatives. Decisions must be approved unanimously, although if a member country wishes to abstain, it does not upset the rule of unanimity. Decisions are binding on a member state, but not until it has complied with the requirements of its own constitutional procedures. If a member state abstains from voting on a decision, it is not bound by that decision; but its abstention does not prevent the decision from binding the other members. Matters to be submitted to the Council are first considered by the Executive Committee, composed of representatives designated annually by the Council. The Executive Committee may also be called upon by the Council to carry out specific tasks, such as to co-ordinate extensive or protracted studies.

Several Committees work under the direction of the Council and the Executive Committee. The Economic Policy Committee keeps under review the economic and financial policies of member countries in order to adapt them to common objectives; the Economic and Development Committee studies the development problems of developing member countries; the Development Assistance Committee compares and improves methods of providing under-developed countries with capital; the Technical Co-operation Committee deals with technical assistance programmes for developing countries; and the Trade Committee studies how world trade can be expanded and national trade policies reconciled. Other committees cover invisible transactions, agriculture and fisheries, industry and energy, manpower, science, technology and education. The Secretariat under the control of the Secretary-General has similar functional divisions.

There are two subsidiary bodies of OECD: the Board of Management which was set up under the European Monetary Agreement (EMA), and the European Nuclear Energy Agency (ENEA).

The Headquarters of the OECD are in Paris.

RELATIONS WITH THE COMMUNITIES

In the early days of the EEC, the Community took part in discussions on the possibility of a European free trade area to link the EEC and the ECSC with the other member states of OEEC. The European Parliament accepted this in principle on 27 June 1958, but the idea was never put into practice.

Subsequent formal relations were founded on the supplementary protocol to the OECD Convention of 30 September 1961, which gave the Commission the right to take part in the work of OECD, and to be a member of the Development Assistance Committee. The provisions of the Supplementary Protocol were more precise than those of Article 231 of the EEC Treaty, specifying not only some of the 'details to be determined by common accord', but also that the Commission was to act as the Community's agent.

The Commission maintains liaison with the OECD at permanent representative level (Director or Director-General). It is represented at most of the meetings of OECD's committees and subsidiary bodies. The finalising of Generalised Tariff Preferences involved the Commission in the work of the Trade Committee. The Commission takes a particularly active part in the affairs of the Development Assistance Committee, and lays before it an annual memorandum giving a summary of EEC technical, financial and food aid to the developing countries during the previous year.

4 The General Agreement on Tariffs and Trade (GATT)

The General Agreement on Tariffs and Trade came into force in January 1948, and by 1971, 78 countries were party to it, while another 15 applied its provisions *de facto*. Apart from Ireland, all the member states of the Communities adhere to the Agreement. The Headquarters of the GATT Secretariat are in Geneva. The main aim of the Agreement is the liberation of world trade from restrictions and controls; it also attempts to encourage economic development and to reduce and stabilise tariffs. The Kennedy Round negotiations completed in June 1967 resulted in an agreement which sought to reduce world industrial tariffs by about one-third by January 1972. Since GATT covers some 80 per cent of world trade, it has become an important forum for the exchange of views as well as for promotion of its aims. In 1964, GATT set up an International Trade Centre, the main aim of which was to assist developing countries in export promotion, and in the running of which UNCTAD[1] has since shared.

Community liaison with GATT is maintained at permanent representative level. The Commission delegation represents the Communities on the GATT committees, such as those on trade in industrial products and on agriculture.

When the EEC came into being in 1958 the member states already accounted for 23 per cent of world trade. It was thus natural that the Community should play an important part in the affairs of GATT. In particular, GATT became a forum for the expression of international views on Community policy.

Just before the formation of OECD in 1961, the Community agreed to extend its first 10 per cent reduction in internal tariffs to all countries party to GATT. This followed the spirit of the rules of the Agreement, which stipulate that any reduction in tariffs must be extended to all Members. A strict interpretation of this would make an organisation such as the EEC incompatible with GATT. However, such a reconciliation is made possible by Article XXIV of the Agreement, which lays down that a free trade area or customs union may be established between two or more countries provided that it covers the bulk of trade between them and that all tariffs and quantitative restrictions are scheduled to be removed by a prior and detailed timetable. The tariff reductions which the Community allowed to the GATT countries as a result of the Kennedy Round were implemented in five instalments, the last beginning on 1 January 1972. The Fifth General Report noted that as a result 'the Community has thus honoured its commitments in GATT with regard to close on 98 per cent of CCT industrial product headings and about 55 per cent of the agricultural product headings, including processed agricultural products'. By the end of 1971, there were 977 tariff headings (920 complete and 57 partial) on which the Community

[1]See page 58.

and the other member countries of GATT applied a common system.

In the early years of the EEC, the rules of GATT tended to dictate the Community's external policy. Thus preferential arrangements not part of a free trade area or customs union were not seriously considered, and the first mooted preferential agreements with Iran and Israel were refused. The growing strength of the Community led to more forthright behaviour; and in recent years aspects of Community external policy have met with strong criticism from some of the countries party to GATT. In 1971 GATT conducted an examination of agreements between the EEC and Spain, and the EEC and Israel, and initiated procedures for the examination of the Arusha agreement, the agreement between the EEC and Malta and the additional protocol to the agreement between the EEC and Turkey.[1] The Fifth General Report noted that 'this general situation gave ample opportunity to those countries which are resolutely opposed to what they call the proliferation of the Community's preferential agreements' to argue that such a process tends towards the formation of economic blocs incompatible with post-war ideas of international co-operation.

The United States Government has been particularly critical of the Community's preferential commercial policy within the framework of GATT. At the 27th Session of the Contracting Parties (November 1971) it was agreed that a programme for the examination of agreements should be drawn up on a two-yearly basis. However, the USA proposal for an evaluation of the effects of preferential trade agreements on a most-favoured-nation system was rejected by the Community. As a result of Community policy towards the Mediterranean citrus-exporting countries, the USA has also invoked the consultation procedure allowed for under Articles XXII and XXIII when the exporters of one country have suffered loss because of the preferential treatment accorded to another country.

The position that emerged as a result of the 27th Session seemed to be that countries sharing the USA's view looked upon the enlargement of the EEC (both by membership and association) as an erosion of their trading rights. The Community position is embodied in a declaration adopted by the Council on 11 December 1971: 'In conformity with the provisions of the General Agreement on Tariffs and Trade, the Community will notify GATT of all adhesion treaties and agreements concluded with the EFTA countries immediately after signature; the negotiations under Article XXIV – 6[2] will be undertaken immediately after ratification'.

Despite some disagreements, the Community has been an active member of GATT. In 1971 the Community played an important part in

---

[1]For details of these Association Agreements see Chapter V.
[2]This Article provides a procedure for ascertaining whether such agreements are compatible with GATT.

the negotiation for the adhesion of Rumania to GATT, and it was at a meeting of the Ministers of GATT that the Community suggestion of generalised tariff preferences for the developing countries was first made.

5 The European Free Trade Association (EFTA)

After the failure of the attempted linking of the EEC with the remaining member states of the then OEEC in a Free Trade Area, the European Free Trade Association was formed in 1959. Its convention came into force on 3 May 1960. The founder-Members were Austria, Denmark, Norway, Portugal, Sweden, Switzerland and the United Kingdom. Finland became an associate member in 1961 and Iceland became a full member of the Association in 1970. EFTA's aims are economic expansion, fair competition and equality of conditions of raw material supply for countries of the Association, and the removal of barriers to world trade. Successive tariff reductions have resulted in the establishment of a near-free trade area, although the fixing of external tariffs is at the discretion of member states. Each state provides one member of the Council whose decisions must normally be unanimous and are binding on member countries.

The problem of future relations between the enlarged Community and those members of EFTA not joining it was the subject of a Commission Opinion of 1 October 1969. The Communiqué issued after the Conference of the Heads of State or Government of the Community at The Hague in December 1969 noted that 'as soon as negotiations with the applicant countries have been opened, discussions will be started with such other EFTA member countries as may request them on their position in relation to the EEC'. From December 1970 to April 1971, exploratory talks were held between the Commission and Switzerland, Sweden, Austria, Finland, Portugal and Iceland; one of the considerations borne in mind was the necessity of retaining the Community's character and power of decision while avoiding the creation of new barriers in intra-European trade.

On 16 June 1971, the Commission submitted to the Council an 'Opinion on the enlarged Community's relations with the EFTA member and associated States not applying for membership'. The opinion offered a choice between maintenance of the status quo for two years and the establishment of free trade arrangements for industrial products with each of the non-applicant countries. These arrangements would not be applied to agricultural products. The non-applicant EFTA countries had asked that close co-operation should not be limited to trade; but the Commission felt that this was undesirable at that time. On 26 July 1971 the Council decided against maintaining the status quo, and as a result on that basis negotiations were opened with the six non-applicant EFTA countries. On 22 July 1972 Special Relations Agreements between the European Communities and each of the non-

E

candidate countries were signed in Brussels.[1] They provided for a transitional period followed by free trade in industrial goods. A slower rate of tariff dismantling was agreed for certain commodities, as for example, paper, some processed foodstuffs and some special steel products. There were no agricultural provisions except in the agreement with Portugal, and in the case of certain special concessions, for example that on Austrian farm produce.

[1]Since Norway had not at this time decided against entry into the Communities, it was not included in these arrangements.

Chapter VII

The relations of the Communities with the United Nations and its specialised agencies

1 General

Co-operation between the European Communities and the various subsidiary bodies of the United Nations has developed in scope as well as intensity. Early work on matters of purely economic, industrial or nuclear energy interest has broadened into activity on social and environmental considerations.

Articles 229 of the EEC Treaty and 199 of the Euratom Treaty declared that the Commission should ensure the maintenance of all appropriate relations with the organs of the United Nations, and of its specialised agencies. Under the wide reference of 'all appropriate relations', mere monitoring of items of Community interest has developed into co-operation and then active participation. This was reflected in the Fourth General Report on the Activities of the Communities (1970) which said that 'the Commission is aware that the Community's internal development is adding to its international responsibilities'.

The Fourth Report of the EEC in 1961 had also noted that relations had 'evolved within the framework of practical arrangements made with the various organs of the United Nations and their Specialised Agencies'. Under these arrangements publications and documents can be exchanged and officials of the Commission can attend meetings organised by the United Nations in the framework of its economic and social activities.

The Communities' particular concern with the Associated African States and Madagascar resulting from an Agreement of Association (the Yaoundé Conventions of 1963 and 1971) has given a recent opportunity of co-operation with the UN on perhaps its major interest, the subject of the developing countries.

2 The United Nations (U N)

The Charter of the UN came into force on 24 October 1945, and was ratified by fifty-one states. In July 1972 there were 132 member states, including all the member states of the Communities apart from the Federal Republic of Germany. The European Headquarters of the UN are in Geneva.

In 1971, efforts were made to find a solution to the problem of how the Community was to participate in the work of the Second of the

General Assembly's seven main committees, that on economic and financial affairs. Following the lack of success at the 26th Session of the General Assembly in 1971, the Council of Ministers gave the European Commission a mandate to pursue the matter further.

Under the authority of the General Assembly is the Economic and Social Council (ECOSOC), which works through commissions and other subsidiary bodies. The subsidiary body of the greatest interest to the European Communities is the Trade and Development Board of the United Nations Conference on Trade and Development, which reports to the General Assembly through the Economic and Social Council.

A distinction should be made between the subsidiary bodies and the specialised agencies. Co-ordination of the agencies, both mutual and with the United Nations, is achieved through the Economic and Social Council, but unlike the subsidiary bodies they have their own memberships, budgets and secretariats. The European Communities have participated in the work of the following agencies:

United Nations Educational, Scientific and Cultural Organisation (UNESCO)

World Health Organisation (WHO)

United Nations Commission on International Trade Law (UNCITRAL)

International Maritime Consultative Organisation (IMCO)

World Meteorological Organisation (WMO)

United Nations Organisation for International Law (UNOIL)

International Atomic Energy Agency (IAEA)

International Labour Organisation (ILO)

Food and Agriculture Organisation (FAO)

The United Nations Industrial Development Organisation (UNIDO) and the United Nations High Commissioner for Refugees (UNHCR) with both of which the Communities have co-operated, are subsidiary bodies of the United Nations. They are under the overall control of the Secretary-General, and have no separate budget. UNHCR has developed increasingly close contacts with the Communities. It is worth noting the separate agreement concluded between the Federal Republic of Germany and UNHCR in the earlier days of the Communities; in October 1960 the Federal Republic established a fund of $10 million with which UNHCR could assist refugees who had been persecuted at the time of the Nazi régime. The fund has since been closed. Under the Second Food Aid Convention, which came into force in July 1971, the Community has a commitment to supply the developing countries with 1,035,000 tons of wheat or coarse grain annually for three years.

The following sections list some of the organisations, both subsidiary bodies and autonomous agencies, with which the Communities' contacts have been formalised or particularly active.

3 The Economic and Social Council (E C O S O C)

The Council is responsible for the economic, social, cultural, educational and health functions of the United Nations. It has six functional Commissions, concerned with such things as Population and Human Rights, and four continental Economic Commissions, including the Economic Commission for Europe (ECE). In July 1972, the Council had 27 members; the proposed enlargement to 54 members, involving an amendment to Article 61 of the UN Charter, was awaiting ratification by the General Assembly. The isolation of Community dealings with ECOSOC is rather artificial in view of the Council's wider co-ordinating role.

Representatives of the European Commission have usually attended meetings of ECOSOC to act as observers and to present the views of the Communities. They have also outlined Community policy on development co-operation. The Fourth General Report on the Activities of the Communities (1970) noted that the Commission had collaborated with ECOSOC on a study of long-term economic forecasts, and, significantly, that 'the ever-growing tendency towards regional economic integration has led many international organisations and, in particular, the regional commissions of ECOSOC to place this problem on the agenda of their meetings'.

4 The Economic Commission for Europe (E C E)

The ECE was established by ECOSOC in 1947, replacing the three emergency European economic organisations. Its aim was 'to initiate and participate in measures for facilitating concerted action for the economic reconstruction of Europe, for raising the level of European economic activity, and for maintaining and strengthening the economic relations of the European countries, both among themselves and with other countries of the world'. Later, the task of supplying governments with economic, technological and statistical analyses and information was added. There were 32 members in July 1972, including all the member states of the Communities; Switzerland, not a member of the United Nations, takes part in an observing and consultative capacity. The Commission has permanent committees on agricultural problems, coal, electric power, gas, inland transport, steel, timber, development of trade, statistics and housing, building and planning. ECE is particularly concerned with the development of East-West trade.

For some time Community representatives (from the Commission) have been taking part in committee meetings, notably in the Development of Trade Committee, but at the 26th annual session of the ECE, a Community representative spoke for the first time to explain the Communities' ideas on common commercial policy and to analyse problems in East-West trade. The Commission, working through ECE, has consistently tried to improve trade relations with Eastern Europe, but has met with opposition from the Soviet Union. In this connection it is worth noting the draft resolution tabled at the 10th Session (March 1971) of the UN Trade and Development Board by a group of Eastern European countries, criticising the Communities for what was described as a discriminatory commercial policy towards the Eastern European countries. At an ECE informal meeting in September 1971, the Community representative answered the queries of Eastern European countries on commercial policies and practices.

The Communities have also participated in the work of the other three economic commissions; those for Latin America (ECLA), Africa (ECA) and Asia and the Far East (ECAFE).

5 The United Nations Conference on Trade and Development (UNCTAD)

In August 1962, ECOSOC decided to convene a UN Conference on Trade and Development. The Conference met in Geneva from March to June 1964, and agreed to set up a permanent organisation to carry out the recommendations it then made. UNCTAD was accordingly established a few months later by a resolution of the UN General Assembly, agreed to on 30 December 1964. The Second Conference met in New Delhi in March 1968, and the Third in Santiago in May 1972. The Commission was represented at both meetings.

Before the Third Conference, the European Parliament debated a report from its Committee on External Trade Relations on possible strategy for the Conference.[1] A resolution was adopted listing subjects to be raised there, noting the necessity for a common Community standpoint, and seeking to stress at the Conference the work already undertaken by the Communities for the economic progress of the developing countries.

As an organ of the General Assembly UNCTAD has no independent budget, although it does have its own secretariat, with permanent headquarters at Geneva. In July 1972 it had 141 members. The Trade and Development Board of UNCTAD normally meets twice a year, and has committees on Manufactures, Commodities, Invisibles and Financing related to Trade, and Shipping. There has been active Community participation in the first two of these.

[1] On 14 March 1962.

The subject of generalised tariff preferences is of particular interest. The member states of the EEC and the Associated States took the initiative in raising the idea of preferences at the meeting of the Ministers of GATT in 1963. Preliminary agreement on preferences for manufactures and semi-finished goods from the developing countries was subsequently reached in the Special Committee on Preferences established by UNCTAD, on which the European Commission was represented. This agreement was later endorsed by the Trade and Development Board of UNCTAD and ratified by the UN General Assembly in December 1970. The European Parliament expressed its approval of generalised tariff preferences in a resolution passed on 6 October 1970 and approval of detailed measures designed to implement preferences was embodied in a further resolution of 9 June 1971. The measures themselves were adopted by the Council of Ministers of the Communities at the session of 21 and 22 June 1971.

In its Fifth General Report on the activities of the Communities in 1971 (paragraph 455) the European Commission said that the Community decisions on the implementation of tariff preferences demonstrated the spirit animating the Community and the member states in their relations with the Third World, and Sr. Malfatti, the Commission's President, said that this step should be thought of as only the beginning of an even more active policy towards world development problems. M. Maurice Schumann, the French Foreign Minister, has described agreement in the field of generalised tariff preferences as the most important step in commercial policy since the conclusion of the Kennedy Round. Implementation of tariff preferences seems likely to play an important part in the United Nations Second Development Decade. Community representatives also took an active part in the Committee for Development Planning (the Tinbergen Committee) and sat as observers on the Preparatory Committee for the Second Development Decade.

The active part taken by the Community in the Trade and Development Board was illustrated at the 10th Session of the Board (March 1971) by the energetic refutation of the criticisms of the Eastern European countries alleging that discriminatory policies had been practised against them by the Communities.

The Communities have participated in some of the international agreements and consultation sponsored by UNCTAD with the aim of securing an international commodity policy. Among these have been the International Coffee Agreement of 1968, followed by representation in an observing capacity on the Executive Committee of the International Coffee Council, and the International Tin Agreements (starting in 1966), a renewal of which was signed on 27 January 1971. An important aspect of this Fourth Agreement was the Commission's negotiation of it for the Communities as a whole; previously the member states had negotiated on their own. In 1971 the Commission pressed for an international agreement on cocoa, and a Commission representative has recently been a member of the Food and Agriculture Organisation's working party on the possibility of an International Tea Agreement. The Communities have so far been unable to participate in the International Sugar Agreement as its terms have proved incompatible with internal Community economic policies.

6 The International Labour Organisation (I L O)

The ILO was founded in 1919 as an autonomous agency attached to the League of Nations, but became the first specialised agency of the United Nations in 1946. By July 1972 it had 123 members including all members of the Communities. Its aim is the promotion of peace through social justice, and annexed to its constitution is the Declaration of Philadelphia adopted by the International Labour Conference in 1944, part of which reads 'all human beings, irrespective of race, creed or sex, have the right to pursue both their material well-being and their spiritual development in conditions of freedom and dignity, of economic security and equal opportunity'.

The organisation consists of representatives of governments, employers and labour. The deliberative body, the International Conference, meets annually at the ILO headquarters in Geneva. The European Commission takes part in these sessions. There is an EEC-ILO Contact Committee which ensures continuity of co-operation between the two organisations. An annual financial contribution is made by the Communities to the International Institute for Labour Studies and to the International Safety Centre. The ILO has given technical assistance to the EEC Administration Committee for the Social Security of Migrant Workers. The Communities have participated in the work of the International Confederation on Social Welfare, the International Social Security Association, the International Association for Mutual Assistance, and the International Housing Committee. Under an agreement between the Commission and the ILO, the Commission participates in the work of the International Centre for Advanced Technical and Vocational Training in Turin.

7 The International Atomic Energy Agency (I A E A)

The Agency was set up on 29 July 1957; according to its Statute its aims are to 'seek to accelerate and enlarge the contribution of atomic energy to peace, health and prosperity throughout the world'. The Statute goes on to say that assistance provided by the IAEA shall not be used for any military purpose, which recalls the aims of Euratom. The Commission is represented at the Annual General Conference, which is held at the IAEA headquarters in Vienna. In 1969 a contract was concluded between the Commission and the Agency for the launching of the International Nuclear Information System (INIS). The Fourth General Report of the Communities described the results as 'satisfactory'. In 1970, the IAEA General Conference decided to enlarge the IAEA Board of Governors from 25 to 33 countries. The Fourth General Report observed that this would give the non-nuclear members of the Communities more say.

At the 15th General Conference in September 1971, it was announced that the Council of Ministers had given a mandate to the Commission to negotiate an agreement on guarantees with the IAEA concerning the application of Article III of the Nuclear Non-Proliferation Treaty. Paragraph 1 of Article III lays down that all control and checks on nuclear installations shall be the responsibility of the IAEA. Under the terms of the Euratom Treaty, such controls have been under the authority of Euratom. All the members of the Communities except for France signed the Nuclear Non-Proliferation Treaty in 1970, but ratification will not take place until negotiations between the Commission and the Agency ensure that Article III will respect the provisions of the Euratom Treaty.

Chapter VIII

The Parliament's links with the Council of Europe, Western European Union and the North Atlantic Assembly

The relations of the European Parliament with the Consultative Assembly of the Council of Europe, the Assembly of Western European Union and the North Atlantic Assembly have a substantial impact on its own practice and procedure, partly because its Members may be or have been members of the three other Assemblies, and partly because in the case of the Consultative Assembly, an annual joint meeting is held with the European Parliament in the House of Europe at Strasbourg.

Before these relations are described in more detail, it will be convenient to refer to the institutional framework of the three Assemblies.

1 The Council of Europe

The Council of Europe was formed in 1949, on the recommendation of a Committee appointed by the Brussels Treaty Consultative Council 'to consider and report to Governments on the steps to be taken towards securing a greater measure of unity between European countries'. The signatories (United Kingdom, France, Belgium, Netherlands, Luxembourg) of the Brussels Treaty of 1948 invited Denmark, Italy, Ireland, Norway and Sweden to confer with them in drafting a constitution; and Austria, Iceland, the Federal Republic of Germany, Greece, Malta, Turkey, Cyprus and Switzerland were later invited to become Members, bringing the number of member states of the Council of Europe to eighteen.[1]

The Council of Europe differed from the Communities of the Six (Belgium, France, the Federal Republic of Germany, Italy, Luxembourg and the Netherlands) in the width of its membership and its general interest in all forms and fields of non-military co-operation. Its principal aim is set out in Article 1 of the Statute of the Council of Europe, which was signed in London in May 1949.

Article 1 states that

'(a) the aim of the Council of Europe is to achieve a greater unity between its members for the purpose of safeguarding and realising the ideals and principles which are their common heritage and facilitating their economic and social progress.

'(b) This aim shall be pursued through the organs of the Council by

---

[1] Greece was suspended from membership in December 1970 so that there are now only seventeen members.

discussion of questions of common concern and by agreements and common action in economic, social, cultural, scientific, legal and administrative matters and in the maintenance and further realisation of human rights and fundamental freedoms.'

The conditions for membership of the Council of Europe are set out in Article 3 of the Statute. Every member state must accept the principles of individual freedom, political liberty and the rule of law as the basis of its internal policy. Strasbourg is named in the Statute as the seat of the Council and has been the meeting place of the Assembly since its inauguration.

The Council of Europe is constituted with the following governmental and parliamentary bodies:

THE COMMITTEE OF MINISTERS

The Committee of Ministers is composed of one representative from each member state, and that representative is the Minister for Foreign Affairs or an alternate 'nominated to act for him, who shall whenever possible, be a member of his Government'. The Chairmanship of the Committee of Ministers is held in turn by its members.

According to Article 21 of the Statute, the Committee of Ministers must meet 'before, and during the beginning of, every session of the Consultative Assembly and at such other times as it may decide'. In addition to this regular meeting, the Committee of Ministers may meet at any other time, if requested to do so by any of its members or by the Secretary-General, provided that two-thirds of the members agree. In practice the Committee of Ministers meets twice a year. The Chairman fixes the exact date, after consulting the members of the Committee.

Under Article 13 of the Statute, the Committee of Ministers is 'the organ which acts on behalf of the Council of Europe'. The Committee of Ministers' executive function is largely complementary to the deliberative function of the Assembly. Under Article 15 (a) of the Statute, the Committee has the duty of considering, either on the recommendation of the Assembly or on its own initiative, the action required to further the aim of the Council of Europe. Such action includes the conclusion of conventions or agreements, and the adoption by Governments of a common policy with regard to particular matters. The Committee of Ministers is empowered to make recommendations to member governments, and subsequently to enquire what action has been taken on its recommendations. Such recommendations, being put forward by eighteen Foreign Ministers, are authoritative, but they are not binding on governments.

The Committee of Ministers approves the budget of the Council, and allocates its expenditure between member states in proportion to their population.

Under Article 20 of the Statute, decisions of the Committee of Ministers require unanimity for certain important matters, including the adoption of recommendations to governments and the amendment of certain fundamental articles of the Statute. Questions arising under the Rules of Procedure or under the Financial and Administrative Regulations may be decided by a simple majority and other questions by a majority of two-thirds. The Committee rarely takes decisions by majority vote. It has preferred the course of endeavouring to reach unanimous agreement on the subjects under discussion, in order that its decisions might gain a ready acceptance by every member State.

To maintain and facilitate contact between the Council of Europe and the governments of member states, the Committee of Ministers in 1951 agreed to a resolution enabling member States to be permanently represented at the seat of the Council. Since that date each government has appointed a permanent representative to act as Minister's Deputy.

For expert advice, the Committee of Ministers relies on a number of expert Committees dealing with the various aspects of the Council's work, such as cultural affairs, social affairs, crime problems, public health and legal affairs.

The agenda of the Committee of Ministers is made up of Recommendations, Opinions, and certain Resolutions of the Consultative Assembly; reports of committees of experts; questions put forward by a Minister on behalf of his government; and administrative and financial proposals concerning the working of the Council of Europe, submitted by the Secretary General of the Council.

Although the Committee of Ministers has the power either to accept or to reject recommendations of the Assembly, it has to give, in annual reports to the Assembly prepared in accordance with Article 19 of the Statute, 'statements of its activities' and therefore of the action it has taken on the proposals put forward by the Assembly. This Report is now presented once a year, normally at the spring part-session by the Chairman of the Committee of Ministers, who then answers oral questions on it. This is followed by a debate on the report.

THE CONSULTATIVE ASSEMBLY

The Consultative Assembly is the parliamentary institution of the Council of Europe. Ordinary sessions are held every year, and are usually divided into three part-sessions, each lasting for about one week. The Assembly is a deliberative body, but the Committee of Ministers may give effect to its recommendations.

(i) Representation

The Consultative Assembly consists of 140 Representatives from seventeen nations, with a President elected by the Assembly annually from among their number. The number of Representatives from each of the first ten member States was laid down in the Statute, and subsequently when a country has been invited by the Committee of Ministers to become a member, the number of Representatives which it is entitled to send has been indicated in the letter of invitation. Generally speaking the entitlement to Representatives is roughly in proportion to the member States' population; but no state has fewer than three Representatives, in order to enable as many political parties as possible to be represented. A member of the Committee of Ministers is disqualified from membership of the Consultative Assembly.

In 1972, the number of Representatives was Austria 6, Belgium 7, Cyprus 3, Denmark 5, France 18, Federal Republic of Germany 18, Iceland 3, Republic of Ireland 4, Italy 18, Luxembourg 3, Malta 3, Netherlands 7, Norway 5, Sweden 6, Switzerland 6, Turkey 10, United Kingdom 18. Since 1951, the United Kingdom Representatives have been appointed annually by the Prime Minister, after consultation with the political parties, and broadly reflect the comparative party strengths.

Credentials of Representatives and substitutes must be in the hands of the Secretary General not later than a week before the opening of a session.

A Representative's term of office expires at the beginning of the ordinary session after that in respect of which he was appointed. If a Representative loses his seat in his national Parliament, the governments of member states have authority in terms of the Statute to make a fresh appointment, if they wish to do so. There is also authority to make new appointments to fill vacancies caused by death or resignation.

A Representative who is prevented from attending a sitting of the Assembly may be replaced by a substitute of the same nationality. Substitutes are appointed in the same manner as Representatives, they are subject to the same disqualifications, and in the absence of a Representative a substitute may sit, speak and vote in his place and enjoy the same rights in the Assembly. Substitute Representatives may be full members of committees.

(ii) *Powers of the Consultative Assembly*

The general competence of the Consultative Assembly extends to the discussion of any matter within the scope of the Council of Europe and the Assembly may thereafter agree to an Opinion or a Resolution, or make a Recommendation.

Communications to the Assembly, whether from the Committee of Ministers or from any other body, and motions tabled by Representatives are normally referred to the appropriate committee before being debated in the Assembly. Debate subsequently takes place on the report of the Committee and the Draft Recommendations, Opinions or Resolutions it contains.

(iii) *Languages*

The official languages of the Assembly are English and French; all its documents are produced in these two languages. Speeches in the Assembly, however, may be made in German and Italian. Simultaneous interpretation is provided from French, German and Italian into English, and from German, Italian and English into French. The Assembly is laid out in a half circle. Representatives normally speak from their own places. There is a 'tribune' on the continental pattern which is reserved for Ministers who wish to address the Assembly and for other speakers who are not members of the Assembly.

(iv) *Political groups*

Seating in the Assembly is arranged in alphabetical order with the aim of preventing Representatives from sitting in national delegations, and the formation of political groups amongst the whole body has made possible to a limited degree the development of European, non-national shades of opinion on political questions. The Christian Democrat, Socialist, Liberal and right-wing 'Independent' groups have gained recognition as such, and suitable arrangements have been made for them during the Session.

(v) *Committees*

At the beginning of each ordinary Session, the Assembly appoints thirteen general committees which have the duty of considering and making reports on the main categories of Assembly business. General committees include those on political affairs, economic affairs and development. Special committees may be appointed for specific purposes. The representation of member states on committees is roughly proportionate to their representation in the Assembly. At the same time as it nominates Representatives to committees, the Assembly also nominates an alternate for each member.

Committees sit in private. Committees and Sub-Committees have met between sessions or part-sessions at Strasbourg and in many other cities of member states.

(vi) *Contacts between the Assembly and Committee of Ministers*

The President of the Assembly has access to meetings of the Committee of Ministers as spokesman of the Assembly. In addition a Joint Committee co-ordinates the activities of the Assembly and the Committee of Ministers.

(vii) *Relations between the Assembly and national parliaments*

One of the general committees appointed sessionally by the Assembly is the Committee on Parliamentary and Public Relations which selects texts for transmission to national Parliaments from among those adopted by the Assembly. Each national delegation is represented on the Committee; and in addition spokesmen are appointed to bear responsibility for relations between national parliamentary delegations and the Committee in all questions concerning links between the Assembly and national Parliaments. The Secretariat regularly publishes information on the action taken in support of Assembly texts in national Parliaments.

2 Western European Union

The Assembly of the international organisation known as Western European Union has a close relationship with the Council of Europe since its entire membership is composed of the Representatives from the seven WEU countries to the Consultative Assembly.

THE COUNCIL OF WEU

Protocols modifying and extending the Brussels Treaty of 1948 for military and defensive purposes were signed in Paris in October 1954 by seven Western European Governments, viz.: Belgium, France, the Federal Republic of Germany, Italy, Luxembourg, the Netherlands and the United Kingdom. These Protocols provided for the creation of the Council of Western European Union which superseded the Consultative Council of the Brussels Treaty Organisation.

The Council of Western European Union was directed to establish an Agency for the Control of Armaments and was given new powers of decision by majority vote in this field.

The Council meets at either Ministerial level composed of the seven Foreign Ministers, or, more frequently, at Ambassadorial level, composed of the Ambassadors in London of the six continental countries, and a representative of the same rank from the British Foreign Office. At Ministerial level, the chairmanship of the Council is held by each country in turn for three months, in alphabetical rotation. At Ambassadorial level, the Secretary General of WEU is the permanent Chairman.

The Chairman of the Council is regularly invited to make an oral presentation of the Council's annual report to the Assembly. He may reply to matters raised in the general debate on the report which follows his presentation. The Council may receive questions from Representatives in writing on any matter which is relevant to the Brussels Treaty, or which has been submitted to the Assembly for an Opinion.

THE ASSEMBLY OF WEU

(i) *Representation*

Under the revised Brussels Treaty (see above) the Council of WEU 'shall make an annual report on its activities, and in particular concerning the control of armaments, to an Assembly composed of Representatives of the Brussels Treaty Powers in the Consultative Assembly of the Council of Europe'. The Assembly of Western European Union is composed of the same Representatives of the seven Brussels Treaty Powers as those appointed to the Consultative Assembly of the Council of Europe. Substitutes appointed for Representatives to the Consultative Assembly may replace those Representatives in the WEU Assembly, should the latter be prevented from attending a meeting of that Assembly.

The Assembly normally meets in the chamber of the French Economic and Social Council in Paris. The term of office of Representatives and substitutes takes effect from the ratification of their credentials in the Consultative Assembly. Where the WEU Assembly meets prior to the beginning of a Consultative Assembly session, the term of office dates from the appointment of the Representative or substitute by the member state; and it is subject to subsequent ratification of credentials by the Consultative Assembly. The term of office ends in accordance with the rules of the Consultative Assembly.

The Assembly must meet at least once, and in practice meets twice during each calendar year; the President may also convene extraordinary sessions either on his own initiative or at the request of the Council or of at least a quarter of the Representatives.

(ii) *Powers of the Assembly*

Under the terms of its Charter, the WEU Assembly carries out the parliamentary function arising from the application of the Brussels Treaty. The Charter authorises the Assembly to proceed on any matter arising out of the Brussels Treaty and upon any matter submitted to the Assembly for an Opinion by the Council.

The Assembly may make Recommendations or transmit Opinions to the Council or adopt resolutions on matters within its competence. Discussions of such matters by the Assembly usually takes place on the report of the relevant committee.

The WEU Assembly is a consultative body and has no power to overthrow the Council of Ministers, the executive organ to which it is related. It is, however, empowered by its Charter to adopt a motion under a special procedure to disagree to the content of a report from the Council of WEU.

The draft budget of the Assembly is prepared in committee, considered by the Assembly, and then transmitted to the Council for approval. The Assembly may thereafter express its views on the approved budget, when it has been communicated to the Assembly.

(iii) *Committees*

The Assembly is directed by the Statute to set up four committees—Defence Questions and Armaments, General Affairs, Budgetary Affairs and Administration, and Rules of Procedure and Privileges. Other committees may be appointed as necessary and committees have been set up on Scientific, Technology and Aerospace Questions, and for Relations with Parliaments. Besides examining questions and documents referred to them by the Assembly, committees are also required to examine any action taken on Recommendations and Resolutions adopted by the Assembly.

The number of Representatives and alternates on each committee is limited according to a formula which takes account of the size of national delegations.

(iv) *Languages*

Speeches in the Assembly or its committees may be made in the official language of any of the member states. Documents are published in English and French.

(v) *Relations with the Consultative Assembly*

In view of the wide character of some of the provisions of the revised Brussels Treaty, co-operation between the WEU Assembly and the Consultative Assembly of the Council of Europe was clearly necessary to define the competence of each and to avoid overlapping both in the field of defence and in the cultural and social work which Western European Union had inherited when it assumed control of the Brussels Treaty Organisation.

On matters of defence the two Assemblies agreed in October 1956 that no report should be transmitted by the WEU Assembly to the Consultative Assembly because such an action might cause difficulties in view of the terms of the Statute of the Council of Europe. It was also agreed that both Assemblies should limit their activities in debating defence matters, the Consultative Assembly to military questions, possibly with related political implications. However, the creation of the Common Market resulted in the political debates of the WEU Assembly extending into the field of relations between Britain and the Six Powers which originally formed that community.

In 1959 the Committee of Ministers decided to transfer to the Council of Europe the social and cultural work of Western European Union in order to avoid overlapping in the activities of the two organisations.

3 The North Atlantic Assembly

The NATO Parliamentarians held their first conference in 1955. From

F

this beginning the North Atlantic Assembly, the forum for parliamentarians of NATO member states has developed. The North Atlantic
Assembly, unlike similar bodies previously mentioned in this chapter,
has no statutory basis as the official consultative organ of the related
intergovernmental organisation. On the other hand, links between the
Assembly and the North Atlantic Treaty Organisation (NATO) have
been strengthened; and in particular the North Atlantic Council
(the highest authority of NATO) examines and comments on the recommendations and resolutions of the Assembly. The Assembly's expenses
are met by the governments of the delegates involved, as also are those
of the delegates themselves in the same way as for the other two
Assemblies previously mentioned.

As the North Atlantic Treaty of 1949 not only brought into being a
military alliance, but also committed the signatories to developing
political, economic, social and cultural co-operation among themselves,
so the aims of the North Atlantic Assembly are to strengthen understanding and co-operation among the member States of NATO.

The North Atlantic Assembly meets annually.

MEMBERSHIP

The Assembly is composed of delegates from the national Parliaments
of the fifteen member states. There is no limit to the size of the dele-
gations, but voting strengths are restricted. The Member nations with
their current voting strengths are Belgium 7, Canada 12, Denmark 5,
France 18, Federal Republic of Germany 18, Iceland 3, Italy 18,
Luxembourg 3, Netherlands 7, Norway 5, Portugal 5, Turkey 10,
United States of America 36, United Kingdom 18. The membership of
Greece has been suspended. The United Kingdom delegation is ap-
pointed by the Lord Chancellor and the Speaker of the House of
Commons.

STRUCTURE

The North Atlantic Assembly meeting in its annual plenary session
appoints a President for the ensuing session from among the delegates.
The Assembly hears addresses by Ministers and leading representatives
of Atlantic and European organisations; it debates and adopts reports
and recommendations made by its committees, and may forward them
to NATO Member governments and to the North Atlantic Council and
other intergovernmental organisations.

There are at present five committees – Political, Military, Economic,
Scientific and Technical, and Education, Cultural Affairs and Information. Sub-Committees may also be appointed. Committees meet normally at the time of plenary sessions, and at other times during the year.

In addition, the Assembly appoints a Standing Committee, composed
of one delegate from each member state. This committee is responsible

for policy decisions, for assigning working programmes to other committees, and for arranging the organisation and agenda of plenary sessions.

The official languages of the Assembly are English and French.

4 Formal links of the European Parliament and the Communities with the Council of Europe

Relations between the European Coal and Steel Community and the Council of Europe are governed by a Protocol to the Treaty setting up the Community signed on 18 April 1951. As a result of the provisions of this Protocol the Common Assembly and subsequently the European Parliament have made an annual report to the Consultative Assembly on their activities. At the beginning of every Session of the Parliament, a Rapporteur is appointed to prepare this report. When approved by the Parliament it is sent to the President of the Consultative Assembly in accordance with Rule 52 of the Rules of Procedure of the European Parliament.

Under another provision of the Protocol the High Authority submitted an annual report on its work to the Committee of Ministers and the Consultative Assembly. Members of the High Authority have appeared before the Consultative Assembly's Economic Committee, and Committees of the Consultative Assembly and the High Authority have exchanged observers. The Committee of Ministers of the Council of Europe and the High Authority on occasion held joint meetings to discuss common problems.

When the European Economic Community and Euratom were set up in pursuance of the Treaties of Rome, the Foreign Ministers of the six member states made clear their desire for the closest links both between the new Communities and the Council of Europe and between their respective Assemblies. Article 230 of the EEC Treaty and Article 200 of the Euratom Treaty themselves expressly provide that 'the Community shall co-operate with the Council of Europe whenever desirable'.

The Consultative Assembly and the Committee of Ministers of the Council of Europe expressed their views in the same sense[1] and instructed the Secretary General to examine with representatives of the Communities how to make relations closer.

As a result, arrangements for collaboration (other than for joint meetings of the two Assemblies described below) were made with the Commissions of both Communities. The Commissions and the Committee of Ministers have exchanged the reports which they are by treaty and Statute respectively required to prepare; and copies of the Com-

---

[1]Consultative Assembly's Recommendation 146 (1957) and Resolution 130 (1957); Committee of Ministers' Resolution (57) 27.

missions' reports are also sent to the Consultative Assembly. The official reports of the debates of the Consultative Assembly on European economic integration have also been transmitted to the Commissions. The Committee of Ministers must invite the Commissions to take part in discussion at the level of Ministers, on problems of mutual interest; and similarly the experts of the Commissions may meet with the governmental experts of the Council of Europe or the members of its Secretariat to exchange views on matters of common concern.

Since the merger of the Commissions of EEC and Euratom and the High Authority of ECSC, these arrangements for collaboration have in practice been continued with the new Commission, though no formal instrument of collaboration has been made.

5 Joint meetings of Members of the European Parliament and Representatives of the Consultative Assembly

At the first meeting of the Common Assembly of the ECSC in September 1952 several representatives proposed that British Members of Parliament should be invited to attend its meetings as observers. This proposal was referred for an opinion to three independent jurists who concluded that within the parliamentary structure of the Common Assembly there could be no legal justification for the presence of observers.

To overcome this difficulty Mr. Monnet, then President of the High Authority, and Lord Layton, then a Vice-President of the Consultative Assembly, proposed that joint meetings of Members of the Common Assembly and of Representatives of the Consultative Assembly should be held. This proposal was accepted by the two Assemblies.

The first joint meeting was held at Strasbourg on 22 June 1953, and joint meetings were held each of the four following years until 1957. No joint meeting was held in 1958, the year in which the EEC and Euratom Treaties came into force.

The first joint meeting between Representatives of the Consultative Assembly and of Members of the European Parliament was held on 16 and 17 January 1959; it was the first to last for more than one day. Joint meetings have been held in every year since 1959 and have usually lasted for one or two days.

PROCEDURE AT A JOINT MEETING

The procedure followed at a joint meeting was originally devised by the Clerk of the Consultative Assembly and the Secretary General of the Common Assembly of the ECSC, after consultation between the Bureaux of the two Assemblies. It is still used for joint meetings of Representatives of the Consultative Assembly and of Members of the European Parliament. The procedure which has been used since 1953 is as follows:

(i) Representatives attending a joint meeting who are members of both bodies cannot be replaced as members of the Consultative Assembly by their substitutes.

(ii) The object of a joint meeting being to allow a free exchange of views, no agenda is distributed and no vote is taken.

(iii) The Chair is taken alternately by the Presidents of the Parliament and of the Common Assembly.

(iv) The Rules of Procedure are those of the Consultative Assembly. Secretarial services for the joint meetings are provided by the two Secretariats in collaboration.

(v) The Clerk to the Consultative Assembly with his staff sits on the right of the President-in-Office. The Clerk and staff of the European Parliament sit on the President's left.

(vi) The report of the debates of the joint meetings are published in accordance with the practice observed for the debates of the European Parliament: every speech is set out *in extenso* and the report is published in five languages.

(vii) The corrected and definitive report of these debates is printed by agreement between the two Secretariats and published in five languages.

SUBJECTS OF DEBATE

Since 1963 it has been the practice of the two Assemblies at their annual joint meetings to debate a subject of interest to both bodies. The subject is agreed upon by their respective Bureaux. At the meeting held on 8 June 1971, for example, the subject chosen was 'the function of an enlarged Community in the European context'. At the session, four reports were presented, two by the Rapporteurs of the Political Affairs Committee and the Committee on Economic Affairs and Development of the Consultative Assembly and two by the Rapporteurs of the Political Committee and Committee on External Trade Relations of the European Parliament. The European Parliament, following its usual practice, also submitted a report to the Consultative Assembly on its activities during the previous year.

Before 1963, debate at joint meetings was largely restricted to the reports made by the European Parliament and by the Communities, and related subjects which could only have a limited interest for the members of the European Parliament. The selection of a more generally interesting theme resulted from an agreement between the Presidents of the two Assemblies.

PARTICIPATION BY THE COMMISSION

At the joint meeting in June 1971, in accordance with the usual practice, the Commission of the Communities was represented by its President and Vice-President. M. Malfatti, the President of the Commission, contributed to the debate. The Committee of Ministers of the Council of Europe has not been represented at the joint meeting since September 1961.

6 Other links with the Council of Europe and with Western European Union

There are several other ways in which the Parliament and the Consultative Assembly are brought into contact. Not least of these is their common heritage and origins, the European Coal and Steel Community growing out of initiatives partly sponsored by the Council of Europe. A further point of contact between the Consultative Assembly and the Parliament is their common meeting place for plenary sessions, the House of Europe at Strasbourg.

On the other hand, there has been little or no formal contact between the European Parliament and the Assembly of WEU. In two ways, however, informal relations exist. First the Members of the Parliament, being members of national legislatures, may also have been nominated to serve concurrently on their national delegation to the Assemblies of the Council of Europe and WEU. Other Members of Parliament may have previously served on the delegation to the two Assemblies. Conversely, Representatives of the two assemblies may formerly have been Members of the Parliament. A second point of contact between the Parliament and the Assemblies has been the liaison of the Secretariats. Members of the Secretariats may attend as observers at meetings of the other bodies.

7 Relations between the Parliament and the North Atlantic Assembly

The European Parliament has no formal relations or regular contacts with the North Atlantic Assembly. Because of the importance of Atlantic economic co-operation, however, some Members of the Parliament and its secretariat have developed an *ad hoc* interest in the work of the North Atlantic Assembly.

Eight of the nine member states of the enlarged Communities take part in the activities of the Assembly, to which the United States and Canada also belong. There is also some overlapping of the national delegations to the Parliament and to the North Atlantic Assembly from the parliaments of Community member states. Several influential members of the Parliament have also been members of the Assembly.[1] Furthermore, the Secretariat of the Parliament customarily sends

[1]In 1972 Herr Lange, the Chairman of the Economic Committee of the European Parliament and Mr. Van der Stoel, Rapporteur of the North Atlantic Assembly's Political Committee, were members of both bodies.

observers to the meetings of the North Atlantic Assembly and its Committees, especially the Economic Committee.

In March 1972, the Standing Committee of the North Atlantic Assembly considered a proposal that the Assembly and its committees should pursue the possibility of greater co-operation between the enlarged Communities and North America, since the Assembly was the only parliamentary body apart from the Inter-Parliamentary Union in which both spheres were represented.

Part III

Procedure of the
European Parliament

Chapter IX

Constitution of the Parliament and status of its Members

The European Parliament consists of a number of Members from the parliaments of member states of the European Communities with a President elected each year from amongst those Members. The European Parliament is able to decide its own agenda according to the procedures laid down in its Rules of Procedure and may pass resolutions on any matter falling within the sphere of activities of the three Communities. In practice the Parliament frequently considers other matters falling outside the strict limits of the Treaties. The Parliament is also charged by Article 137 of the Treaty of Rome with exercising the advisory and supervisory powers which are conferred upon it by the ~~President elected each year from amongst those Members. The Euro-~~ Treaty, and to this end it is consulted by the Council of Ministers on the legislative proposals of the Commission. In addition, the European Parliament possesses certain powers in respect of the Community budget and, unlike many national parliaments, enjoys budgetary autonomy in respect of its own administrative expenditure. During periods when the Parliament is not sitting the Bureau (see pp. 86–92) or the enlarged Bureau may, in accordance with the Rules of Procedure of the Parliament, act on behalf of its Members.

1 Number of Members

The development and enlargement of membership of the Communities has been described in Chapter I. The number of representatives in the Common Assembly of the European Coal and Steel Community for each of the six original member states was laid down in Article 21 (2) of the ECSC Treaty. This was superseded in 1957 when the number of Members of the Assembly was increased under Article 138 (2) of the EEC Treaty and Article 108 (2) of the Euratom Treaty from 78 to 142. The result of the changes was that the representation of France, the Federal Republic of Germany and Italy was doubled and that of Belgium, the Netherlands and Luxembourg increased to a smaller extent.

Under the arrangements laid down in Article 10 of the Act of Accession annexed to the Treaty of Accession, the representation of the six original member states in the Parliament remains the same. The present number of Members from each of the member states is as follows:

Belgium .	.	.	.	14
Denmark	.	.	.	10

Germany	.	.	.	36
France	.	.	.	36
Ireland	.	.	.	10
Italy	.	.	.	36
Luxembourg	.	.		6
Netherlands	.	.		14
United Kingdom	.	.		36
Total membership	.	.		198[1]

The number of Members in each delegation is not decided in strict mathematical proportion to the size of the population of each country. It varies roughly according to population, but no country has fewer than six members to enable even the smallest state to have a delegation representative of all its principal political parties. The smaller countries, therefore, are allotted a number of seats larger than they would have on a strictly proportional basis. The four largest countries each have equal representation, although their populations vary somewhat in size.

2 Appointment and terms of office

Members are appointed to the Parliament in accordance with the procedure laid down in the Treaties establishing the Communities. The Treaty of Rome provides that the European Parliament shall consist of delegates who shall be designated by the respective Parliaments from among their Members in accordance with the procedure laid down by each member state (Article 138 (1)).

The Treaty of Rome also instructed the European Parliament to draw up proposals for elections by direct universal suffrage in accordance with a uniform procedure in all member states. The Council, acting unanimously, was to lay down the appropriate provisions which it would recommend to member states for adoption in accordance with their respective constitutional requirements (Article 138 (3)).

The Parliament adopted a draft convention on 17 May 1960, in compliance with the provisions of the first paragraph of Article 138 (3). The Council of Ministers, however, has not yet taken any action on this. Consequently the representatives of the peoples of the member states are still drawn from among the members of national parliaments according to the procedure which each thinks fit.

Rule 4 of the Rules of Procedure lays down certain limits to the term of office of a Member. He holds office from the time of his appointment conferred upon him by his national parliament and may continue to do so until the expiry of his appointment. Appointments are made by the national parliaments of member states for differing lengths of time according to their prevailing law or practice. The terms of office of Members have also been cut short by death; on resignation submitted

[1]The Act of Accession also provides for a delegation of 10 Members from Norway.

to the President of the Parliament; on disqualification by the European Parliament; or on a Member losing his seat in his national parliament.

Because of political difficulties in Italy, its delegation to the European Parliament was not re-nominated between 1961 and 1969 despite two national elections having taken place in that time. Consequently, the delegation included some Members who had lost their seats in the Italian Parliament. As a result of this anomaly, the European Parliament passed a resolution on 11 March 1969 that any Member losing his seat in his national parliament could continue to sit in the European Parliament only until the appointment of his successor or until the expiry of a maximum period of six months, provided that his original appointment from his national parliament had not expired. This provision is now incorporated as Rule 4 (2) of the Rules of Procedure.

Within the conditions established by the Treaty of Rome and the Rules of Procedure, the parliaments of member states nominate Members of the Parliament in various ways. In the Parliament of the six member states, Belgium and Italy took their delegations equally from their two Houses; France and the Netherlands predominantly from their lower Houses but with their Upper Houses represented; and Germany only from the Lower House, the Bundestag.[1] All Luxembourg Members came from the Chamber of Deputies since it is a unicameral Parliament.

3 Political Groups

The balance of political parties within each national delegation in general reflects the proportions in which the parties sit in their national parliament although it is left to each member country to appoint its own delegation in the manner it considers appropriate. For many years no communist members were appointed although in both Italy and France on a proportional basis the communist party might have had several members. In 1969, however, seven communists were appointed to the Italian delegation together with two allied members. The French communists are still not represented.

On 21 March 1958 a resolution of the Parliament at its constituent meeting provided that Members of the Parliament should sit with the political groups to which they belonged. Within each group Members sit in alphabetical order but with the bureau of the group at the head. The groups in general transcend national boundaries. Only one group is composed of members of one country only, the European Democratic Union being composed solely of French Members. The Bureau of the Parliament decides the place of seating in the chamber of the various political groups and of the members of the Commission and Council of the Communities.

In accordance with Rule 36 of the Rules of Procedure, a political

[1]The Bundestag is the only elective Chamber of the German Federal Parliament. The Bundesrat is composed of representatives of the *Land* Governments.

group must consist of at least fourteen members. To establish a group its members must submit to the President a statement giving the name of the group, the signatures of its members and the composition of its Bureau. No member may belong to more than one group. The statement is published in the Official Journal of the Communities.

Originally the number of members required to establish a political group was set at seventeen. After a report prepared by M. Weinkamm (Doc. 118/1964–65), the Parliament voted by resolution on 20 January 1965 to amend the rule so that thereafter only fourteen members were required.

Since the early sessions of the Parliament, progress has been made towards the development of different shades of European opinion on Community questions, irrespective of often conflicting policies of member governments. Membership of the groups is of course not compulsory. In April 1972, in the Parliament of the six member countries comprising 142 Members, the following groups existed:[1]

Christian Democrats . .	50
Socialists . . .	37
Liberals and Allies . .	22
European Democratic Union .	19

In addition there were eleven unattached Members who belonged to no political group. Nine of these Members were communists or their allies who were not, on their own, sufficiently numerous to constitute a separate group. The membership of groups is set out in a handbook (known as the *Vademecum*) issued by the Parliament from time to time.

In 1958, at the beginning of the life of the Parliament, three groups, the Christian Democrats, Socialists, and Liberals and their allies were established. However, in 1962, the UDR members of the French delegation (Gaullists) left the Liberal group and established a separate group called the European Democratic Union. It was following the pressure of the new group that the rule concerning the minimum number of members to establish a group was changed in January 1965.

The activities of the groups have from the outset been directed towards the selection of candidates for important posts in the Parliament and its committees and, through the membership of the chairman of each group of the enlarged Bureau, the organisation of the work of the Parliament. The representatives of the groups play a very important part in the deliberations of the enlarged Bureau, the work of which is described in Chapter X on the President and Bureau. The groups meet before every meeting of the Parliament to decide on common positions in debate. Political groups are also accorded priority in the organisation of debates[2] and in the tabling of oral Questions with debate.[3] In

---

[1]In April 1972 there were only 139 current Members of the Parliament.
[2]See pages 99 and 100.
[3]See pages 135 and 136.

committees, when a member wishes to be replaced by a substitute, it is the political group which nominates his replacement.

In addition to the procedural privileges granted to the political groups, the organisation of the groups is materially assisted by the Parliament in several ways. Offices and other rooms are made available to the secretariats of the political groups both at the European Centre at Luxembourg, and during sessions at the House of Europe at Strasbourg. The secretariat of each political group is paid for directly from the Parliament's budget. An annual grant is made to each group which is calculated on the basis of a fixed sum and a small *per capita* payment for each member of the group. This is meant to cover travel expenses, postage and other miscellaneous group costs. Also paid directly from the Parliament's budgets are the expenses of members of the group for two one-day meetings in Brussels, Luxembourg or Strasbourg in between sessions of the Parliament. Exceptionally four days of such meetings each year may be held away from these places, such as in Rome.

4 Verification of credentials

The names of the Members appointed to serve on the delegations of national parliaments at the European Parliament are addressed to the President of the Parliament. The length of the appointment of Members is at the discretion of national parliaments.

The Parliament verifies the credentials of its Members in accordance with the procedure laid down in Rule 3 of the Rules of Procedure and on the basis of a report from the Bureau; the Bureau checks whether the appointments fall within the provisions of the Treaty. Disputes concerning credentials are referred to the Legal Affairs Committee which is bound to report to the Parliament as soon as possible. Disputes concerning the validity of the appointment of a member whose credentials are in order are also referred to the Legal Affairs Committee which must report to the Parliament not later than at the beginning of its next part-session.

It is also provided in Rule 3 (3) that a Member whose credentials have not yet been verified may provisionally take his seat in Parliament or on its committees and may exercise the same rights as other Members.

5 Privileges and immunities

Articles 8 to 10 of the Protocol on Privileges and Immunities annexed to the Merger Treaty of 1965 establishing a single Council and a single Commission of the European Communities set out the immunities granted to members of the Parliament.[1]

[1]This Protocol replaced the Protocols on Privileges and Immunities annexed to the EEC, ECSC and Euratom Treaties.

No administrative or other restriction may be imposed on the free movement of Members of the Parliament, travelling to or from the place of meeting of the Parliament.

Members of the Parliament must, in respect of customs and exchange control, be accorded:

(*a*) by their own Government, the same facilities as those accorded to senior officials travelling abroad on temporary official missions;

(*b*) by the Governments of other member states, the same facilities as those accorded to representatives of foreign Governments on temporary official missions (Article 8).

Members of the Parliament are not subject to any form of inquiry, detention or legal proceedings in respect of opinions expressed or votes cast by them in the performance of their duties (Article 9).

During the sessions of the Parliament, its Members enjoy:

(*a*) in the territory of their own state, the immunities accorded to members of their parliament:

(*b*) in the territory of any other member state, immunity from any measure of detention and from local proceedings.

Immunity likewise applies to Members while they are travelling to and from the place of meeting of the Parliament.

Immunity cannot be claimed when a Member is found in the act of committing an offence and does not prevent the Parliament from exercising its right to waive the immunity of one of its Members (Article 10).

The duration of a session of the Parliament materially affects the immunities granted under Article 9. In a decision of the Court of Justice on 12 May 1964[1] the Parliament was deemed to be in session, even when not sitting, from the opening of the annual session until its close shortly before the opening of the next annual session. The judgement arose out of a suit of defamation brought against two Luxembourg members of the Parliament, MM. Fohrman and Krier in 1962 in the Luxembourg courts. In order to decide the matter, the applicability of the immunities of the Parliament had to be established. A request was made to the Parliament by the Foreign Minister of Luxembourg that the Parliament waive its immunities in this case. The Legal Affairs Committee, to which the matter was referred, recommended in a report prepared by M. Weinkamm[2] that immunities and privileges should apply only outside a member's country of origin where he is covered by the immunities of his national parliament.

Rule 51 of the Rules of Procedure also amplifies the provisions of the Protocol. It was under its provisions that the Foreign Minister of Luxembourg requested the Parliament, through the President, to waive

[1]Case No. 103–63.
[2]Doc. 27, 1964–65.

the immunity of the two Members referred to above. It is also provided that if a Member has been found in the act of committing an offence, arrested or held in custody, any member of the Parliament may request that proceedings be suspended or that the Member be released. The Legal Affairs Committee must consider such a request without delay but may not enter into the merits of the case. The Member concerned or a Member representing him may appear before the committee if the Member so wishes. The report of the committee takes priority over the business on the agenda of the first sitting after the date on which it is laid before the Bureau of the Parliament. Debate on the report is confined to argument for and against the waiver of immunity. The President is bound to communicate the decision as soon as possible to member states concerned.

Passes (*laissez-passer*) are issued by the President to Members of the Parliament on their appointment to allow them to travel without hindrance within the states of the Communities.

G

Chapter X

President and Bureau of the Parliament

1 Constitution of the Bureau

The European Parliament elects its President and its officers from among its own Members.[1] Rules 5, 6 and 7 of the Rules of Procedure provide that there shall be a President and eight Vice-Presidents[2] who are elected at the beginning of the session, which starts on the second Tuesday in March, and who remain in office until the opening of the next annual session. These nine officers constitute the Bureau of the Parliament. At the moment when the annual session is opened, the Bureau of the previous session becomes *functus officio*.

Rule 6 of the Rules of Procedure lays down that the oldest Member present at the opening sitting takes the chair. While he remains in the chair no business may be transacted unless it is concerned with the election of the President or the verification of credentials.

Under the terms of Rule 5 (2) of the Rules of Procedure no Member who is a member of a national government may be a member of the Bureau.

2 Election of the President and Vice-Presidents

The founding Treaties allow the Parliament to determine the manner of the election of the President and other members of the Bureau. The Parliament is however bound by the requirement in Article 141 of the EEC Treaty, that decisions should be taken by an absolute majority of the votes cast.

The procedure for electing the President and Vice-Presidents is laid down in Rule 7 of the Rules of Procedure. Elections are held by secret ballot. The votes cast are counted by four tellers who are chosen by lot.

If it is necessary for a President or a Vice-President to be replaced in the course of a session, his successor is elected in a like manner.

ELECTION OF THE PRESIDENT

The Parliament is bound by Rule 9 (2) of the Rules of Procedure first to elect its President, before proceeding to the election of the Vice-Presidents. If there is only one candidate for the office of President then the Parliament may elect him by acclamation. This procedure is often used when a President is re-elected for a second or even third term.

[1] Article 140 of the EEC Treaty.
[2] The number of Vice-Presidents may be altered after 1 January 1973.

The first President of the Parliament of the Communities, M. Robert Schuman, was elected by acclamation. Contested elections are often avoided by an agreement of the political groups on a candidate beforehand.

Nominations are handed before each ballot to the oldest Member who announces the names of the candidates to the Parliament. In a contested election, no candidate is successful at the first ballot unless he receives an absolute majority of the votes cast. A contested election for the office of President under this Rule took place in 1971, when Herr W. Behrendt of the Federal Republic of Germany was successful.

If after three ballots no candidate has obtained an absolute majority of the votes cast, the fourth ballot is confined to the two Members who have obtained the highest number of votes in the third ballot. In the event of a tie, the older candidate shall be declared elected.

The result of the election of the President is announced from the tribune by the oldest Member, who then vacates the chair which is taken by the newly elected President.

It is usual for the successful candidate in the presidential election to be elected for a second year. Exceptionally, as in the case of M. Poher (France) from 1966–69, a President may serve three years. The Presidents of the Parliament since 1958 have been:

1958–60   M. Robert Schuman (France)
1960–62   Professor Furler (Germany)
1962–64   Dr. Gaetano Martino (Italy)
1964–65   M. Jean Duvieusart (Belgium)
1965–66   M. Victor Leemans (Belgium)
1966–69   M. Alain Poher (France)
1969–71   Signor Mario Scelba (Italy)
1971–   Herr Walter Behrendt (Germany).

ELECTION OF VICE-PRESIDENTS

If the number of candidates does not exceed the number of offices to be filled, the Parliament may elect the Vice-Presidents by acclamation. This frequently occurs since the political groups often support an agreed list of candidates. If there are more candidates than places to be filled, then voting by secret ballot takes place on a single ballot paper containing the names of all candidates. Those who on the first ballot obtain an absolute majority of the votes cast are declared elected. Should the number of candidates elected be less than the number of seats remaining to be filled, a second ballot is held among the candidates, following the same procedure. If a third ballot is necessary, the candidates who obtain the greatest number of votes are declared elected. In the event of a tie for the remaining place or places, the older candidates are declared elected.

The Vice-Presidents take precedence in the order in which they are elected. If successful candidates for the office of Vice-President are elected on a tied vote, they rank according to age.

If a seat on the Bureau becomes vacant during a break in the session, the political group to which the Member whose seat has fallen vacant belonged may nominate a candidate for interim membership of the Bureau, pending the election to fill the vacancy which takes place under the procedure already described. Such a nomination must be submitted to the enlarged Bureau for ratification. An interim member of the Bureau enjoys the same rights as a Vice-President.

It was usual in the Parliament of the six countries that France, Germany and Italy had two places on the Bureau and Belgium, Luxembourg and the Netherlands one place each.

3 Duties of the President and Vice-Presidents

DUTIES OF THE PRESIDENT

The President of the Parliament has two main roles, both of which are recognised in the Rules of Procedure. Rule 8 declares that 'the President shall direct all proceedings of the Parliament and of its organs, subject to the provisions of these Rules'. Rule 53 defines the other main function of the President: he represents the Parliament as a whole in its dealings with the Commission, Council and other institutions.

To discharge his procedural duties, Rule 8 grants to the President 'all powers necessary to preside over the proceedings of the Parliament and to ensure that they are properly conducted'. His powers are elaborated in the Rules of Procedure and are dealt with in detail in the appropriate chapters. In the course of his duties the President is responsible for the opening, adjourning and closing of sittings; the scrutiny of Questions, resolutions and amendments to ensure their compliance with the rules of order; and the calling of speakers. He puts questions to the vote and announces the results of such votes; and he refers business to the appropriate committees. He is also responsible for signing the Minutes of Proceedings and laying them before the Parliament for approval.

When he is in the chair, the President may not take part in a debate. His only interventions may be to sum up or to call speakers to order. The President on election may give an inaugural address. In addition he has addressed the Assembly on formal occasions.

The President may leave the chair and speak in debate, though if he does so, he is bound by Rule 8 (3) of the Rules of Procedure not to resume the chair until that debate has been concluded.

In his capacity as the representative of the Parliament the President has participated in international delegations, ceremonial occasions, and in the administrative, legal and financial organisation of the Parliament and the Communities. The President is the natural channel for the formal communications with outside authorities or persons. The President is the formal recipient of requests for consultation by the Council of Ministers and the Commission. He is also bound to transmit to the Presidents of the other institutions the opinions of the Parliament on proposals being considered by the Council. As President of one of the Community institutions, the President may also declare adopted the Community budget if the Parliament has agreed to the draft budget submitted by the Council.

In his capacity as a representative of the Parliament Herr Behrendt led a delegation from the Parliament on an official visit to the United Kingdom Parliament in February 1972.

DUTIES OF THE VICE-PRESIDENTS

The duty of a Vice-President is to take the chair at plenary meetings when the President is unable to be present, when he is otherwise unable to discharge his duties or when the President wishes to speak in a debate. While he is in the chair, a Vice-President may exercise the powers and is subject to the obligations laid upon the President. The substitution of the President by Vice-Presidents at plenary meetings is done by agreement between the President and the Vice-Presidents.

4 Duties of the Bureau

The Bureau meets frequently, both before and during sessions of the Parliament. Together with the enlarged Bureau (see page 91) and the Presidential Committee, to which bodies members of the Bureau automatically belong, the Bureau is the central organisational and administrative committee of the Parliament. Regardless of the subject under discussion and of the division of functions between the Bureau and enlarged Bureau, Members of the enlarged Bureau take part in all the work of the Bureau.

(i) *Preparation of the meetings of the Parliament*

Members of the Bureau participate in the preparation of the agenda for each part-session of the Parliament. This is done by the enlarged Bureau on information provided by the Presidential Committee. The Bureau is responsible for deciding whether proceedings of the Parliament are simultaneously interpreted into any language other than the official languages.

According to Rule 3 of the Rules of Procedure, the Bureau prepares reports on the credentials of Members, taking special note that appointments comply with the provisions of the founding Treaties. A further important procedural function of the Bureau is to take decisions on points of parliamentary practice which thereafter are followed by the Parliament.[1]

(ii) *Administration of the Parliament and its Secretariat*

Under the terms of Rule 49 of the Rules of Procedure, the Parliament is assisted by a Secretary-General appointed by the Bureau. The Secretary-General gives a solemn undertaking before the Bureau to perform his duties conscientiously and impartially. This makes the Secretary-General responsible to the Bureau for the discharge of his functions.

The composition and organisation of the Secretariat, headed by the Secretary-General, is determined by the Bureau within the framework of the Communities' Statute of Personnel. The Bureau decides the number and grades of staff and lays down service regulations relating to their administrative and financial status. This is done after consultation with the appropriate committee of the Parliament. The Bureau also decides the status of servants and officials of the Parliament under the terms of Articles 12 and 14 of the Protocol on the Privileges and Immunities of the European Communities annexed to the Merger Treaty of 1965.

The Bureau plays an important part in the financial procedures of the Parliament. The Bureau prepares the first preliminary draft of the provisional estimates of the Parliament on the basis of a report by the Secretary-General and after consultation with the Committee on Finance and Budgetary Affairs. Thereafter, the budgetary process is continued by the enlarged Bureau and the Parliament itself. The Bureau also issues the internal financial regulations of Parliament.

(iii) *Control of the committees of the Parliament*

The Bureau plays a large part in the nomination of Members to serve on committees. Nominations for election to committees are addressed to the Bureau, which is charged each session with the task of submitting to Parliament proposals designed to ensure fair representation of member states and of political views. The Bureau may also fill vacancies on committees with the consent of the Member concerned provided that the principle of fair representation of member states and political groups is followed. These proposals are subject to ratification by the Parliament.

Reference of matters to committees is done by the Parliament on the advice of the Bureau. The President may refer matters to committees on behalf of the Bureau during a break in the session.

The Bureau is the authorising body for study or fact-finding journeys

---

[1]The more important of these decisions are published in the Handbook (*Vademecum*) issued to Members of the Parliament from time to time.

by committees. The number of members of such a mission is fixed by the Bureau according to the size of the committees and membership is limited to members of the sponsoring committee itself. Committees must also apply to the President for the Bureau to consider whether they should be allowed to meet other than at the seat of the Parliament; this procedure is generally only a formality.

5 The enlarged Bureau

Under the terms of Rule 5 (2) of the Rules of Procedure, an enlarged Bureau is appointed. This body has in practice taken over many of the functions of the Bureau proper and has become the principal organising committee of the Parliament. It consists of the members of the Bureau proper together with the chairmen of political groups. The chairman of a political group may appoint a member of his group to represent him. As is the case in the Bureau, the President has a casting vote.

The principal task of the enlarged Bureau, laid down by Rule 12 of the Rules of Procedure, is to prepare the draft agenda for sittings of the Parliament on the basis of information passed to it by the Presidential Committee. An important aspect of this work is the responsibility for deciding whether Questions which have been tabled should be for oral answer with debate, for oral answer without debate or for written answer, in accordance with the procedure laid down in Rules 46 and 47 of the Rules of Procedure.[1]

Among the other powers given to the enlarged Bureau is the right to alter the duration of the breaks in the session by a reasoned decision of a majority of its members at least two weeks before the Parliament is due to meet. It is also the body to which nominations for interim vacancies on the Bureau must be submitted for ratification.

The enlarged Bureau also has a role in the preparation of the provisional estimates of the Parliament. After receiving the opinion of the appropriate committee, the enlarged Bureau adopts the preliminary draft of the provisional estimates.[2]

The formal powers of the enlarged Bureau were substantially increased to their present level in the revision of the Rules of 19 October 1967.[3]

6 The Presidential Committee

The Presidential Committee is also concerned in the organisation of the agenda. As constituted according to the provisions of Rule 12 (1) of the Rules of Procedure, the Committee consists of the members of the enlarged Bureau together with the chairman or vice-chairman of each

[1] See also Chapter XVII on Questions and Petitions.
[2] See Rule 50 of the Rules of Procedure.
[3] See page 132.

of the parliamentary committees. Representatives of the Commission and the Council may, at the invitation of the President, attend meetings of the Presidential Committee.

Whenever possible the Presidential Committee prepares for the enlarged Bureau the information from which the draft agenda for each part-session is drawn up.[1] The other principal function of the Committee is, at the beginning of the session in March each year, to appoint a rapporteur to prepare the report to the Consultative Assembly of the Council of Europe on the activities of the Parliament.[2] Before transmission to the President of the Consultative Assembly, the report must be approved by the Presidential Committee and by the Parliament.

[1]For the preparation of the agenda, see Chapter XI pp. 95–97.
[2]See Rule 52 of the Rules of Procedure.

Chapter XI

Sittings and agenda of the Parliament

1 Date and duration of the Session

Ordinary sessions of the Parliament are held every year. The Parliament was bound by Article 139 of the EEC Treaty to meet once a year on the third Tuesday in October. Under the earlier ECSC Treaty of 1951 the date of the opening of the annual session was given as the second Tuesday in May. In practice these requirements were disregarded to the extent that as early as 1960 the formal opening of the annual session took place in March.[1] The formal opening was recognised as taking place in March in Article 27 of the Merger Treaty of 1965 establishing a single Council and a single Commission of the European Communities. The opening takes place on the second Tuesday in March.

Under Rule 1 (2) of the Rules of Procedure the Parliament determines its own times of meeting and meets for approximately eleven part-sessions per year amounting to about forty days in all. These meetings are generally spread out throughout the months of the year except the month of August. In 1972 there were eleven meetings lasting forty-three days in all. In a judgement of the Court of Justice in 1964, it was held that the Parliament was in continuous session from its opening in March until its close shortly before the next annual opening (see page 84).

The dates of the meetings of the Parliament are determined by the Parliament itself on a proposal of the Bureau. Following a decision of the Bureau of 22 September 1969, the calendar of periods of a session includes, besides the firmly fixed meetings, two brief periods for which the Parliament might meet. These periods must be confirmed by the Bureau at least twenty days before the provisional date of meeting. The enlarged Bureau may alter the duration of breaks between part sessions by a reasoned decision of a majority of its members taken at least two weeks before the date previously fixed by Parliament for resuming the session; the date of resumption may not, however, be postponed by more than two weeks. In practice the dates of each part-session are confirmed by the Parliament itself at the end of the preceding part-session.

Ordinary sessions are normally held in Strasbourg in the Chamber of the Consultative Assembly of the Council of Europe. Rule 2 (1) of the Rules of Procedure lays down that for plenary sittings the Parliament

[1] Official Journal, 27 April 1960.

shall meet at the place fixed as its seat under the provisions of the Treaties. Strasbourg, the original place of meeting, was confirmed as the place of meeting in a Decision of the Representatives of the Governments of Member States on the provisional location of certain institutions and departments of the Communities of 8 April 1965.[1] Since 1967, the Parliament has held a number of its shorter part-sessions at the European Centre in Luxembourg where the General Secretariat is sited. This recent development is sanctioned by Rule 2 (2) which allows that, by resolution adopted by a majority of its members, the Parliament may decide to hold one or more plenary sittings elsewhere than at its seat.

The Parliament each year holds a joint meeting with the Consultative Assembly of the Council of Europe either at the time of a meeting of the Parliament or of the Consultative Assembly. When such a meeting takes place during a part-session of the Consultative Assembly, the Members of the European Parliament must be convened for a special meeting.

Extraordinary sessions of the Parliament may be held according to the provisions of Rule 1 (4) of the Rules of Procedure.[2] The President may on behalf of the enlarged Bureau summon the Parliament at the request of a majority of its current members or at the request of the Council or of the Commission. This rule was utilised for convening the meeting of 8 January 1968 which was called to allow the Parliament to give its opinion in response to a request for consultation within the time limit laid down by the Treaties in the draft Budget for research and investment of Euratom and on the supplementary draft budget of the European Communities.

2 Sittings of the Parliament

DAYS OF SITTING

The Parliament normally sits from Monday to Friday. As far as possible, committees of the Parliament do not meet during the hours when the Parliament itself is sitting. The authority of the President (or the Vice-President taking his place) is required before a committee may meet during a sitting. Meetings of political groups may also take place at the time of Parliamentary sessions, but not while the Parliament is actually sitting.

HOURS OF SITTING

The date and time of the beginning of each sitting is fixed by the Parliament on the proposal of the President. The hours of sitting may then be varied by the President with the approval of the Parliament, taking

[1] Official Journal 1967 p. 18.
[2] And Article 139 of the EEC Treaty.

account of the volume of business. On days when sittings of the Parliament occur before and after luncheon, these sittings are formally counted as one.

OPENING, SUSPENDING AND CLOSING THE SITTING

It is the duty of the President, or a Vice-President acting on his behalf to open, suspend and close the sitting.

Bells are rung continuously for one minute at the opening or the resumption of the sitting. The suspension and the end of the sitting are signalled by the ringing of bells for three short peals. These signals were established by a decision of the Bureau of 16 November 1964.

At the entrance to the Chamber an attendance register is placed for each day of plenary meetings, which Members are obliged to sign. The register is put in place half an hour before the opening of a meeting and is removed half an hour after the end of the meeting.

3 Composition and settlement of the agenda

The Parliament is able to debate any matter within the aims and scope of the Communities as defined by the founding Treaties. Moreover the jurisdiction of the Communities has been extended on the basis of Article 235 of the EEC Treaty so that the field of debate of the Parliament is extremely wide. The discussion of new areas by the Parliament was encouraged by the heads of state of member governments at the Bonn summit meeting on 18 July 1961.

There are four principal ways in which matters come on to the agenda of the Parliament. Firstly, the Parliament must be consulted by the Council of Ministers before the Council takes a decision on proposals from the Commission to make regulations or issue directives which have the force of law in member states of the Communities. Such requests for consultation are referred to committees of the Parliament for report. Secondly, any member of the Parliament may table a motion for a resolution on matters within the sphere of activity of the Communities. In accordance with Rule 25 of the Rules of Procedure, such a motion is also referred to the competent committee for a report. Thirdly, a committee may take the initiative in studying any matter within its field of responsibility and, having obtained the approval of the Bureau, present a report to the Parliament. Finally, oral Questions with or without debate must be found a place on the agenda if the enlarged Bureau so decides.

In addition to Questions and the reports from committees which originate under the procedure outlined above, there are certain annual events on the parliamentary calendar which must be accommodated. In February of each year, the President of the Commission presents the annual general report of the Communities and the future programme of the Commission. Also presented in February by a member of the Commission is a statement on the social situation in the Community. In the following months debates must take place on these matters, in particular on the report of the Parliament on the general report of the Communities. In May or June of each year the President in office of the Council of Ministers makes an annual statement to the Parliament on which a debate takes place. In October and November, the Parliament debates the budget of the Communities. Finally, the annual colloquy with the Council of Ministers and the annual joint meeting with the Consultative Assembly of the Council of Europe must be fitted in at some point during the year.

Rule 12 of the Rules of Procedure lays down the procedure by which the draft agenda for sittings of the Parliament is prepared. According to the Provisions of Rule 12 (1) the enlarged Bureau prepares the draft agenda on information passed to it by the Presidential Committee. The Commission and Council may attend meetings of the Presidential Committee at the invitation of the President. The President submits the draft agenda to the Parliament at the opening of each part-session for approval and if necessary for amendment.

In practice, it is not always possible for the Presidential Committee to meet to prepare the information which it should supply to the enlarged Bureau. In this case the Secretariat prepares an analysis of the business waiting to be considered by the Parliament, on the basis of which the enlarged Bureau may draw up the draft agenda. It is also useful in dividing business between the days of part-sessions for the enlarged Bureau to know which Commissioners are available to attend and reply to debates. This information is also provided as far as practicable by the Secretariat after consulting the Commission.

The secretariats of the committees provide information about the state of preparation of their reports. In some cases where consultation has been requested by the Council, reports may have to be placed on the agenda within a time limit so that Parliament can give its opinion before the Council has taken a decision.

In preparing the draft agenda, the enlarged Bureau must take into account that, in accordance with Rule 13 of the Rules of Procedure, no debate may take place on a report unless it has been circulated at least twenty-four hours previously. In order to make this provision effective, the Bureau extended its scope in a decision taken on 26 April 1967 and communicated to the Parliament on 11 May 1967. It said:

> In Order to allow Rule 13 of the Rules of Procedure to be respected, only reports which have been tabled at least ten days before the opening of a part-session may be put on the agenda for that part-session: i.e. the Friday before the week preceding the week of the opening of the part-session.

Where such conditions cannot be complied with, and consultation has been requested by the Council, it is possible that a report may be taken by urgent procedure (see below). This was done on 21 and 22

February 1968 when all three reports debated were taken under the urgent procedure.

After the agenda has been approved by the enlarged Bureau, it is published in the *Bulletin* of the European Parliament. When the Parliament meets, the President proposes any amendments made necessary by the delay in the production of a report or the appearance of reports or Questions to be dealt with by urgent procedure. Once it has been approved by the Parliament the agenda may only be amended by a decision of the Parliament.

4 Urgent Procedure

It is necessary in any parliamentary assembly to have a procedure under which it is possible to discuss important matters which require urgent consideration. On the other hand the use of such a device must be limited to avoid unnecessary disturbance of the order of business which has been agreed to and which Members expect to be followed.

In the Parliament, a proposal that a debate be treated as urgent may, according to the provisions of Rule 14 of the Rules of Procedure, be made to the Parliament by the President, by at least ten Members, or by the Commission or Council of Ministers. The urgent procedure is also adopted where it has been requested in writing by one-third of the current members of the Parliament. It is most frequently invoked when consultation has been requested by the Council in a limited time. Following the precedent of 19 October 1967, when the urgent procedure was invoked for the discussion of the Report of Mr. Bech on the Rules of Procedure,[1] there is no limit on the number of speakers or on the length of speeches on a request for an urgent debate.

Where the adoption of urgent procedure has been decided upon by the Parliament, debate may take place without a report or on the basis of an oral report by the appropriate committee. Once it has been decided that the urgent procedure shall be invoked, the matter to be dealt with under the procedure is given absolute priority over the other items on the agenda.

[1]Document 131/1967.

Chapter XII

Rules of debate and languages

1 General

According to Rule 16 of the Rules of Procedure, debates in the Parliament are held in public unless the Parliament decides otherwise. There has been difficulty in giving full weight to this provision since the meeting place in Luxembourg used for up to ten days each year has no room for the public.

The Parliament may transact its business, adopt its agenda and approve the Minutes of Proceedings of the previous sitting whatever the number of Members present. However, if a vote by roll call is requested, the number of Members taking part must include a majority of the current Members of the Parliament for the decision to be valid.

The President has the general responsibility for the direction of all proceedings of the Parliament. His duties are to open, suspend and close sittings; to ensure observance of the Rules, maintain order, call upon speakers, close debates, put questions to the vote and announce the results of votes; and to refer business to the appropriate committees.[1]

A Vice-President has the same powers and duties when replacing the President in the chair.

The debates of the Parliament are conducted according to the general principles observed in the national parliaments of the founding members. As a result, the rules of debate on the whole allow speakers considerable scope in addressing themselves to the subject under discussion.

2 Languages

The official languages of the Parliament are Danish, Dutch, English, French, German and Italian. All documents of the Parliament are drawn up in these official languages.

A speech delivered in an official language is simultaneously interpreted into each of the other official languages. Thus all members of the Parliament may hear a simultaneous interpretation of every speech in their own language by means of the headphones installed in each place.

[1]Rule 8 (2) of the Rules of Procedure.

Interpretation in any language other than the official languages is a matter for the Bureau. In the Parliament of the six countries, as well as the official languages of Dutch, French, German and Italian, speeches were simultaneously interpreted into English.

The position of the Irish language is somewhat different from that of the other national languages. Some documents have been translated into Irish, and the matter will be further considered after the enlargement of the Parliament in January 1973.

3 Time and manner of speaking

A Member may speak only if he is called to do so by the President, Members may give notice of their intention to speak in a forthcoming debate. The names of Members who ask to speak are entered in a speakers' book in the order in which their requests are received, but the President is not bound to call speakers in that order, nor is the right to speak restricted to those who have registered their intention to do so. It is quite usual for Members to indicate their wish to speak by notifying the President informally during the course of the debate or by endeavouring to catch his eye.

The President is bound by Rule 31 (2) of the Rules of Procedure to call Members to speak ensuring as far as possible that speakers of different political views and using different languages are heard in turn. On request, however, priority has been given to the chairman of a political group who wanted to speak on its behalf or to a speaker deputising for him for the same purpose. By a decision of the Bureau, confirmed on 22 September 1969, communicated to the Parliament on 6 October 1969, only one spokesman for each political group can exercise this right. To do so, the chairman of the political group concerned must write to the President or Vice-President in the chair.

No Member is allowed to speak more than twice on the same subject except by leave of the President. But the chairmen and the rapporteurs of committees concerned are allowed to speak at their own request more frequently. The number of Members who may take part in any debate is not limited, except in debates on procedural motions considered below. In such debates, only the proposer of the motion, one supporter, one opposer, and the chairmen or rapporteurs of the committees concerned may speak.

In accordance with Rules 31 (4) and 28 of the Rules of Procedure, the Parliament may propose, in agreement with the chairmen of political groups, that speaking time be apportioned in a particular debate. If the Parliament decides to organise a debate in such a manner, the President convenes a meeting of the chairmen of political groups and the chairmen of the committees directly concerned and of the committees asked for their opinions. Speaking time is divided among the political groups within the limits of the number or length of sittings provided for in the agenda.[1] A time is also fixed by which a vote is to be taken.

According to a decision of the Bureau communicated to the Parliament on 6 October 1969, no speech should normally be made by the rapporteur in the presentation of a report which has been distributed in advance in accordance with the rules unless there is a need to elucidate matters of complexity or if new information has since come to light; but in practice this decision is frequently disregarded. In such debates only the rapporteur or the chairman of the committee may exercise the priority accorded to them to intervene in the debate whenever necessary.

A speaker may not be interrupted except on a point of order. He may, however, with the leave of the President, give way during his speech to allow another Member, or a member of the Commission or of the Council, to put to him a question on a particular point in his speech. A Member may rise at any time to speak on a point of order, to move an adjournment or other dilatory motion or to move the closure (see below). The reading of speeches has been discouraged in several decisions issued by the Bureau, the last of which was taken on 22 September 1969, and delivered to the Parliament on 6 October 1969.

A Member who wishes to make a personal statement may only do so at the end of the sitting.

4 Speeches in the Parliament by members of the Commission and the Council of Ministers

Members of the Commission of the Communities have the right of access to the Parliament and its committees and a prior right to speak whenever they wish to intervene in the debates. They cannot of course vote since they are not Members.

The rights extended to the Commission are widely used. At least one and usually several of the Commissioners attend the meetings of the Parliament to reply to debates and when necessary to answer questions.[2] Participation of Commissioners in debates is not restricted to the debate on the annual report on the activities of the Communities.

Members of the Council of Ministers may also address the Parliament at their request. This right is exercised infrequently, although the Council of Ministers is often represented at meetings of the Parliament by one of its members. Each year the President in office of the Council presents an account of the Council's activities in the preceding year.

[1]The usual allocation of speaking time is as follows: rapporteurs and one spokesman for each political group may speak for fifteen minutes; other speakers are allotted ten minutes and speakers on amendments five minutes.
[2]See pages 134–138.

5 Content of speeches and scope of debate

The Parliament only considers matters which fall within the sphere of the activities of the Communities. It therefore follows that any speech or remark dealing with other matters would not be in order.

A speaker must address himself to the subject before the Parliament. If a Member persists in speaking out of order, the President can use a succession of measures which may be taken with him (see below). If a speaker has been called to order twice in the same debate, the President may, on the third occasion, forbid him to speak for the remainder of the debate.

Without prejudice to his other disciplinary powers, the President can have the speeches of Members who have not been called by him to speak or who continue to speak beyond their allotted time deleted from the official report of debates.

6 Rules of order

The rules which govern the conduct of members of the Parliament have not been frequently invoked. Under the terms of Rule 10 of the Rules of Procedure, it is the duty of the President to call to order any Member who creates a disorder or who otherwise departs from the Rules of Order. If the Member repeats the breach of order at the same sitting the President must again call him to order and the fact is recorded in the Minutes of Proceedings. In the event of the Member repeating the offence a third time, the President is empowered to exclude the offender from the Chamber for the remainder of the sitting.

If it appears to the President that the seriousness of the case demands more severe action on behalf of the Parliament, he may move that the Parliament pass a vote of censure on the Member concerned. A vote of censure must be taken by sitting and standing and without debate. However, any Member against whom such a motion has been tabled has the right to be heard first. A Member on whom a vote of censure is passed is immediately excluded from the Chamber and is suspended for a period of from two to five days at the discretion of the Parliament.

In accordance with Rule 11 of the Rules of Procedure, no person shall enter the Chamber during a sitting unless he is a member of the Parliament, a member of the Commission or the Council, the Secretary-General of the Parliament, a member of the staff whose duties require his presence there, or an expert or official of the Communities. Only holders of an admission card duly issued by the President or Secretary-General are admitted to the gallery under arrangements made by the Secretary-General. They must remain seated and silent. Any person expressing disapproval is removed by the ushers immediately.

H

7 Procedural motions

A Member of the Parliament who wishes to raise a point of order or who asks leave to move a procedural motion has a prior right to do so.

Under the terms of Rule 32 (1) of the Rules of Procedure, such procedural motions include, in particular, the reference of a matter to a committee, the closure of debate, the adjournment of debate, and the moving of the previous question.

Such procedural or 'dilatory' motions are debatable and take precedence over the proceedings on the item on the orders of the day which is under discussion. The discussion on the main question is suspended until the dilatory motion has been disposed of.

In accordance with Rules 31 (5) and 32 (3) of the Rules of Procedure, debate on dilatory motions is limited. Only the proposer of the motion, one other speaker for the motion and one against it, and the rapporteur or chairman of any committee concerned are entitled to speak in the debate on the motion. Their speeches must be limited to five minutes. The Parliament must then come to a decision on the motion by its customary methods of voting.

8 The Closure

A motion for the closure of a debate which is in progress may be moved by any Member of the Parliament who has the same prior right to do so as is the case with any other dilatory motion. The proposer of the motion, one speaker for and one against the motion, and the chairman or the rapporteur of each of the committees concerned may speak on the motion. Following this, the motion is voted upon by show of hands unless a vote by roll call has been requested. If the motion is agreed to, the main question must then be put to the vote.

9 Methods of voting

Voting on questions, except those which concern appointments, takes place by one of three methods, each of which in certain circumstances may be used in turn.

Rule 35 of the Rules of Procedure provides that normally the Parliament votes by show of hands. The President first calls upon those in favour of the proposition to raise their hands, and then those against to do so. If the result of a vote by show of hands is doubtful a second vote may be taken by sitting and standing. According to a decision of the Bureau of 13 May 1964 it is for the President to decide the validity of a vote by show of hands. In a vote by sitting and standing, the President first calls upon those in favour of the proposition to stand and then those against.

If the result of a second vote by sitting and standing is adjudged doubtful by the President, or if a qualified majority is required, or if at least ten Members request it, a vote by roll call is taken. The names of the Members requesting a vote by roll call are recorded in the Minutes of Proceedings.

In a vote by roll call, the names of Members are read in alphabetical order, beginning with the name of a Member chosen by lot. The President is the last to be called to vote. Voting is done by word of mouth, Members expressing their votes 'yes' or 'no' or 'I abstain'. The votes are recorded and counted by the officials at the Tribune with the President, but the President alone is responsible for the count, and announces the result to the Parliament giving the number of votes for and against the proposition and the number of abstentions. In calculating whether a motion has been adopted or rejected, account is not taken of abstentions. The votes are recorded in the Minutes of Proceedings of the sitting in the alphabetical order of Members' names.

Roll call votes are not valid unless the number of Members voting includes a majority of the current Members of the Parliament. If this has not been so, the vote is taken at the next sitting. The names of Members voting in a void vote are not recorded in the Minutes of Proceedings. The request for a roll call vote may be withdrawn so that a decision may be reached without a quorum present. On 22 March 1968, such a request was withdrawn before the vote had begun.

On 21 and 22 February 1968, the vote on an amendment to a text produced considerable difficulty. On 21 February, an amendment tabled by Mr. Pleven was voted on by roll call at the request of eleven Members led by Mr. Pleven. The result revealed the lack of a quorum so the vote was deferred until 22 February. The following morning, the request for a roll call vote was withdrawn and the amendment was rejected by show of hands.

If a request for a roll call vote is made only relating to some of the amendments to or paragraphs of a resolution, the paragraphs and amendments not requiring a roll call vote can be disposed of while a quorum is not present.

The election of the President and Vice-Presidents has been described in Chapter XI. For appointments, only ballot papers bearing the names of persons who have been entered as candidates shall be taken into account in calculating the number of votes cast.

10 Majorities

Article 141 of the EEC Treaty stipulates that except where otherwise provided in the Treaty, the 'Assembly' shall take decisions by an absolute majority of the votes cast. This requirement is repeated in Rule 35 (5) of the Rules of Procedure which provides that

'Motions put to the vote shall be declared adopted only if they have secured a majority of the votes cast'.

The most important exception to the general rule of majorities is the two-thirds majority required for the adoption of a motion of censure on the activities of the Commission. The motion is carried if it is supported by a two-thirds majority of the votes cast, representing a majority of the Members of the Parliament.[1]

Another instance of a variation of majority provided for in the EEC Treaty is the majority required for adoption and amendment of the Rules of Procedure. Article 142 states that this is done by a 'majority vote of its members'. This is applied in Rule 54 (2) which provides that amendments must secure the 'votes of the majority of the Members of the Parliament', but in practice this does not preclude the Parliament from amending its Rules of Procedure by acclamation.

Other matters which require an absolute majority of the Members of the Parliament are proposals for holding plenary sessions elsewhere than the seat of the Parliament (Rule 2 (2) of the Rules of Procedure), the election of the President and Vice-Presidents (Rule 7 (2 and 4)) and resolutions proposing amendments to the ECSC Treaty (Rule 24 (3)).

Proposals from the Commission or Council for the amendment of the ECSC Treaty require the support of a two-thirds majority of the current members of the Parliament and a three-quarters majority of the votes cast.[2]

11 Quorum

A quorum exists when a majority of the current Members of the Parliament is present. If all delegations are at full strength, then a quorum is one hundred Members.

All votes other than votes by roll call are valid whatever the number of Members voting, unless before the voting has begun the President has been requested by at least ten Members to ascertain the number of those present.

The Parliament may deliberate, adopt its orders of the day and approve the minutes of proceedings of the previous sitting, whatever the number of Members present.

A vote by roll call may be requested by at least ten Members for any item of business. In 1969 it was decided that even for the approval of the orders of the day and the adoption of the minutes of proceedings, a vote by roll call could be requested. A vote by roll call must also be taken after two votes by other procedures which are not conclusive or if a qualified majority is required.

If when the result of a vote by roll call is announced it appears that a quorum is not present and voting, the vote is postponed until the next sitting. For the purpose of calculating the number of Members present, abstentions are not counted with the votes for and against the matters before the Parliament.

[1]See Article 144 of the EEC Treaty and Rule 21 (4) of the Rules of Procedure.
[2]Rule 24 (2) of the Rules of Procedure.

Chapter XIII

Decisions of the Parliament and advice to the Council of Ministers

1 The powers of the Parliament

The role of the European Parliament within the Communities is almost exclusively advisory and supervisory.[1] The only present exception to this situation is the power, by a two-thirds majority, to dismiss the Commission, a power which has not so far been exercised or invoked by the members of the Parliament (see Chapter III). Under the terms of a Treaty signed in Luxembourg on 22 April 1970, establishing new procedures for dealing with the budget of the Communities, the Parliament has also acquired for a transitional period to the end of 1974 powers to recommend modifications to the budget which can be overridden only by a qualified majority[2] of the Council. After 1 January 1975, the Parliament will also have the power to take binding decisions in respect of certain parts of the budget against the opposition of the Council of Ministers.[3]

As the deliberative and advisory institution of the Communities, the Parliament is charged with discussing matters defined by the Treaty of Paris (establishing the ECSC) and the Treaties of Rome (establishing the EEC and Euratom). For the most part, and with the exceptions noted above, the powers conferred by the Treaties give the Parliament the right to be consulted on Community legislation. Thus, the Parliament gives its opinion on the proposals of the Commission before the Council makes decisions or issues directives and regulations having the force of law within the Communities. This right of consultation extends to many areas of Community legislation, and to all proposals to amend the Treaties,[4] but it is not automatic in all cases. The procedure for seeking the advice and opinions of the Parliament at present takes the form of a request for advice submitted by the President of the Council of Ministers to the President of the Parliament.

> Since in the original languages the Treaties are ambiguous on the question of whether the Council or the Commission should consult the Parliament in those cases where consultation is required, the Parliament decided, on

[1] Article 137 of the EEC Treaty; Article 20 ECSC; Article 107 Euratom.

[2] For voting procedure in the Council see p. 10.

[3] These budgetary powers are described in full on pages 21–24.

[4] ECSC: Treaty amendments under Article 95 only. For EEC: under Articles 7, 14, 43, 54, 56, 57, 63, 75, 87, 100, 126, 127, 201, 203, 228, 235, 236 and 238. For Euratom: under Articles 31, 76, 85, 90, 96, 98, 173, 177, 203, 204 and 206.

the occasion of the first consultation under the Euratom Treaty in 1958, that it should always be consulted by the Council of Ministers, and this practice has been followed ever since. After considerable criticism that this procedure often leaves little time for parliamentary discussion because of the need to expedite decisions by the Council, the Bureau and the Legal Affairs Committee of the Parliament reconsidered the situation in the autumn of 1969 and the spring of 1970, and considerable support was expressed for the view that the Parliament could, if it wished, be consulted by the Commission instead. The Legal Affairs Committee, however, came to the conclusion that the relevant articles of the Treaties tended to support the view that the process of consultation should be initiated by the Council, and recommended that the process could best be changed, if so desired, by agreement between the Council and Commission under Article 162 of the EEC Treaty (which provides for consultation between the Council and Commission to establish their methods of co-operation). No positive action has since been taken on the proposal.

In addition to giving its opinion in response to requests for advice under the Treaties, the Parliament may also consider motions tabled by Members on any matter falling within the sphere of activities of the Communities (Rule 25 of the Rules of Procedure); motions for resolutions addressed to the Commission and the Council of Ministers proposing amendments to the Treaties (Rule 24); the annual general report of the Commission (Rule 20); and matters raised by committees on their own initiative (though reports on such matters are only included on the agenda with the approval of the Bureau).

At a summit meeting held in Bonn on 18 July 1961 the heads of government of the Six invited the European Parliament (then the Parliamentary Assembly) 'to extend the field of its deliberations, in collaboration with the governments, into new areas', thus effectively releasing the Parliament from the limitations imposed by the Treaties.

With the exception of motions of censure and motions for resolutions following debates on oral Questions,[1] all matters are usually referred first to a committee or committees and are not debated without the relevant reports of the committees to which they are referred. The normal procedure by which decisions of the Parliament are formulated may therefore be described in four stages:

1 Tabling of motions and references to committees

2 Consideration by committees

3 Debate and examination of reports and motions from committees

4 Final vote and resolutions.

[1]See page 136.

2 Motions of censure

The Parliament may remove the Commission as a body in accordance with Article 144 of the EEC Treaty, Article 24 of the ECSC Treaty and Article 114 of the Euratom Treaty.

In its original form, Article 24 of the ECSC Treaty provides for a motion of censure only on the annual report of the High Authority. Article 24 was amended by Article 27 of the Merger Treaty of 1965 to bring it into line with the provisions of the Rome Treaties.

According to Rule 21 of the Rules of Procedure, any member of the Parliament may table a motion of censure[1] on the Commission by handing the appropriate text to the President of the Parliament. The motion must be in writing, it must be supported by reasons, and it must be labelled 'motion of censure'. As soon as the text is received by the President it is printed and distributed in the official languages and is brought to the notice of the Commission. The President announces the tabling of the motion immediately he receives it, if the Parliament is sitting, or else at the beginning of the next suitable sitting.

The debate on a motion of censure may not be opened earlier than twenty-four hours after its receipt is announced by the President, and, in accordance with the Treaty articles mentioned above, may not be voted on until at least three days after the announcement. Voting on such a motion must be by open roll-call vote, and it is only deemed to be adopted if it secures a two-thirds majority of the votes cast and a majority of the current membership of the Parliament. If fractions appear in the results of these calculations, the required numbers are rounded up to the nearest whole number.[2]

The result of the vote is notified to the President of the Council and the President of the Commission, and if the motion has been carried with the required majorities the members of the Commission must thereupon resign, although they continue to handle current business until their successors are appointed.

3 Consideration of the Community budget

On 17 May 1971, the Parliament adopted new Rules of Procedure (Nos. 23 and 23A) concerning the consideration of the budget of the Communities by the Parliament and its committees, following the ratification of the Treaty of Luxembourg of 1970.[3] The same rules also apply to supplementary budgets which may be submitted from time to time by the Commission.

The financial year of the Communities runs from 1 January to 31 December. The Commission must submit the draft administrative budget to the Council of Ministers by 1 September, and the Council

[1]No such motion has ever been tabled.
[2]Decision of the Bureau, 25 May 1965.
[3]See pages 21–24.

must submit it to the Parliament by 5 October in the year preceding the
financial year to which it applies.[1] In addition to the draft budget, the
Parliament also receives the report of the board of auditors of the
Communities; the report of the ECSC auditor; and the documents drawn
up by the Commission in pursuance of Articles 49 and 50 of the ECSC
Treaty, including the report of the Commission to the Council, on the
basis of which the Council adapts the portion of expenditure covered
by the ECSC levies to the budget of the Communities.[2] All these documents are printed and circulated and referred to the Committee on
Finance and Budgets. Other committees are also asked for their
opinions on relevant parts of the budget, and the President fixes a
time-limit for the submission of these opinions to the Committee on
Finance and Budgets.

According to Rule 23A of the Rules of Procedure, any member of
the Parliament may propose amendments to the draft budget of the
Communities, but the President fixes a time-limit for their submission.
Amendments must be signed by at least five Members, and must
specify the budget head to which they relate. They are referred to the
Committee on Finance and Budgets or other appropriate committees
and are not debated in plenary session until the opinion of the com-
mittee concerned has been reported. Proposals for amendments to the
Parliament's own budget (which forms a part of the budget of the
Communities) which are similar to proposals rejected by the Parliament
when the provisional estimates were drawn up are debated only if the
Committee on Finance and Budgets has reported favourably on them.

When the budget is considered in plenary session the basis for the
debate is the report of the Committee on Finance and Budgets. In
contrast with proceedings on reports from other committees[3] the
Parliament votes not only on the motions for resolutions accompanying
the report, but also on each proposed amendment, each section of the
draft budget, and the draft budget as a whole.[4] If the budget is approved
by the Parliament without amendment, it is deemed to have been finally
adopted in accordance with the provisions of the Treaty. If amendments
have been made to the budget, however, it is returned as amended to the
Council and the Commission is notified of the changes proposed.[5] By a
qualified majority the Council may subsequently reject the amendments
made by the Parliament.

In discussions in the autumn of 1971 the Council and the Parliament
agreed to increase collaboration between the two institutions on

[1]Articles 78 and 78A of the ECSC Treaty, Articles 203 and 203A of the EEC Treaty, Articles
177 and 177A of the Euratom Treaty, all as amended by the Luxembourg Treaty of April
1970.
[2]Rule 23 (1) of the Rules of Procedure.
[3]Rule 26 (1).
[4]*e.g.* Official Journal (C) 124, 1971, pp. 56–58 (Sitting of 18 November 1971).
[5]*e.g. ibid.* p. 61.

budgetary matters beyond that formally provided for in the Treaties. The arrangements were approved by the Parliament on 18 November 1971. They cover the three phases of the budgetary work of the Council and the Parliament.

(i) The Council forwards to the Parliament the preliminary draft of the budget as soon as it has been received from the Commission, and in advance of the timetable for parliamentary consultation established by the Luxembourg Treaty of 1970. This allows the Parliament to proceed with a first examination of the political aspects of the preliminary draft, and to offer advice to the Council before the budget is formally laid before the Parliament. To this end a meeting is arranged between representatives of the Parliament and the President in office and other members of the Council. The Council has nevertheless emphasised that this arrangement cannot be allowed to retard its work in drawing up the budget.

(ii) After the formal submission of the budget to the Parliament, members of the Council of Ministers attend the meetings of the Committee on Finance and Budgets during its discussion of the budget. Ministers are also present during the debate and voting on the budget in the plenary sessions.

(iii) When the Council considers the budget after its return from the Parliament, a delegation from the Parliament presents reasons for the amendments proposed and discusses them with the Council before the Council considers what action to take on the amendments.

Throughout the discussions on the budget close contacts are maintained with the European Commission, whose representatives attend meetings of the parliamentary committees and the plenary sessions on the budget.

> Some modification will be necessary to the procedure of the Parliament and the methods of collaboration between the Council and the Parliament when the responsibilities of the Parliament in budgetary matters are extended at the end of the transitional period on 1 January 1975.[1]

After the signature of the Treaty of Luxembourg in 1970, the Council of Ministers agreed, with certain conditions, that it would not amend the estimates submitted by the Parliament for its own administrative expenditure, thus allowing the Parliament autonomy in the matter of its own budget.

4 Consideration of the annual general report of the Commission

Until 1967 the High Authority and the Commissions published separate reports in respect of the three Communities. Since 1968 the single European Commission has published an annual report on the activities of all three Communities. The report is published not later than one month before the opening of the annual session of the Parliament in

[1]See pages 21–24.

March of each year.[1] The consideration of the annual report is shared
by all the Parliament's committees and has been one of the principal
means by which the Parliament exercises its power of supervision over
the activities of the Commission. Regular and increasing collaboration
between the Commission and the Parliament, however, has made the
examination of the Commission's report of less importance than the
process of continuing scrutiny of the Communities' activities. Since
1970, moreover, the Commission has presented an annual programme
of future Community activity which allows the Parliament to comment
on Community policies before, rather than after, they have been
implemented.

The annual report is printed and circulated to Members of the
Parliament as soon as it is issued by the Commission.[2] The various parts
of the report are allocated to the committees of the Parliament in
accordance with the division of functions between committees described
in Chapter XIV. The opinions of the various committees are embodied
in a single report and motion for a resolution prepared on behalf of
the Parliament, rather than of any one committee, by a general
rapporteur. The rapporteur is elected at the first sitting of each annual
session under the provisions of Rule 37 (2) and (3) of the Rules of
Procedure, on the nomination of the Bureau. Subsequently, the annual
report of the Commission is debated in plenary session of the Parliament on the basis of the report of the general rapporteur, and the
Parliament votes only on the general motion for a resolution proposed
in the latter report.

Each year in February or March the Parliament passes a separate
resolution establishing the detailed procedure and timetable to be
followed in considering the Commission's report, and providing for
the appointment of the general rapporteur.[3] In the resolution of
7 March 1966 in respect of the Ninth General Report of the EEC Commission, provision was made for the report of the general rapporteur
to be approved for submission to the Parliament by the Presidential
Committee. In the resolution of 11 February 1972 in respect of the
Fifth General Report of the European Commission provision was made
for the approval of the general rapporteur's report by the Political
Affairs Committee in the presence of the drafters of the opinions of the
parliamentary committees. In 1966 the general rapporteur's report was
not approved by the Presidential Committee until 22 September. The
procedural resolution in 1972 required the plenary debate on the report
to be held on 8, 9 and 10 May, and the submission of the general
rapporteur's report not later than two weeks before the start of the
May part-session of the Parliament.

---

[1]Merger Treaty, 1965, Article 18.
[2]Rule 20 of the Rules of Procedure.
[3]*e.g.* Official Journal (C) 19, 1972 (Sitting of 11 February 1972).

Members of the Commission attend and participate in meetings of the committees and in the debates in plenary session.

5 Consideration of Community legislation

When the Parliament receives notice of a proposed piece of legislation, the draft of the legislation is published in the Official Journal (Communications) Series and referred to the appropriate committee.[1] In accordance with Rule 38, drafts are formally referred to committees by the Parliament or, during a break in the session, by the President on behalf of the Bureau. In practice, draft legislative proposals are usually forwarded to the Parliament by the European Commission at the same time as they are formally submitted to the Council of Ministers. While receipt of the proposals at this stage is for information only, and formal proceedings cannot begin until consultation is requested by the Council, the committees' officers and secretaries are able to make prior arrangements for the consideration of the proposals and to decide on the distribution of work to the committees.

The appropriate committee makes its report to the Parliament in a single document (published as a working document of the European Parliament[2]) which contains:

(i) (a) a motion for a resolution by the Parliament expressing absolute or qualified approval or disapproval of the draft submitted to the Council by the Commission; and

   (b) where appropriate, a copy of those parts of the Commission's text to which amendments have been proposed by the committee, printed in parallel with the new text proposed by the committee (this formally constitutes a part of the motion for a resolution); and

(ii) an explanatory memorandum (*exposé des motifs*) prepared by the committee rapporteur, which sets out the committee's reasons for the proposals in the resolution and the amendments to the text, and where the committee is not unanimous explains also the views of the minority.

In accordance with Rule 42 of the Rules of Procedure the report must also include the results of any votes taken in the committee. In decisions of 26 April 1967 and 22 September 1969 the Bureau ruled that explanatory memoranda must be concise, must not include, for example, a history of the problems considered, and must be restricted to a paragraph by paragraph commentary on the motion for a resolution.

Rule 26 of the Rules of Procedure provides that the Parliament's debate and detailed examination shall be based on the report of the responsible committee. Except in cases of urgency[3] no debate may be held on a report until it has been in circulation for at least twenty-four hours.

[1] Rule 22 of the Rules of Procedure.
[2] *e.g.* Doc. 156, 1971 (Report by M. Vals).
[3] See page 97.

COURSE OF DEBATE

The normal course of debate is as follows:

(i) *General debate on the committee report:* This is opened by the committee rapporteur, followed by representatives of the political groups and other Members who have asked to speak. A time limit on speeches is usually agreed to in advance of the debate under the provisions of Rule 31 (4) of the Rules of Procedure.[1] It is usual for the responsible member of the Commission, and sometimes for a member of the Council of Ministers, to speak towards the end of the general debate, which is wound up by the rapporteur and occasionally also by representatives of the political groups. No vote is taken at this stage.

(ii) *Examination of the motion for a resolution:* The Parliament considers the motion for a resolution. Amendments may be proposed and voted on before a decision is taken on the resolution as a whole. In practice this part of the debate is usually deferred until the legislative draft has been considered.

(iii) *Examination of the proposed legislation:* In accordance with continental practice the Parliament examines the text of the legislation as proposed by the committee, and not the original draft submitted by the Council. Amendments to the text are proposed and voted on, but no vote is taken on the individual articles of the legislative draft.

(iv) *Adoption of a resolution:* The Parliament finally votes on a resolution, embodying the text of the legislation as amended by the committee and approved by the Parliament. Representatives of the political groups and other Members may give explanations of the votes of their groups or themselves before the final vote is taken. Rule 31 (5) of the Rules of Procedure limits these explanations to a maximum of five minutes each.

> On 10 March 1970 the Parliament decided that if the Parliament rejected amendments proposed by a parliamentary committee to a regulation submitted by the Council, this would not involve the automatic acceptance of the Commission's text but would involve the automatic reference back of the regulation to the committee. Texts of resolutions are also referred back to committee if the texts as amended appear to contain contradictions.

In accordance with Rule 22 (2) of the Rules of Procedure, a resolution adopted by the Parliament following a demand from the Council for consultation or a request from the Council or any other institution for advice is forwarded immediately to the President of that institution. Should the request have originated with the Council of Ministers, the resolution is also forwarded to the European Commission.

> On 15 November 1967 the Bureau approved a number of measures to provide a follow-up procedure in cases where the Parliament has proposed important amendments to proposals of the European Commission:
> (i) Where important changes have been proposed, the subject in question is reinstated in an appropriate form on the agenda of the responsible com-

---

[1] *e.g.* Official Journal Annex (Official Report) No. 140, July 1971, p. 8.

mittee; this allows the committee to resume consideration of the subject when the need arises without a further formal reference.

(ii) the Parliament and the responsible committee should be informed immediately by the Commission if, in accordance with article 149 of the EEC Treaty, the Commission has withdrawn its original proposal to the Council of Ministers and replaced it with an amended proposal.

(iii) there will be a periodic examination of the decisions taken by the Council in respect of regulations, directives, and decisions about which the Parliament has been consulted, to ensure that these conform with the advice of the Parliament.

The European Commission has undertaken to give its opinion to the Parliament on all modifications proposed by the Parliament to the Commission's legislative proposals. The opinion is given either by a Commissioner during a plenary session of the Parliament or, if that is impossible, by letter. This arrangement provides the Parliament with an assurance that its modifications will be seriously considered by the Commission, even if no action is ultimately taken on them.

6 Other motions

Any member of the European Parliament may table a motion for a resolution on a matter falling within the sphere of activities of the Communities. Such motions are printed, distributed and referred to the appropriate committees.

Debate in the plenary session of the Parliament is based on the report of the appropriate committee or committees, which must include the text of the motion tabled and any amendments proposed by the committee. Resolutions approved by the Parliament are forwarded by the President to the institutions to which they relate.

7 Amendments

According to Rule 29 of the Rules of Procedure, any member of the Parliament has the right to propose and to speak in support of amendments to resolutions. The right to propose amendments does not include the right to propose amendments to the explanatory memoranda of committee reports.

Amendments must relate to the text of the motion for a resolution or, in the case of consultations and requests for advice, to the legislative texts as amended by the parliamentary committee, and not to the original texts submitted by the Commission. Amendments may not be tabled to proposals for amendments to the ECSC Treaty submitted for approval under Article 95 of the Treaty.[1]

All amendments must be submitted in writing, and the President has the right to decide whether or not they are in order. They must relate to the text which it is sought to amend, and they may seek to replace a

[1]See page 130.

part or the whole of a motion for a resolution.[1] Unless the Parliament decides otherwise, amendments may not be put to the vote until they have been printed and published in the official languages. In practice, manuscript drafting amendments may be accepted. By a decision of the Bureau of the Parliament on 26 March 1965, an amendment is inadmissible if the text which it is intended to amend is unamendable in the form proposed in any one or more of the official languages. In such a case the President is empowered to seek out an appropriate linguistic solution with the help of the interested parties. Amendments to amendments are admissible and are governed by the same rules.

Every amendment which is in order is called by the President and, if not withdrawn,[2] is disposed of by the Parliament after debate. Amendments have priority over the texts to which they relate and must be put to the vote before these texts. Amendments to amendments have similar priority. The majority required to carry an amendment is an absolute majority of the votes cast.[3]

REFERENCE OF AMENDMENTS TO COMMITTEES

Any member of the Parliament may move the reference of amendments to the appropriate committee. Under the terms of Rule 32 (1) such a motion has priority over the discussion in progress. Only the proposer of the procedural motion, one speaker for and against the motion, and the chairman or rapporteur of the committee concerned may speak on such a motion and, according to Rule 31 (5), none may speak for more than five minutes. In accordance with Rule 29 (5) of the Rules of Procedure, however, the reference of amendments to committee is automatic if it is requested by the responsible committee. The Parliament may fix a time-limit within which the committee must report back on the amendment, and the reference of amendments to committees need not interrupt the debate if the Parliament wishes to proceed. In such cases the relevant part or parts of the text are set aside for later consideration.

ORDER OF DISPOSAL OF AMENDMENTS

When two or more mutually exclusive amendments are proposed to the same part of a text, they are considered in an order which accords with continental parliamentary practice.[4] Those furthest in intention from the text submitted by the committee have priority and are put to the vote first. If they are rejected, the amendments next furthest from the text are considered, and so on until all the remaining amendments have been disposed of. If the first or subsequent amendments are adopted, the remaining amendments are considered as rejected. If there is any

[1] Agreed by the Parliament on 16 April 1959 and 8 January 1968.
[2] *e.g.* Official Journal (C) 18, 1968, page 3 (sitting of 21 February 1968).
[3] Rule 35 (5) of the Rules of Procedure.
[4] Rule 29 (4) of the Rules of Procedure.

doubt about the order in which amendments are to be considered and voted on, the President gives a ruling.

8 Final vote

When the examination of a text by the Parliament has been concluded, the final vote on the whole text is taken. Before voting, explanations of vote, not exceeding five minutes in duration, may be made by any Member on his own behalf or on behalf of his political group. The methods of voting are described in Chapter XII. When the Parliament is unanimously in favour of a text, as is often the case, there is no roll-call.

VOTING WITHOUT DEBATE

Rule 27 of the Rules of Procedure lays down a procedure by which debate on a motion for a resolution may be avoided and the Parliament may proceed directly to a final vote. The right of Members to give an explanation of their vote is unaffected.

With the agreement of the European Commission, committees may request that motions for resolutions contained in their reports be put to the vote without further discussion after consideration of the reports. If such a request is made the political groups are notified, and at the first sitting of each part-session, or at the latest on the day before the sitting on whose agenda they appear, the President announces any texts which can be voted on without debate. If no request to speak has been submitted under Rule 31 (1) of the Rules of Procedure, the President puts them to the vote immediately they are reached on the agenda.

By a decision of the Bureau of 22 September 1969, of which the Parliament was informed at the sitting of 6 October 1969, a similar procedure was established in respect of committee reports as a whole. In accordance with this decision, the President of the Parliament or the Bureau, when referring a consultation to a committee, may propose that the report of the committee concerned should be examined in plenary session without debate. This proposal is deemed to have been approved by the committee concerned unless that committee decides to request an alternative procedure. If the committee does not so decide the proposal is submitted for approval by the Parliament and, if it is approved, the report is placed on the agenda for examination without debate. On the same date the Bureau decided that in all cases the responsible committee should state, during the preparation of the report, the procedure, with or without debate, to be proposed for the examination of its report in plenary session.

Chapter XIV

The system of committees

1 General

Since its session of March 1967, the Parliament has, at the beginning of each session, set up twelve committees which have the duty of considering and making reports on the main categories of the business of the Parliament. According to Rule 37 (1) of the Rules of Procedure, the Parliament may set up standing or temporary, general or special committees and define their powers and duties.

The number of committees has not always been the same. At its constituent meeting in March 1958 the Parliament established thirteen committees: the Committee on Political Affairs and Institutional Questions, the Committee on Commercial Policy and Economic Co-operation with Non-member countries, the Committee on Agriculture, the Committee on Social Affairs, the Committee on the Internal Market of the Community, the Committee on Investments, Financial Questions and long-term Policies, the Committee on the Association of Overseas Countries and Territories, the Committee on Transport, the Committee on Energy Policy, the Committee on Scientific and Technical Research, the Committee on Safety, Industrial Hygiene and Health Protection, the Administrative Committee, and the Committee on Legal Questions, Privileges and Immunities.

The establishment of committees was changed in March 1967 and the following twelve committees were set up:

Political Affairs Committee	
Economic Affairs Committee	
Committee on Finance and Budgets . . .	
Committee on Agriculture	29 Members
Committee on Social Affairs and Public Health .	
Committee on External Trade Relations . .	
Legal Affairs Committee	
Committee on Energy Research and Atomic Problems	
Transport Committee	17 Members
Committee for the Association with Greece . .	15 Members
Committee for the Association with Turkey . .	
Committee on Relations with the Associated African States and Madagascar	18 Members

It is likely that a number of Members of the Parliament from the new member countries will be added to these committees in January 1973 as an interim measure until a new permanent committee structure is established.

From time to time the European Parliament also establishes committees of a temporary nature to deal with specific problems falling outside the ambit of the permanent committees. In January 1961, for instance, a special temporary committee was set up to prepare the opinion of the Parliament on the draft agreement of association between Greece and the Communities.

2 Constitution of committees

In accordance with resolutions of the Parliament of 2 February 1967, 14 March 1967, and 13 March 1969, the membership of the committees has been fixed as described below.

The representation of political groups and of member states on committees is roughly proportionate to their representation in the Parliament, but in the last resort political considerations outweigh national balance in the distribution of seats. Committees are elected at the beginning of the session, which opens each year on the second Tuesday in March. Nominations are given to the Bureau of the Parliament, which is bound by Rule 37 (2) of the Rules of Procedure to submit to the Parliament proposals designed to ensure fair representation of member states and of political views.

The Bureau's proposed list of candidates for membership of committees is published with the draft agenda. The proposals, which derive from the political groups, are usually agreed to without amendment. If any dispute arises over the nomination and election of members of committees, the Parliament votes by secret ballot to decide the matter. The Bureau may also provisionally fill any vacancy on a committee with the agreement of the persons concerned and within the requirements for fair representation of nationalities and political views. Such provisional changes are submitted to the Parliament for ratification at its next sitting.

The nomination of members of committees is made according to the considerations of political and national balance. Seats in committee are first divided among political groups using the d'Hondt system of proportional representation. When this division is made, the national delegations are allotted seats as far as possible in accordance with their numerical strength in the Parliament. Whereas the criterion of political balance is almost invariably followed, the requirement of national balance cannot always be respected within each committee; but within the whole group of committee appointments each national delegation receives seats according to its strength.

I

In the committees established in March 1972, while the political balance was virtually the same in each committee of 29 Members (Christian Democrats 10 or 11, Socialists 8, Liberals and Allies 5, European Democratic Union 4, unattached 1 or 2), national representation on these committees varied between seven and ten Members for France, six and eight Members for Germany, four and seven Members for Italy, two and three Members for Belgium, two and four Members for Holland, and one and two Members of Luxembourg. The theoretical overall distribution of seats on these largest committees was seven each for France, Germany and Italy, three each for Belgium and Holland, and two for Luxembourg.

3 Appointment of committee bureaux

Each committee elects its own bureau which consists of a chairman and one or two vice-chairmen. No Member who belongs to a national government may be a member of the bureau of a committee, in accordance with Rule 37 (1) of the Rules of Procedure.

4 Appointment of sub-committees

Committees are empowered by Rule 39 (2) of the Rules of Procedure in the interest of their work to appoint one or more sub-committees. The composition and scope of a sub-committee are laid down by the main committee when it is appointed.

The procedure followed by sub-committees is the same as that which applies in full committees. A sub-committee reports to the committee which set it up.

The use of sub-committees is now infrequent.

5 Substitutes

Any member of a committee may arrange for his place to be taken at meetings of the committee by another member of the Parliament in accordance with the provisions of Rule 40 (3) of the Rules of Procedure. The name of the substitute must be notified in advance to the chairman of the committee. Substitutes may also sit on sub-committees under the same conditions.

The object of appointing substitutes to attend committee meetings is to ensure that a quorum is always present. While the responsibility for nominating a substitute is nominally under the control of the individual member, in practice this is done under the aegis of political groups, whose secretariats maintain lists of Members who are interested in attending committees to which they have not been nominated as full members. Thus the balance of nationalities on a committee can be substantially altered by the use of substitutes, but the political balance is likely to be maintained.

Substitute members have full voting and speaking rights while formally replacing a full member of the committee.

6 Division of functions between committees

Committees have no formal terms of reference under the Rules of Procedure, and in the last resort the power to refer individual matters to committees rests, under Rule 38 of the Rules of Procedure, with the Parliament or, during a break in the session, with the President on behalf of the Bureau. Nevertheless, there is an accepted division of functions between the committees, which is usually followed in the reference of matters to the committees.

Between 1961 and 1967 the responsibilities of committees were determined by reference to a catalogue of functions printed as an annex to the report of M. P.A. Blaisse (of the Legal Affairs Committee) of 24 February 1961.

On 8 March 1968, following the committee reorganisation of the previous year, the Bureau of the Parliament issued a directive to members of the Parliament on the division of functions between committees. The Bureau stressed that, in view of the powers contained in Rule 38 of the Rules of Procedure, the directive was of an 'indicative character' only.

The main subjects for which the committees are responsible are as follows:

(i) *Political Affairs Committee:* the general structure of the Communities; relations with other Community institutions; the political and institutional aspects of association agreements etc., of popular representation and the direct election of members of the Parliament, of the siting of Community institutions, and of relations with other international organisations and with non-member countries; cultural exchanges; the European university; harmonisation of educational courses and qualifications.

(ii) *Economic Affairs Committee:* overall functioning and development of the common market (in particular the application of Articles 9 to 37 of the EEC Treaty); competition, combines and monopolies; dumping; grants-in-aid; markets, prices, combines etc. in the coal and steel market; problems of the nuclear common market; co-ordination and harmonisation of economic policies; conjuncture[1]; coal and steel objectives; regional policies; mid-term economic planning and the co-ordination of investments in coal, steel and nuclear energy; monetary policy, balance of payments, and capital movements.

(iii) *Committee on Finance and Budgets:* examination of Community budgets; budget, administrative operation and accountability of the Parliament; financial resources of the Communities; financial and accounting methods; status of Community employees; budgetary and financial control of the use of special funds (e.g. European Social Fund); co-ordination of budgetary systems of member states; European Investment Bank.

(iv) *Committee on Agriculture:* all questions relating to Title II (Agriculture) of the EEC Treaty; common market in agricultural and fisheries products; common agricultural policy; price regulation; productivity, etc.

[1]See Article 103 of the EEC Treaty (Appendix A).

(v) *Committee on Social Affairs and Public Health:* amelioration and equalisation of conditions of life and labour; harmonisation of social systems, equal pay, holidays and overtime; circulation of labour; employment policy; professional training and rehabilitation; housing; activities of European Social Fund; social problems of underdeveloped regions; industrial safety; industrial health; radiation hazards; public health.

(vi) *Committee on External Trade Relations:* commercial and economic aspects of relations with international organisations such as EFTA, GATT, and OECD; common external tariff; co-ordination of national commercial policies; general problems of trade with non-member countries.

(vii) *Legal Affairs Committee:* elaboration, application and interpretation of the Rules of Procedure of the Parliament; privileges and immunities; juridical questions related to the activities of the Parliament; creation and application of Community law; co-ordination of national legislation in the fields of freedom of establishment and the provision of services, company law, and the application of Article 220 of the EEC Treaty.

(viii) *Committee on Energy Research and Atomic Problems:* all aspects of Community energy policy; scientific and technical research; technological co-operation; patents; industrial property; agronometric research (in co-operation with the Agriculture Committee). The committee also has a general right to consider any other matters which may influence short, medium or long-term energy policy.

(ix) *Transport Committee:* all questions relating to transport; development of a common transport policy; liberalisation of international transport; air, marine and pipeline problems; conflicts between a common transport policy and other Community policies (e.g. regional policies).

(x) *Committee for the Association with Greece:* all problems concerning the application of the association agreement between the Community and Greece. The members of the committee form the delegation to the joint parliamentary committee established between the Economic Community and Greece (the joint committee is at present suspended).

(xi) *Committee for the Association with Turkey:* all problems concerning the application of the association agreement between the Community and Turkey. The members of the committee form the delegation to the joint parliamentary committee established between the Economic Community and Turkey.

(xii) *Committee on Relations with the Associated African states and Madagascar:* implementation of the Yaoundé Convention and the activities of the European Development Fund; relations with African states, whether associated or not; general development problems, where these affect Africa and Madagascar. The prime responsibility for development problems outside Africa rests with the Committee on External Trade Relations. The members of the committee form the delegation to the joint committee of the Parliamentary Conference of the Association between the EEC and the African States and Madagascar.

In marginal cases where the interests of two or more committees overlap, arrangements have been made to provide what amounts to multiple responsibility for the committees concerned. In accordance with Rule 38 (3) of the Rules of Procedure, one of the committees is named as the committee responsible and the others as committees asked for their opinions.

While the Legal Affairs Committee is responsible for problems arising under Articles 52 to 66 of the EEC Treaty (the right of establishment, free provision of services, etc.), the committee is required to receive the opinions of the Economic Affairs Committee or other committees which may be concerned with specific problems in these fields.

The Economic Affairs Committee must receive the opinions of the Committee on Finance and Budgets on matters relating to monetary policy, balance of payments, and the movement of capital, and must include these opinions at an appropriate place in its own reports. The Finance and Budgets Committee is free to take the initiative in these matters.

The Committee on Agriculture and the Committee on Social Affairs and Public Health have a general right to submit opinions to other committees on any matter falling within the responsibility of other committees which touch upon the interests of agriculture or of social affairs and public health. Similar arrangements exist to deal with the overlapping jurisdiction of other committees.

Chapter XV

Powers and procedures of committees

The procedure of committees is governed by Rules 39 to 44 of the Rules of Procedure which lay down the practice of committees. Rules 7 (2), 29 to 32 and 35 (4), (5) and (6) are also applied to committees. These rules have also been amplified by a body of practice and decisions which has been built up since committees were first appointed by the Parliament.

1 General scope

The twelve general committees of the Parliament do not have specific terms of reference; but they do work in the specialised fields of inquiry described in Chapter XIV. Within this framework and within the provisions of the Rules of Procedure, committees of the Parliament have examined several different categories of business.

There is a general obligation in Rule 38 of the Rules of Procedure to examine questions referred by the Parliament, or during a break in the session by the President on behalf of the Bureau. If a committee decides that it is not competent to consider a question, or if there is a dispute between two or more committees, the question of which is the competent committee is placed on the Parliament's agenda on a motion of the Bureau or at the request of one of the committees concerned. If it is decided that more than one committee has a responsibility, one committee is named as primarily responsible and the other committee or committees are asked to give opinions. In general, not more than three committees may deal with one topic at the same time unless the Parliament decides otherwise.

The first category of business referred to committees consists of requests from the Commission or the Council of Ministers for consultation. Such requests must be printed and distributed as soon as they are received by the Parliament. In the case of the general report on the activities of the Communities, the Parliament agreed in 1972 that each committee could submit their opinion to the general rapporteur.

A second category of business dealt with by committees includes motions for resolutions tabled by Members on matters falling within the sphere of activities of the Communities under Rule 25 of the Rules of Procedure. Such motions are printed and distributed, and, unless urgent procedure has been requested, referred to the appropriate committee. In reporting to the Parliament, the committee must include in the report the original text of the motion.

Two other types of business which are referred to committees are petitions to the Parliament (see Chapter XVII) and the draft Budget (see Chapter XIII).

Since 1963 committees have made studies and produced working documents for their own use without the consent of the Bureau. A committee may also apply to the Bureau to be allowed to submit a report to the Parliament on a particular subject. Such initiatives have been taken after the production of working documents.[1]

2 Meetings of committees

Meetings of committees are convened by the chairman on his own initiative or at the request of the President of the Parliament. Committees may meet during meetings of the Parliament or in between part-sessions. But following a decision of the Bureau of 24 April 1964, committees cannot meet while the Parliament is sitting without the authorisation of the President or the Vice-President in the chair. The secretary of the committee is responsible for circulating to Members summonses to meetings together with the draft agenda. He is also responsible for seeing that all documents required by the committee are prepared and distributed.

Committees meet at the time of sessions of the Parliament at the place of meeting, either Strasbourg or Luxembourg. Between sessions, they usually meet at the Palais des Congrès in Brussels where it is convenient for the officials of the Commission to be present. Any committee may decide to request that it be allowed to hold one or more meetings away from Strasbourg, Luxembourg or Brussels. A reasoned request must be submitted to the President for consideration by the Bureau. If an urgent decision is required, then the President may take the responsibility himself. If such a request is rejected by the Bureau or the President, the reasons for it must be given. It has become customary for a week of committee meetings to be held in Italy each year because Italian members have the longest journey to reach the other places of meeting.

3 Election of chairmen and rapporteurs

In accordance with Rules 41 (5) and 42 (1) of the Rules of Procedure, each committee elects its own chairman and two vice-chairmen and appoints a rapporteur for each subject under discussion. The election of the Bureau, which consists of the chairman and vice-chairmen, takes place by secret ballot without debate. The chairman is elected

[1]See Doc. 111/1967 Report of M. Bech.

first. Nominations for that office are handed to the oldest member of the committee who takes the chair during the election. If more than one nomination is received for the position of chairman, one, or if necessary, two secret ballots are held. To be elected a candidate, requires an absolute majority of the votes cast on the first ballot. Should a second ballot be necessary, a simple majority is sufficient. As soon as the chairman has been duly elected he takes the chair. The same procedure is followed in the election of the vice-chairmen. Contested elections are often avoided by agreement on candidates between political groups before the election takes place.

When the bureau of a committee is established, the committee may then proceed with business. Where the committee has several subjects to consider, a separate rapporteur is appointed to prepare the committee's report on each subject. Appointments may be made by general agreement among the members of the committee or by election by secret ballot if necessary. The chairman and vice-chairman of the committee may also accept appointment as rapporteurs.

4 Attendance at meetings by witnesses, observers and the public

Committee meetings are not held in public unless a committee decides to the contrary. Unless committees decide otherwise, members of the Parliament may attend meetings of the committees of which they are not members but may not take part in their deliberations.

Members of the Commission and of the Council of Ministers may take part in meetings of committees if invited to do so by the chairman on behalf of a committee. By special decision a committee may invite any other person to attend a meeting of the committee, and to take part in the discussions. Under the terms of a decision of the Bureau of 13 April 1965, special invitations may only be issued with the approval of the Bureau of the Parliament.

Committees frequently take evidence informally from officers of the Commission who are responsible for the drafting of Regulations, etc., which are before committee. Attendance of the officers is arranged through the Parliamentary Liaison Division of the Commission.

5 Study or fact-finding missions

Any committee may, with the agreement of the Bureau of the Parliament, instruct one or more of its members to go on a study or fact-finding mission.

The Bureau of the Parliament has laid down guidelines at various times about the composition and conduct of such missions.

The number of Members attending such visits was fixed at a maximum of nine for a large committee and six for a small committee, on 21 September 1961. At the same time it was deicded that the members of such missions could only be replaced by a member of the same committee and then only on the recommendation of the chairman of the political group concerned. In the case of journeys organised by the Committee for Relations with the Associated African States and Madagascar, the Bureau decided on 27 February 1967 that, if a member of such a mission needed to be replaced and a member of the committee could not be found, a substitute could be chosen from among the European members of the Conference of the Association.

Following decisions of the Bureau of 15 June and 5 November 1962, after each journey a report on the visit is made to the enlarged Bureau. At the head of the report are given the names of the Members nominated to go on the mission, the names of those Members who took part at the different stages of the visit and the names of those Members who were present at the different meetings during the visit as well as the names of officials accompanying the Members. Thereafter, the programme of the visit and a statement of the problems examined must be given. After each mission is completed by a parliamentary delegation, the list of Members who took part is communicated to the Parliament.

6 Privacy of documents

Documents issued by a committee are not publicly available because they are deemed to be part of the proceedings of a committee from which the public are excluded. A committee may decide to make public all its working documents; but unless a decision to that effect is taken, only reports adopted for presentation to the Parliament and statements prepared on the responsibility of the chairman are publicly available.

7 Languages

Simultaneous interpretation into all official languages is provided. All committee documents are also translated into all official languages.

8 Quorum

A committee may deliberate or vote when one-third of its members is present. There is no rule that a committee cannot adopt a report unless a majority of the members are present.

If, however, a request is made by one-sixth of the members of a committee before voting begins, a vote is not valid unless the number voting represents an absolute majority of members of the committee.

9 Methods of voting and majorities

Voting in committee is normally by show of hands. If a member requests it, a vote by roll call is held. When a vote by roll call is taken, proceedings follow the procedure laid down in Rule 35 (4) and (5) for voting in the Parliament. The roll is called in alphabetical order beginning with a name drawn by lot. Members vote by word of mouth expressed by 'yes', 'no' and 'I abstain'. Only votes for and against the proposition count in calculating a majority. The chairman is responsible for counting votes and announcing the result. The result is recorded in the Minutes of Proceedings, with voters listed in alphabetical order.

The chairman may vote but has no casting vote. He may also take part in discussions of a committee. An absolute majority of the votes is required for a question to be decided. If one-sixth of the members of a committee so request before the commencement of a vote, the vote is not valid unless the number of members present and voting represents an absolute majority of the members of the committee.

10 Rules of order in debate

The rules of the Parliament concerning the right to speak and the maintenance of order in debate are applied to committee proceedings 'as appropriate' by Rule 41 (1) of the Rules of Procedure. In practice the proceedings in committee are much less formal than those of the Parliament itself.

11 Procedural motions

Rule 32 of the Rules of Procedure of the Parliament concerning procedural motions is applied to committees. However since a less formal approach to proceedings is adopted in committee, such motions are rarely used.

12 Minutes of proceedings

Minutes of proceedings of each meeting of a committee containing a record of the decisions taken are drawn up by the secretariat of the committee. The minutes are circulated to members of the committee and are formally submitted to the committee for its approval at its next meeting. In addition a summary report may be compiled. Unless the committee decides to the contrary, the summary report is not distributed but is kept available for all members. In practice, summary reports are no longer kept since the minutes of proceedings of a committee contain a short summary of arguments presented.

13 Committees asked for an opinion

If a committee to which a matter has been referred wishes to obtain the views of another committee, or if another committee wishes to make known its views on the report of the responsible committee, the President may be requested to designate one committee as the committee primarily responsible and the other committee as the committee asked for its opinion.[1]

The committee asked for an opinion may communicate the opinion to the responsible committee either orally through its own chairman or rapporteur or in writing. The opinion must relate to the text referred to the committee and not exceed ten pages of roneo typescript. The result of the vote in the committee must be given as well as a summary of minority views.

The Bureau decided on 22 September 1969 that the committee primarily responsible may fix a time limit by which opinions must be submitted and before the expiry of which the main report may not be completed. The committee primarily responsible must incorporate in the main report the views of committees asked for an opinion.

If a committee asked for an opinion is unable to deliver it before the main report is finally adopted, the chairman or rapporteur may present the opinion to Parliament in the debate on the report provided that they have notified the President of their intention before the opening of the debate.

An opinion may include proposed amendments to the text referred to the committee. The opinion may also include suggestions for parts of the motion for resolution to be submitted by the responsible committee. It may not include a separate motion for a resolution.

The chairman and rapporteur of a committee asked for an opinion may take part in an advisory capacity in the discussions of the responsible committee provided that the discussions relate to the matter of joint interest. In special circumstances the committee asked for an opinion may nominate up to five other members, with the approval of the chairman of the main committee, to take part in an advisory capacity in the meetings of that committee for matters of joint interest.

14 Reports

The final report of a committee falls into two parts: a motion for a resolution and an explanatory statement. In a decision of 26 April 1967 communicated to the Parliament on 11 May 1967 it was decided that the motion for a resolution must precede the explanatory statement.

Following a decision of the Bureau of 22 September 1969 announced by the Parliament on 6 October 1969 only the text of the resolution is considered and voted upon paragraph by paragraph by a committee after the conclusion of a general debate. For the adoption of the explanatory statement, which sets out the reasons for the proposed text and the arguments preceding its adoption, the committee votes

[1]Rules 35 (3) and 44 of the Rules of Procedure.

only once. The report includes the result of the vote on the report as a whole. If the committee is not unanimous, the report also states the views of the minority.

If the bureau of a committee so decides, a time limit may be fixed within which the appointed rapporteur must submit his draft report to the committee. Although the time limit may be extended, once it has finally expired the committee may instruct its chairman to ask for the matter to be placed on the agenda of the next sitting of the Parliament. Debate may then take place on the basis of an oral report.

15 Amendments

Amendments are dealt with according to the procedure laid down in Rule 29 of the Rules of Procedure which is applied by Rule 41 (1) to proceedings in the committee. Amendments must relate to the motion for a resolution in the report which is before a committee.

Under Rule 29 (5) of the Rules of Procedure amendments proposed to a report at a plenary meeting may be referred to a committee. The Parliament may fix a time limit within which the committee must reach its conclusions on the amendments. The debates are not necessarily adjourned for their consideration.

Chapter XVI

Revision of the Treaties and of the Rules of Procedure of the Parliament

1 General

The procedure of the Parliament stems from two sources. Certain basic matters are governed by the founding Treaties of the Communities, the provisions of which can only be altered by the procedures laid down in Article 236 of the EEC Treaty 1957, Article 204 of the Euratom Treaty 1957 and Articles 95 and 96 of the ECSC Treaty 1951. But the main body of procedure is governed by the Rules of Procedure which were drawn up by the Parliament and can be amended only by the Parliament itself.

2 Revision of the E E C and Euratom Treaties

Article 236 of the EEC Treaty and Article 204 of the Euratom Treaty provide for the amendment of the two Treaties by agreements between the Council of Ministers and the governments of member states. Proposals for amendment may be submitted to the Council of Ministers by the Commission or by any of the individual member governments. The Council must consult the Parliament, and when the proposal has come from a member state, must also consult the Commission. Thereafter the Council may convene a conference of the representatives of the governments of member states for the purpose of determining the amendments to be made to the Treaty or Treaties concerned.

An amendment to one of the Treaties agreed in this way may alter member states' rights and obligations in international law. A treaty to establish such rights and obligations must be ratified by all member states in accordance with their respective constitutional requirements. In this context, an agreement might be made by several different instruments such as a Treaty, Convention or Protocol. In the United Kingdom a treaty must be laid before the House of Commons and ratified according to the procedure established by the Ponsonby Rule (see page 29).

Under the procedure of treaty revision, the powers of the European Parliament are similar to its powers in relation to the making of community law by the Council of Ministers.[1] It has the right to be consulted, but has no power to reject the proposals submitted to it. Conversely, any member of the Parliament may table a motion for a

[1] See pages 20–21, 105–106 and 111–113.

resolution to the Council and the Commission proposing amendments
to the Treaties; and such a motion may be adopted as a resolution by a
simple majority of the members voting.

On two occasions when (before the enlargement of the Communities by the
Treaty of Accession) the three Treaties (including the ECSC Treaty)
were amended, the amendments were adopted under the terms of Article
236 of the EEC Treaty, Article 204 of the Euratom Treaty and Article 96
of the ECSC Treaty. The Merger Treaty establishing a single Council and
a single Commission of the European Communities was signed in Brussels
on 8 April 1965. The Treaty amending certain Budgetary Provisions of
the Treaties establishing the European Communities and of the Treaty
establishing a single Council and a single Commission of the European
Communities was signed in Luxembourg on 22 April 1970.

3 Revision of the E C S C Treaty

Article 95 of the ECSC Treaty of 1951 provides that where unforeseen
difficulties or fundamental economic and technical changes affecting
the coal and steel market require changes in the rules affecting the High
Authority's exercise of its powers, amendments to the Treaty may be
proposed jointly by the High Authority (now the Commission) and the
Council acting by a five-sixths majority of its members. Such proposed
amendments may not conflict with the provisions of Articles 2, 3 and 4
of the Treaty (which lay down the primary tasks and objectives of the
Coal and Steel Community), and must be submitted to the European
Court of Justice for consideration.

If the Court finds the proposals compatible with the Treaty, they are
forwarded to the European Parliament and only enter into force if
approved by a majority of three-quarters of the votes cast and two-thirds
of the members of the Parliament.

In accordance with Rule 24 of the Parliament's Rules of Procedure,
proposals from the Commission and the Council for the amendment of
the ECSC Treaty under Article 95 are printed and distributed at the
same time as the assenting opinion on the proposals delivered by the
Court of Justice. In conformity with the Parliament's usual practice,
the proposals are referred to the Legal Affairs Committee, whose report
may only recommend either adoption or rejection of each proposal as a
whole, but may not recommend amendments.

In the debate in plenary session of the Parliament, no amendments
to proposals for the revision of the Treaties may be moved, and each
proposal must be voted upon as a whole, and not item by item. If
fractions appear in the results of the calculations of the necessary
majorities the required numbers are rounded up to the nearest whole
numbers.[1] Abstentions are not included in the calculation of the results
of such votes.

[1]Decision of the Bureau, 25 May 1965.

Any Member of the Parliament may also table a motion for a resolution proposing to the Commission and the Council that amendments be made under Article 95 of the ECSC Treaty. After consideration by the appropriate committee or committees, such a motion is only deemed to be adopted as a resolution to the Commission and the Council if it secures the votes of a majority of the current members of the Parliament.[1]

The ECSC Treaty may also be revised (under Article 96) by negotiation between the member states at a conference convened by the President of the Council of Ministers in the same way as laid down by the Treaties of Rome. The Parliament is not given the right of consultation on revisions of the Treaty under this article, although in practice the Parliament has been consulted on the amendments to the Treaty which have been adopted.

4 Revision of the Rules of Procedure

Since the first session of the Parliament in March 1958, the Rules of Procedure have been continually revised. The Provisional Rules used initially were those of the former Common Assembly of the European Coal and Steel Community; these Rules were reviewed by the Committee on Rules of Procedure, Legal Affairs, and Petitions and Immunities of the Parliament and new Rules of Procedure were adopted on 23 June 1958.

Under the terms of Rule 54 of the Rules of Procedure any Member may table a motion for a resolution to amend the Parliament's Rules of Procedure; such a motion is printed and referred to the Legal Affairs Committee. After a report from the Legal Affairs Committee, the Parliament votes on a resolution to amend the Rules prepared by the Committee. No such motion is adopted unless it has the support of a majority of the members of the Parliament.

Since 1958, amendments have been made by resolutions adopted on 25 September 1959, 21 November 1959, 31 March 1960, 28 June 1960, 26 June 1961, 27 June 1962, 28 June 1963, 20 January 1965, 20 September 1967, 19 October 1967 and 17 May 1971. These amendments have sprung from several sources. Some have resulted from the need to bring the Rules of Procedure into conformity with amendments to the Treaties.[2] Others have followed motions for resolutions tabled by Members or political groups.[3] Amendments have also been made following a report made by the Legal Affairs Committee on its own initiative.[4]

Several important amendments have been made since the adoption of the original Rules of Procedure on 23 June 1958. Initially the Rules required that the annual session should open 'after 31 December'; this

[1]Rule 24 (3) of the Rules of Procedure.
[2]*e.g.* Resolution of 17 May 1971.
[3]*e.g.* Resolution of 19 October 1967 and Report 131/1967.
[4]*e.g.* Resolution of 20 September 1967 and Report 111/1967.

was altered by the amendment of 21 November 1959,[1] which provided that the session opened 'after 1 March in each year'. A further change of the timing of the opening of the session was made in the major revision of 19 October 1967. The current position in conformity with that amendment and the Merger Treaty requires that the opening of the session takes place on the second Tuesday in March.

An addition to the Rules of Procedure was made on 31 March 1960[2] in relation to the work of committees. It was provided that where several committees had a legitimate interest in a matter, one committee was to be designated as primarily responsible and the others as required to give their opinions. The resolution of 29 June 1962[3] included the redrafting of the Rules relating to Questions, and removed the primary responsibility for the agenda from the Presidential Committee to the Bureau. Finally, the minimum number of Members constituting a political group was reduced by the amendment of 20 January 1965.[4]

REVISION OF 19 OCTOBER 1967

In 1965 the Bureau asked the Legal Affairs Committee to examine the procedures and working methods of the Parliament. The Committee was also asked to consider the motion for a resolution tabled by M. Esteve on behalf of the European Democratic Union Group (Doc. 20/65) and the motion for a resolution tabled by MM. Carboni and Moro (Doc. 109/65). The Committee's report (Doc. 131/67) was debated on 19 October 1967 and its resolution was unanimously adopted.

A large number of important changes were made. The functions of the committee for the verification of credentials were transferred to the Bureau under the revised terms of Rule 3. The Bureau had in practice already begun to discharge those duties (see page 83). The role of the Presidential Committee was also reduced because of its large membership, which included all members of the Bureau and the chairmen of committees and political groups. On the other hand the position of the enlarged Bureau was enhanced. The enlarged Bureau was thus given duties in relation to the summoning of extraordinary sessions, the drawing up of the agenda, and the inclusion on the agenda of oral Questions without debate (see page 135). Two new provisions were adopted to speed up the work of the Parliament: the procedure of voting without debate (Rule 27) and the organisation or time-tabling of debates (Rule 28) were introduced into the Rules of Procedure for the first time.

An important change was also made in the calculation of the quorum. It was clearly established in Rule 33 that a quorum consisted of a

---

[1]Official Journal, 1959, p. 1253.
[2]Official Journal, 1960, p. 702.
[3]Official Journal, 1962, p. 1798.
[4]Official Journal, 1965, p. 292.

majority of current members of the Parliament and not of the maximum number (142) then laid down by the Treaties. Finally, committees were empowered in a new Rule 43 to fix a time limit within which a rapporteur must submit his first draft report.[1]

The revision of October 1967, the main elements of which are outlined above, remained the basis of the Rules of 1972. Amendments, however, were made by resolution on 17 May 1971, to adapt the financial procedures of the Parliament to the provisions of the Luxembourg Treaty of 1970 (see page 107).

[1]For a complete list of changes made and the reasons for them, see Doc. 131/167.

K

Chapter XVII

Questions and Petitions

1 Questions

The right of members of the Parliament to put Questions to the Commission was established in Article 140 of the EEC Treaty 1957. It provided that:

'The Commission shall reply orally or in writing to questions put to it by the Assembly[1] or by its Members'.

In the case of the Council the provisions of Article 140 were much more restricted since the Council had only to 'be heard by the Assembly[1] in accordance with the conditions laid down by the Council in its Rules of Procedure'. The Council's Rules of Procedure did not enlarge on this requirement except to provide that any member of the Council could represent it at meetings of the Parliament or alternatively that the Council's views could be presented in writing. At the session of the Council of March and April 1960 the President of the Council announced that it had been decided to forward replies to Parliamentary Questions on matters which the Council had already considered.

From these beginnings the practice of the Parliament with regard to Questions has developed. The detailed rules are set out as Rules 45 to 47 of the Rules of Procedure. There are three types of Question which may be asked: Questions for written answer, Questions for oral answer without debate, and Questions for oral answer with debate. In the last three complete sessions, 1969–70, 1970–71 and 1971–72, there have been 508, 583 and 641 written questions and 17, 16 and 23 oral Questions, with or without debate.

2 Questions for written answer

Any Member may table Questions for written answer by the Commission or the Council of the Communities. Rule 45 of the Rules of Procedure lays down that Questions shall be brief and relate to specific points; they are passed in writing to the President who must communicate them to the institution concerned.

According to Rule 45 (3) of the Rules of Procedure, written Questions

---

[1]The European Parliament adopted its present title on 30 March 1962.

should be answered by the Commission within one month, and by the Council within two months. Questions to which answers have been given are published, together with the answers, in the Official Journal of the Communities (C) series, giving both the date when the Questions were tabled and the date on which the answers were given. A Question to which no reply has been given in the specified period may be published in the Official Journal without a reply. This may be done only with permission of the Member concerned, and Members have not often made use of this sanction.

3 Questions for oral answer without debate

Any Member may table Questions for answer by the Commission or the Council and request that they be placed on the agenda of the Parliament and dealt with by oral procedure without debate. Such Questions must be sent in writing to the President who lays them before the enlarged Bureau at the next meeting held to establish the agenda of the Parliament. Under the terms of Rule 46, the enlarged Bureau decides whether a Question is to be answered in writing or orally without debate. The decision of the enlarged Bureau must be notified immediately to the Member who has put down the Question and also the institution concerned. In the case of Questions addressed to the Commission, at least one week's notice must be given; and for Questions to the Council, notice of six weeks is required before the opening of the sitting at which the Question may be put.

As in the case of Questions for written answer, Questions must be brief and relate to specific matters and not to problems of a general nature. Under the terms of Rule 46 (2) of the Rules of Procedure, the Parliament may set aside not more than half a day in each part-session for answers to oral Questions. Questions left unanswered after this are carried forward to the next part-session or answered in writing according to the choice of the questioner. In plenary meetings, the Member putting a Question reads it out and may speak upon it for up to ten minutes. The Commissioner or member of the Council replying may give a brief reply. If a Question is directed to the Commission, the Member putting it may ask one or two supplementary questions, to which the Commissioner may give a brief reply.

4 Questions for oral answer with debate[1]

Questions may be addressed to the Commission and Council by a committee, by a political group or by five or more Members for inclusion on the agenda of the Parliament to be answered orally with

---

[1] The procedure for oral Questions with debate is similar to the 'interpellation' procedure commonly used in continental parliaments.

debate. Such Questions must be sent in writing to the President who puts them before the enlarged Bureau at its next meeting held to estab-lish the agenda of the Parliament. The enlarged Bureau must decide whether or not the institution concerned should be consulted and whether the Question is to be answered in writing, orally without debate as set out above, or orally with debate. Questions from political groups are automatically answered orally with debate. As soon as the enlarged Bureau has determined the status of a Question, its decision is sent to the group which has tabled the Question, and the institution to which the Question has been directed.

Oral Questions with debate may be wider in scope than the other types of Question since they may deal with problems of a more general nature. Rule 47 (2) allows that the procedure for oral Questions with debate may be proposed only where notice can be given of at least one week to the Commission and at least six weeks to the Council before the opening of the sitting on the agenda for which the Question is to be placed. In urgent cases, the President may propose direct to a plenary meeting of the Parliament that a Question, unable to be considered by the enlarged Bureau, should be placed on the agenda. Such an arrange-ment may only be made with the agreement of the institution concerned as is also necessary when the customary period of notice has not otherwise been complied with.

In putting a Question, one of the Members concerned may speak for up to twenty minutes. A member of the institution addressed gives a reply. Members who wish to do so may speak once for up to ten minutes. One of the sponsors of the Question may, at his request, briefly comment on the reply given. To close a debate on a Question put to the Commission, the committee, a political group or group of Members concerned may table a motion for a resolution with a request for a vote to follow immediately. When a motion for a resolution has been distributed, the Parliament must first vote on whether a vote shall be taken on the motion immediately. One of the proposers of the motion may speak before the decision is taken. Thereafter only explana-tions of vote are permitted. If an immediate vote on the motion for a resolution is decided upon, the motion is put to the vote without refer-ence to committee. Again, only explanations of vote are permitted.

5 Form of Questions

Questions are printed in the *Bulletin* of the Parliament when they are tabled. Answers to oral Questions appear in the Official Report of Debates of the part-session at which they are answered, together with the original Question. Answers to written Questions are printed in the Official Journal (C) series together with the original Question when a reply is forwarded by the Council or the Commission.

Oral and written Questions are numbered in separate series each session. At the head of each Question are printed its number and the procedure by which it is to be answered. Then follows the name of the Member or group putting the Question, the name of the institution to which it is directed and, in the case of written Questions, the date on which the Question was tabled.

The main body of the Question may contain three parts: first the object of the Question is summarised; second, there may be a statement of fact on which the Question is based; and finally there is a question or a number of questions an answer to which is required.

In the case of oral Questions, a reply is given in the form of a short speech by a member of the Commission or the Council. For written Questions the answer is printed beneath the Question in the Official Journal (C) series. The answer to a written Question may take some months to appear.

In the Official Journal No. C146 of 11 December 1970 replies to Questions tabled between 14 May and 23 October were published. Of eleven Questions answered, nine were to the Commission and two to the Council, including one by M. Califice to the Council on the subject of the negotiations for the entry of Great Britain into the Common Market (299/70). Five of the Questions had been tabled by one Member, there being no limit to the number of written Questions which a Member may put.

6 Practice relating to Questions

Since the early days of the Parliament, the practice of putting Questions to the Commission and the Council has increased three or fourfold.[1] In order to ensure that the practice is not abused certain rules have been developed. According to a decision of the Bureau of 4 July 1968, the enlarged Bureau may ask Members who have tabled Questions to redraft them. This decision has enabled the provisions of Rules 45 and 47 of the Rules of Procedure relating to the scope of Questions to be properly enforced. Questions must relate to matters within the responsibility of the institutions of the Communities. It has also been ruled that Questions must not request statistics readily available.

A problem of parliamentary practice examined early in 1972 was the matter of withdrawal of oral Questions. On 4 July 1968 the Bureau decided that an oral Question could only be withdrawn from the agenda when a written request signed by the Member in charge of the Question had been received. In 1972, the Legal Affairs Committee studied this matter again at the request of the President, and considered the problems created by the withdrawal of an oral Question with debate already sent to the institution concerned and placed on the Parliament's agenda. It was concluded that, following the example of national parliaments,

[1]Only 180 written Questions and 6 oral Questions were answered in 1962, while in 1971, 641 written and 23 oral Questions were answered.

there was no objection to this procedure. Moreover, if another group of Members wished to table a Question in the same terms as one withdrawn, the provision of the rules concerning minimum notice must start again as if a completely new Question was being tabled.

It has also become the practice of the Parliament to group Questions for answer together if the subject matter is the same. In this case, it is not the Commission or the Council which decides, but the political groups from which the Questions emanate.

The Legal Affairs Committee also considered in 1972 the need to establish an hour set aside exclusively for Questions at each part-session of the Parliament. This proposal, accompanied also by a suggestion to set aside an hour at each part-session for the debate of current issues, was endorsed by the Committee and supplementary Rules and draft Orders were prepared for submission to the enlarged Bureau to implement these proposals. The Parliament has not yet taken a decision on this matter.

7 Petitions

According to Rule 48 of the Rules of Procedure, petitions to the Parliament are entered in a register in the order in which they are received provided that they show the name, occupation, nationality and permanent address of each petitioner. The President announces the registration of petitions to the Parliament and is bound to refer them to one of the Committees established under Rule 37 (1) of the Rules of Procedure. The committee within whose field of responsibility the petition falls must first determine whether the petition falls within the scope of the activities of the Communities.

The competent committee may report to the Parliament on the admissibility of the petitions which it has studied. If the committee so recommends, the President sends the petitions declared to be admissible to the Commission or the Council of the Communities together with the opinion of the Committee. Notice of the transmission of a petition to the Commission or Council or of a report on a petition by the relevant committee must be given to the Parliament and recorded in the minutes of proceedings. The petitioner is also informed of the proceedings.

An example of a petition which was passed to the Commission by the Parliament was that of the Municipal Council of St Savin on the creation of a European Currency. It was received by the Parliament and referred to the Economic and Financial Committee on 22 January 1964. On 11 May 1964 the President announced to the Parliament that, in accordance with the advice of the Economic and Financial Committee, the petition was to be referred to the Commission of the EEC together with the opinion of the Committee.

There have been several cases where committees have recommended that petitions be disallowed.

In a statement to the Parliament on 19 March 1971 the President informed the Parliament that he had received two letters from the Legal Affairs Committee concerning Petitions Nos. 2/70 and 2/71.[1] The Committee recommended that Petition 2/70 relating to Isola delle Rosa could not be admitted because the island in question was outside the territory of the Italian Republic and therefore did not fall within the sphere of activities of the Communities.

The Committee also recommended that Petition 2/71 concerning articles published in the weekly magazine *Die Zeit*, should not be admitted since it did not take the customary form of a request or petition to the Parliament.

The texts of petitions entered on the register and the reports of committees thereon are preserved in the archives of the Parliament, where they are available for inspection by Members.

[1]See Official Journal, Annex No. 142, October 1971.

Chapter XVIII

The administration of the Parliament

1 The Secretariat

The Secretariat of the Parliament is based in Luxembourg, where the secretariat has offices in the European Centre at Kitchberg. After the accession to the Communities of the three new members in January 1973, the establishment of the Secretariat will number in excess of one thousand employees. This is considerably larger than the average staff of parliaments at a national level. The size, however, is largely due to the need for translation and interpretation services to allow the Parliament to work in its several languages. The Secretariat is under the direction of a Secretary-General.

Rule 49 of the Rules of Procedure provides that the Parliament is assisted by a Secretary-General who is appointed by the Bureau. On appointment, the Secretary-General must give a solemn undertaking before the Bureau to perform his duties conscientiously and impartially. He is responsible to the Bureau for his administration of the Parliament. Only two Secretaries-General have held office since the foundation of the Parliament. Mr. M.F.F.A. de Nerée tot Babberich (Netherlands) was Secretary-General from 1958 to 1960. Mr. Hans Nord (Netherlands), who was appointed to succeed to the office in 1961, continues to occupy the post.

The composition and organisation of the Secretariat is laid down by the Bureau on behalf of the Parliament. The Bureau must decide the number of staff and determine the regulations relating to conditions of service, after consulting the appropriate committee of the Parliament, and within the limits imposed by the Statute of Personnel adopted by the Communities to apply to all Community institutions. The Bureau must also decide into which categories members of the staff fall with regard to the application of the provisions of Articles 12 to 14 of the Protocol on the Privileges and Immunities of the European Communities.[1] The President of the Parliament informs the appropriate institutions of the Communities of those decisions.

At the beginning of 1972, the Secretariat of the Parliament was divided into four general directorates. The enlargement of the Communities was likely to lead to some redistribution of functions between

[1]The Protocol is appended to the Merger Treaty of 1965 establishing a single Council and a single Commission of the European Communities.

the general directorates,[1] but the functional divisions within them were likely to remain substantially unchanged. In 1972, the four general directorates were: General Affairs; Committees and Parliamentary Studies; Documentation and Information; and Administration.

The General Directorate of General Affairs is headed by a director general and two directors. It is the largest department and performs the task of translation, distribution of documents and the provision of procedural advice. It has four divisions. One division on the Bureau, sessions and Members and another on the verbatim report are concerned with procedural matters. They deal with the conduct of sittings, the preparation of the agenda, and the compilation of the records of the Parliament. The division on Official Documents, Mail, Reproduction and Distribution of Documents, and the Translation division are concerned with the translation and distribution of documents from within the Parliament or from the other Community institutions.

The General Directorate of Committees and Parliamentary Studies, headed by a director general, provides the secretariats of all the parliamentary committees. It is divided into two directorates, each of which, under the supervision of its director, staffs a group of committees. Each committee is assisted by several secretaries, one of whom is ranked as a head of division. There is also a parliamentary studies division[1] which falls within the General Directorate. This division makes *ad hoc* studies of particular problems arising in the course of committee discussions where appropriate information cannot be provided by the Commission or the Council.

The General Directorate of Parliamentary Documentation and Information, headed by a director general, is divided into two directorates each under its own director. The Directorate of Parliamentary Documentation[1] controls the library of the Parliament and prepares digests of information on European problems. The latter duty was undertaken so as to provide Members with statistics and background material which are not available in national parliaments. The second Directorate of Information and Public Relations has as its primary task to increase public awareness of the importance of the Parliament in the European Communities. It has information offices in Brussels, Paris, Rome and London.

The General Directorate of Administration is under the headship of a director general and a director. It is currently divided into three divisions; a Personnel Division, a Financial Division and a Division on Conference and General Services. Its primary tasks are to draw up the annual estimates of the expenditure of the Parliament for submission to the Bureau; to administer the staff of the Secretariat within the terms

---

[1]A fifth General Directorate of Research and Documentation was established in December 1972 incorporating the Directorate of Parliamentary Documentation and the Parliamentary Studies division.

of the Statute of Personnel of the Communities; and to administer the travel, accommodation and expenses arrangements designed to assist Members attending meetings of the Parliament and its committees.

2 Travel, accommodation and expenses of Members

The European Parliament gives assistance to its Members in making travel arrangements to and from meetings of the Parliament and its committees and in booking hotel accommodation. Members' expenses are paid in respect of travel and subsistence, telephone calls and medical treatment. In addition all Members are insured against accidents sustained both in the course of their parliamentary duties and in their private lives. The Bureau of the Parliament issues general regulations from time to time concerning the entitlement of Members to expenses and the rates of expenses to be paid.

TRAVEL AND ACCOMMODATION

Members of the Parliament who require assistance in booking hotel accommodation or tickets for travel may make use of the services of the Parliament's Travel Office, which is situated in the Secretariat's offices in Luxembourg. The services of the Travel Office are provided not only for official meetings of the Parliament and its committees, or for other meetings and visits authorised by the President or the Bureau, but also for travel undertaken by Members in their private capacity. In the latter case Members are charged directly for the bookings made.

A standard booking form is provided by the Office, and tickets can either be collected or are despatched to Members at the addresses from which they are travelling. The Travel Office also provides an official car service during meetings of the Parliament. Members are free to make their own booking arrangements if they do not wish to use the services of the Travel Office.

EXPENSES FOR SUBSISTENCE AND TRAVEL

All expenses of Members in attending both plenary sessions and committee meetings are paid direct to Members by the Parliament. The general regulations issued by the Bureau in January 1964 and April 1967 are amended from time to time to bring the expenses payable up to date. The rates were last increased during the part-session of the Parliament held in July 1972 and are now as follows:

(i) *Subsistence:* Members are paid 2,500 Belgian francs for each day or part of a day spent attending a meeting of the Parliament or a committee meeting. The daily subsistence payment may also be made for days between meetings, but only if the subsistence payment does not exceed the return travel expenses to the Member's national parliament or home, and in any case for not more than four days. The payment will also be made for days when the Parliament does not sit during a part-session (for instance over weekends) but only if the Member has attended the meetings immediately before and after the break in sittings.

(ii) *Travel:* The reimbursement of travelling expenses is based not on actual cost but on mileage, according to the following formula:

11 Belgian francs for each of the first 400 kilometres, and

3 Belgian francs for each subsequent kilometre.

A Member's travelling distance is calculated either from his home or the seat of his national parliament, at his choice. If a Member is obliged to attend two or more consecutive meetings in different places, his travel expenses between meetings are calculated on the basis of the distance between the meeting places. Expenses may be paid either in cash during meetings, or direct into the Member's bank account.

The general regulations of the Bureau concerning Members' expenses make special provision with regard to travel on parliamentary business outside the territory of member states of the Communities. The same principles apply in respect of subsistence allowances, but, where a charter flight is not provided by the Parliament, Members are paid the cost of the first-class return air fare instead of a mileage allowance.

3 The budget of the Parliament

The annual budget of the European Parliament forms part of the general administrative budget of the Communities. After the signature of the Treaty of Luxembourg in 1970, the Council of Ministers agreed that it would not amend the estimates submitted by the Parliament for its own expenditure, thus in practice allowing the Parliament autonomy in the matter of its own budget.[1] The expenditure of the Parliament, which is controlled by regulations issued by the Bureau, is small compared with that of other Community institutions. In 1972, out of a total Community budget of 4,028,814,320 units of account, the expenses of the Parliament amounted to only 14,087,895 u.a.

Each year the Bureau of the Parliament draws up a preliminary draft of the estimates on the basis of a report prepared by the Secretariat. After consulting the Committee on Finance and Budgets, the Bureau adopts the preliminary draft, which is then formally referred back to that committee. The Committee on Finance and Budgets draws up the draft estimates, and submits them to the Parliament. Any Member may propose amendments to the draft estimates, which are considered by the Finance Committee before they are voted on in plenary session. Once agreed to by the Parliament, the estimates are sent to the Council and the Commission, and are embodied in the draft budget of the Communities.

[1]The Parliament's powers over the Community budget, which will be enlarged from 1 January 1975, are described on pages 22–24, and the procedure for considering the budget on pages 107–109.

Chapter XIX

The records and publications of the Parliament

1 General

The European Parliament publishes a wide range of documents during the course of each year. Most of these documents relate to the day-to-day work of the Parliament and its committees. Others are occasional publications issued for the information of Members of the European Parliament and for members of the public in the member states of the Communities. In addition Members of the Parliament may receive many of the regular publications of other Community institutions. Although some restrictions have been placed on the number of documents automatically despatched to Members,[1] all available documents are provided free of charge.

All the documents of the Parliament are published in Danish, Dutch, English, French, German and Italian, and documents may also be published in Irish. In order to distinguish easily between documents in the different languages the Parliament, in common with the other institutions of the Communities, has adopted a system of colour coding, as follows:

Danish	Red
Dutch	Orange
English . . .	Mauve
French	Blue
German . . .	Yellow
Irish	Brown
Italian	Green

Documents are either duplicated on paper of the appropriate colour, or duplicated or printed on white paper with the front cover or the left-hand edge of the front cover in the appropriate colour. Apart from occasional publications, all documents are numbered in series.[2]

2 Agenda and the *Bulletin*

The agenda for future sittings of the Parliament is published in the

---

[1]See page 147.

[2]The number (e.g. EP 29.783) which appears in the bottom right-hand corner of duplicated documents is an internal printing number and not an official serial number.

Official Journal of the European Communities (Communications series) and in a duplicated paper known as the *Bulletin* of the European Parliament, which is circulated to Members each week, By this means Members have before them details of the agenda to be proposed by the enlarged Bureau at the start of each part-session.[1] Apart from the agenda, the *Bulletin* also provides Members with the following additional information.

(i) lists of committees appointed and the Members nominated to them;

(ii) Questions tabled by Members for written reply by the Commission or the Council of Ministers;

(iii) Questions tabled by Members for oral reply by the Commission or the Council of Ministers, indicating whether the Questions are to be answered with or without debate;

(iv) Petitions addressed to the European Parliament;

(v) the time and place of meetings of committees and political groups;

(vi) a list of documents available and an order form for Members to return to the Secretariat.

The *Bulletin* may also contain miscellaneous announcements and information for members of the Parliament. While much of this information may be found in the minutes of proceedings and elsewhere in the Official Journal, it is set out in the *Bulletin* in a form more convenient to Members.

3 Minutes of proceedings

The minutes of proceedings are the authoritative record of the decisions taken by the Parliament. They include a statement of the action taken by the Parliament on the texts of draft resolutions, with amendments made thereto; a list of the names of members of the Parliament (and members of the Council and the Commission) who have spoken in debates; a list of Members who have taken part in roll-call votes; and a list of the documents deposited with the Parliament, including legislative proposals, and the committees to which they have been referred.

> By a decision of the Bureau of the Parliament on 26 March 1965 it was agreed that the minutes of proceedings would in future include only those parts of the legislative drafts of the Commission to which the Parliament has proposed amendments, because the full texts of such drafts are published in the Official Journal in advance of the publication of the minutes of proceedings.

The minutes of proceedings are duplicated for distribution during the sittings of the Parliament and, after the close of a session or one of its

[1]For an account of the drafting of the agenda see p. 94.

parts, are printed in the Official Journal of the European Communities (Communications series) within one month of the date of the sitting to which they relate. In accordance with Rule 17 (4) of the Parliament's Rules of Procedure, a copy of the minutes of proceedings for each sitting is signed by the President and the Secretary-General and preserved in the archives of the Parliament as the authentic record.

Rule 17 of the Rules of Procedure prescribes that the minutes of proceedings of a sitting must be distributed at least half an hour before the opening of the following sitting. At the beginning of each sitting the President lays before the Parliament for its approval the minutes of the previous sitting. The minutes of the last sitting of a part-session are laid before the Parliament for its approval immediately before the sitting is closed, and if no objection is raised they are declared adopted.[1] Rule 17 (3) prescribes that if the minutes of proceedings are challenged the Parliament may, if necessary, vote on the changes requested.

4 Verbatim reports of debates

Rule 18 of the Rules of Procedure of the Parliament provides for the compilation and distribution in the official languages of a summary report of the debates of each sitting. Practical experience soon proved that bringing out a complete summary of debates in all the official languages within a period of time when it could serve a useful purpose, was an almost impossible task, and the summary report was abandoned.

The verbatim record of the debates of the Parliament, required by Rule 19 of the Rules of Procedure, is issued in two forms. A provisional edition is normally issued to Members on the day after each sitting. This is a single multi-language publication containing the complete text of all speeches printed in the original languages in which they were delivered, and is sometimes known as the 'rainbow' edition of the debates. Speakers are required by Rule 19 (2) to return the corrected versions of their speeches to the Secretariat not later than the day following that on which they receive the text. In practice those speakers who are unable to examine the stenographic record of their speeches during sittings are allowed an extra day for the delivery of corrections.

The second and definitive verbatim record of the Parliament's debates is published four or five weeks after each part-session as an annex to the Official Journal (Communications series). These annexes, which are numbered in continuous series, appear in each of the official languages of the Communities and contain the original texts of speeches made in the language concerned and translations of speeches made in other languages. The languages in which translated speeches were originally delivered are indicated in brackets after the name of each speaker. A separate index of the proceedings during each annual session of the

[1] *e.g.* Official Journal (C) Annex (Debates) (No. 142), October 1971 p. 171.

Parliament is also published and distributed to Members. The index is divided into three parts: a subject index, an index of speakers, and a list of documents.

5 Working documents of the Parliament

The working documents of the European Parliament include reports from committees of the Parliament and copies of the legislative proposals of the Commission submitted by the Council of Ministers for consultation or advice. These documents are registered and numbered in a separate series as documents of the Parliament.

In addition, the working documents of the Bureau and the committees of the Parliament are issued and circulated either generally or to committee members only, according to criteria described in the next section. These documents include the minutes of proceedings of the committees (which include a summary of the main points made during each committee's debates as well as a formal record of the committee proceedings), the agenda for future committee meetings, and working papers and statements prepared for the use of the committees or for wider circulation in the Parliament. In accordance with Rule 41 of the Rules of Procedure of the Parliament, the minutes of proceedings of a committee must be distributed to the members of the committee and submitted for approval at the next committee meeting. The same Rule prescribes that unless a committee decides otherwise the only texts made public are reports adopted and statements prepared on the responsibility of the chairman.

6 Distribution of documents

In February 1971 the Bureau of the Parliament adopted new rules concerning the distribution of documents to the members of the Parliament, designed to lighten the burden of paper sent out to Members while keeping them fully informed of the work of the Parliament, to avoid double or triple distributions of the same document, and to reduce expenditure on time, paper, printing and postage. Under the new system, which came into operation on 1 June 1971, documents are divided into three categories, as follows:

(i) *documents distributed automatically to all Members.* The following documents are distributed automatically to all members of the Parliament at their usual addresses:

Treaties
Official Journal (Communications series)
Official Journal (Legislation series)
Debates of the European Parliament – provisional edition.
Debates of the European Parliament – definitive edition annexed to the Official Journal

Rules of Procedure of the European Parliament
Members' Handbook (*Vademecum*)
Annual general report of the European Commission
Preliminary draft budget
Draft budget
Draft supplementary budgets
Amendments to draft budgets
Budgets as amended by the European Parliament
Bulletin of the European Parliament
Minutes of proceedings of the European Parliament
Other documents, such as reports published by the Commission, information bulletins and lists of documents.

(ii) *documents distributed to members of committees only*. The working documents of the committees of the Parliament are sent automatically only to Members of the Parliament who are members of the committees concerned. These include the agenda, minutes of proceedings and other internal committee documents, together with reports and other working documents prepared by the committees for plenary sessions of the Parliament. Despite this rule, public committee documents continue to be sent to the offices of the political groups, and to all members of the Parliament during part-sessions in Strasbourg and Luxembourg.

(iii) *documents sent out only on request*. Other publications of the institutions of the Communities may be obtained only on request from the Secretariat and are not generally distributed. These include press statements of the Council of Ministers, the monthly bulletin and specialised publications of the European Commission, statistical abstracts, and the records and reports of the Economic and Social Committee of the Communities and of the Consultative Committee of the Coal and Steel Community.

Members of the Parliament may at any time place orders with the Secretariat of the Parliament for any of the documents in categories (ii) and (iii) above which are not sent to them by virtue of the offices they hold. Documents may be ordered either by annual standing order, if they are required on a regular basis, or by special individual order if individual copies only are required. In the latter case a list of documents available and a detachable order form are included in the weekly *Bulletin* of the Parliament. A standard form is provided for Members who wish to place annual orders with the Secretariat.

7 Library of the European Parliament

All members of the Parliament have access to the Library of the Parliament, which is situated on the first floor of the Parliament Building in Luxembourg. The Library, under the control of the Directorate of Parliamentary Documentation, houses not only the records of the Parliament, but also a substantial collection of books, journals and newspapers.

Appendix A

Treaty establishing the European Economic Community

Rome, 25 March 1957

NOTES

I: The Rome Treaty of 25 March 1957, establishing the European Economic Community, is reproduced here as amended by:

(i) The Treaty establishing a Single Council and a Single Commission of the European Communities (Brussels, 8 April 1965) (referred to as the Merger Treaty of 1965);

(ii) The Treaty amending certain Budgetary Provisions of the Treaties establishing the European Communities and of the Treaty establishing a Single Council and a Single Commission of the European Communities (Luxembourg, 22 April 1970) (referred to as the Luxembourg Treaty of 1970); and

(iii) The Treaty concerning the Accession of the Kingdom of Denmark, Ireland, the Kingdom of Norway and the United Kingdom of Great Britain and Northern Ireland to the European Economic Community and the European Atomic Energy Community (Brussels, 22 January 1972) (referred to as the Treaty of Accession of 1972) and the Act concerning the Conditions of Accession and the Adjustments to the Treaties forming part of that Treaty (referred to as the Act of Accession of 1972).

The English text reproduced here is not an official text of the EEC Treaty as amended, but is based on the texts of the separate Treaties which became authentic on 1 January 1973 (Cmnd. 4864, Cmnd. 4866, Cmnd. 4867 and Cmnd. 4862).

II: As a consequence of the withdrawal of Norway in the autumn of 1972 from the three Communities, certain further adjustments to this Treaty will be required. Article 2 of the Treaty of Accession of 1972 empowers the Council of Ministers, by unanimous decision, to make whatever adjustments are necessary in such circumstances to the Treaty of Accession, and in particular to Articles 14, 16, 17, 19, 20, 23, 129, 142, 143, 155 and 160 of the Act of Accession forming part of that Treaty.

III: The Treaty establishing the European Economic Community (referred to in the text as 'the Rome Treaty', 'the Treaty of Rome' or 'the EEC Treaty') should not be confused with the Treaty establishing the European Atomic Energy Community (referred to as 'the Euratom Treaty'), which was also signed in Rome on 25 March 1957. The two Treaties together are sometimes referred to as 'the Treaties of Rome'.

CONTENTS OF THE TREATY ESTABLISHING THE EUROPEAN ECONOMIC COMMUNITY

HIS MAJESTY THE KING OF THE BELGIANS, THE PRESIDENT OF THE FEDERAL REPUBLIC OF GERMANY, THE PRESIDENT OF THE FRENCH REPUBLIC, THE PRESIDENT OF THE ITALIAN REPUBLIC, HER ROYAL HIGHNESS THE GRAND DUCHESS OF LUXEMBOURG, HER MAJESTY THE QUEEN OF THE NETHERLANDS,[1]

DETERMINED to lay the foundations of an ever closer union among the peoples of Europe,

RESOLVED to ensure the economic and social progress of their countries by common action to eliminate the barriers which divide Europe,

AFFIRMING as the essential objective of their efforts the constant improvement of the living and working conditions of their peoples,

RECOGNISING that the removal of existing obstacles calls for concerted action in order to guarantee steady expansion, balanced trade and fair competition,

ANXIOUS to strengthen the unity of their economies and to ensure their harmonious development by reducing the differences existing between the various regions and the backwardness of the less favoured regions,

DESIRING to contribute, by means of a common commercial policy, to the progressive abolition of restrictions on international trade,

INTENDING to confirm the solidarity which binds Europe and the overseas countries and desiring to ensure the development of their prosperity, in accordance with the principles of the Charter of the United Nations,

RESOLVED by thus pooling their resources to preserve and strengthen peace and liberty, and calling upon the other peoples of Europe who share their ideal to join in their efforts,

HAVE DECIDED to create a European Economic Community and to this end have designated as their Plenipotentiaries:

HIS MAJESTY THE KING OF THE BELGIANS:

Mr. Paul-Henri SPAAK, Minister for Foreign Affairs,
Baron J. Ch. SNOY et d'OPPUERS, Secretary-General of the Ministry of Economic Affairs, Head of the Belgian Delegation to the Intergovernmental Conference;

THE PRESIDENT OF THE FEDERAL REPUBLIC OF GERMANY:

Dr. Konrad ADENAUER, Federal Chancellor,
Professor Dr. Walter HALLSTEIN, State Secretary of the Federal Foreign Office;

[1]Under the terms of Article 1 of the Treaty of Accession of 1972, the Kingdom of Denmark, Ireland and the United Kingdom of Great Britain and Northern Ireland become parties to this Treaty on 1 January 1973.

THE PRESIDENT OF THE FRENCH REPUBLIC:

Mr. Christian PINEAU, Minister for Foreign Affairs,
Mr. Maurice FAURE, Under-Secretary of State for Foreign Affairs;

THE PRESIDENT OF THE ITALIAN REPUBLIC:

Mr. Antonio SEGNI, President of the Council of Ministers,
Professor Gaetano MARTINO, Minister for Foreign Affairs;

HER ROYAL HIGHNESS THE GRAND DUCHESS OF LUXEMBOURG:

Mr. Joseph BECH, President of the Government, Minister for Foreign Affairs,
Mr. Lambert SCHAUS, Ambassador, Head of the Luxembourg Delegation to the Intergovernmental Conference;

HER MAJESTY THE QUEEN OF THE NETHERLANDS:

Mr. Joseph LUNS, Minister for Foreign Affairs.
Mr. J. LINTHORST HOMAN, Head of the Netherlands Delegation to the Intergovernmental Conference;

WHO, having exchanged their Full Powers, found in good and due form,

HAVE AGREED as follows:

Part One

Principles

ARTICLE 1

By this Treaty, the High Contracting Parties establish among themselves a EUROPEAN ECONOMIC COMMUNITY.

ARTICLE 2

The Community shall have as its task, by establishing a common market and progressively approximating the economic policies of Member States, to promote throughout the Community a harmonious development of economic activities, a continuous and balanced expansion, an increase in stability, an accelerated raising of the standard of living and closer relations between the States belonging to it.

ARTICLE 3

For the purposes set out in Article 2, the activities of the Community shall include, as provided in this Treaty and in accordance with the timetable set out therein:

(*a*) the elimination, as between Member States, of customs duties and of quantitative restrictions on the import and export of goods, and of all other measures having equivalent effect;

(*b*) the establishment of a common customs tariff and of a common commercial policy towards third countries;

(*c*) the abolition, as between Member States, of obstacles to freedom of movement for persons, services and capital;

(*d*) the adoption of a common policy in the sphere of agriculture;

(*e*) the adoption of a common policy in the sphere of transport;

(*f*) the institution of a system ensuring that competition in the common market is not distorted;

(*g*) the application of procedures by which the economic policies of Member States can be co-ordinated and disequilibria in their balances of payments remedied;

(*h*) the approximation of the laws of Member States to the extent required for the proper functioning of the common market;

(*i*) the creation of a European Social Fund in order to improve employment opportunities for workers and to contribute to the raising of their standard of living;

(*j*) the establishment of a European Investment Bank to facilitate the economic expansion of the Community by opening up fresh resources;

(*k*) the association of the overseas countries and territories in order to increase trade and to promote jointly economic and social development.

ARTICLE 4

1. The tasks entrusted to the Community shall be carried out by the following institutions:

– an ASSEMBLY,
– a COUNCIL,
– a COMMISSION,
– a COURT OF JUSTICE.

Each institution shall act within the limits of the powers conferred upon it by this Treaty.

2. The Council and the Commission shall be assisted by an Economic and Social Committee acting in an advisory capacity.

ARTICLE 5

Member States shall take all appropriate measures, whether general or particular, to ensure fulfilment of the obligations arising out of this Treaty or resulting from action taken by the institutions of the Community. They shall facilitate the achievement of the Community's tasks.

They shall abstain from any measure which could jeopardise the attainment of the objectives of this Treaty.

ARTICLE 6

1. Member States shall, in close co-operation with the institutions of the Community, co-ordinate their respective economic policies to the extent necessary to attain the objectives of this Treaty.

2. The institutions of the Community shall take care not to prejudice the internal and external financial stability of the Member States.

ARTICLE 7

Within the scope of application of this Treaty, and without prejudice to any special provisions contained therein, any discrimination on grounds of nationality shall be prohibited.

The Council may, on a proposal from the Commission and after consulting the Assembly, adopt, by a qualified majority, rules designed to prohibit such discrimination.

ARTICLE 8

1. The common market shall be progressively established during a transitional period of twelve years.

This transitional period shall be divided into three stages of four years each; the length of each stage may be altered in accordance with the provisions set out below.

2. To each stage there shall be assigned a set of actions to be initiated and carried through concurrently.

3. Transition from the first to the second stage shall be conditional upon a finding that the objectives specifically laid down in this Treaty for the first stage have in fact been attained in substance and that, subject to the exceptions and procedures provided for in this Treaty, the obligations have been fulfilled.

This finding shall be made at the end of the fourth year by the Council, acting unanimously on a report from the Commission. A Member State may not, however, prevent unanimity by relying upon the non-fulfilment of its own obligations, Failing unanimity, the first stage shall automatically be extended for one year.

At the end of the fifth year, the Council shall make its finding under the same conditions. Failing unanimity, the first stage shall automatically be extended for a further year.

At the end of the sixth year, the Council shall make its finding, acting by a qualified majority on a report from the Commission.

4. Within one month of the last-mentioned vote any Member State which voted with the minority or, if the required majority was not obtained, any Member State shall be entitled to call upon the Council to appoint an arbitration board whose decision shall be binding upon all Member States and upon the institutions of the Community. The arbitration board shall consist of three members appointed by the Council acting unanimously on a proposal from the Commission.

If the Council has not appointed the members of the arbitration board within one month of being called upon to do so, they shall be appointed by the Court of Justice within a further period of one month.

The arbitration board shall elect its own Chairman.

The board shall make its award within six months of the date of the Council vote referred to in the last subparagraph of paragraph 3.

5. The second and third stages may not be extended or curtailed except by a decision of the Council, acting unanimously on a proposal from the Commission.

6. Nothing in the preceding paragraphs shall cause the transitional period to last more than fifteen years after the entry into force of this Treaty.

7. Save for the exceptions or derogations provided for in this Treaty, the expiry of the transitional period shall constitute the latest date by which all the rules laid down must enter into force and all the measures required for establishing the common market must be implemented.

Part Two

Foundations of the Community

TITLE I: FREE MOVEMENT OF GOODS

ARTICLE 9

1. The Community shall be based upon a customs union which shall cover all trade in goods and which shall involve the prohibition between Member States of customs duties on imports and exports and of all charges having equivalent effect, and the adoption of a common customs tariff in their relations with third countries.

2. The provisions of Chapter 1, Section 1, and of Chapter 2 of this Title shall apply to products originating in Member States and to products coming from third countries which are in free circulation in Member States.

ARTICLE 10

1. Products coming from a third country shall be considered to be in free circulation in a Member State if the import formalities have been complied with and any customs duties or charges having equivalent effect which are payable have been levied in that Member State, and if they have not benefited from a total or partial drawback of such duties or charges.

2. The Commission shall, before the end of the first year after the entry into force of this Treaty, determine the methods of administrative co-operation to be adopted for the purpose of applying Article 9 (2), taking into account the need to reduce as much as possible formalities imposed on trade.

Before the end of the first year after the entry into force of this Treaty, the Commission shall lay down the provisions applicable, as regards trade between Member States, to goods originating in another Member State in whose manufacture products have been used on which the exporting Member State has not levied the appropriate customs duties or charges having equivalent effect, or which have benefited from a total or partial drawback of such duties or charges.

In adopting these provisions, the Commission shall take into account the rules for the elimination of customs duties within the Community and for the progressive application of the common customs tariff.

ARTICLE 11

Member States shall take all appropriate measures to enable Governments to carry out, within the periods of time laid down, the obligations with regard to customs duties which devolve upon them pursuant to this Treaty.

Chapter 1: The Customs Union

SECTION 1: ELIMINATION OF CUSTOMS DUTIES BETWEEN MEMBER STATES

ARTICLE 12

Member States shall refrain from introducing between themselves any new customs duties on imports or exports or any charges having equivalent effect, and from increasing those which they already apply in their trade with each other.

ARTICLE 13

1. Customs duties on imports in force between Member States shall be progressively abolished by them during the transitional period in accordance with Articles 14 and 15.

2. Charges having an effect equivalent to customs duties on imports, in force between Member States, shall be progressively abolished by them during the transitional period. The Commission shall determine by means of directives the timetable for such abolition. It shall be guided by the rules contained in Article 14 (2) and (3) and by the directives issued by the Council pursuant to Article 14 (2).

ARTICLE 14

1. For each product, the basic duty to which the successive reductions shall be applied shall be the duty applied on 1 January 1957.

2. The timetable for the reductions shall be determined as follows:

(*a*) during the first stage, the first reduction shall be made one year after the date when this Treaty enters into force; the second reduction, eighteen months later; the third reduction, at the end of the fourth year after the date when this Treaty enters into force;

(*b*) during the second stage, a reduction shall be made eighteen months after that stage begins; a second reduction, eighteen months after the preceding one; a third reduction, one year later;

(*c*) any remaining reductions shall be made during the third stage; the Council shall, acting by a qualified majority on a proposal from the Commission, determine the timetable therefor by means of directives.

3. At the time of the first reduction, Member States shall introduce between themselves a duty on each product equal to the basic duty minus 10 per cent.

At the time of each subsequent reduction, each Member State shall reduce its customs duties as a whole in such manner as to lower by 10 per cent its total customs receipts as defined in paragraph 4 and to reduce the duty on each product by at least 5 per cent of the basic duty.

In the case, however, of products on which the duty is still in excess of 30 per cent, each reduction must be at least 10 per cent of the basic duty.

4. The total customs receipts of each Member State, as referred to in para-

graph 3, shall be calculated by multiplying the value of its imports from other Member States during 1956 by the basic duties.

5. Any special problems raised in applying paragraphs 1 to 4 shall be settled by directives issued by the Council acting by a qualified majority on a proposal from the Commission.

6. Member States shall report to the Commission on the manner in which effect has been given to the preceding rules for the reduction of duties. They shall endeavour to ensure that the reduction made in the duties on each product shall amount:

  – at the end of the first stage, to at least 25 per cent of the basic duty;
  – at the end of the second stage, to at least 50 per cent of the basic duty.

If the Commission finds that there is a risk that the objectives laid down in Article 13, and the percentages laid down in this paragraph, cannot be attained, it shall make all appropriate recommendations to Member States.

7. The provisions of this Article may be amended by the Council, acting unanimously on a proposal from the Commission and after consulting the Assembly.

ARTICLE 15

1. Irrespective of the provisions of Article 14, any Member State may, in the course of the transitional period, suspend in whole or in part the collection of duties applied by it to products imported from other Member States. It shall inform the other Member States and the Commission thereof.

2. The Member States declare their readiness to reduce customs duties against the other Member States more rapidly than is provided for in Article 14 if their general economic situation and the situation of the economic sector concerned so permit.

To this end, the Commission shall make recommendations to the Member States concerned.

ARTICLE 16

Member States shall abolish between themselves customs duties on exports and charges having equivalent effect by the end of the first stage at the latest.

ARTICLE 17

1. The provisions of Articles 9 to 15 (1) shall also apply to customs duties of a fiscal nature. Such duties shall not, however, be taken into consideration for the purpose of calculating either total customs receipts or the reduction of customs duties as a whole as referred to in Article 14 (3) and (4).

Such duties shall, at each reduction, be lowered by not less than 10 per cent of the basic duty. Member States may reduce such duties more rapidly than is provided for in Article 14.

2. Member States shall, before the end of the first year after the entry into

force of this Treaty, inform the Commission of their customs duties of a fiscal nature.

3. Member States shall retain the right to substitute for these duties an internal tax which complies with the provisions of Article 95.

4. If the Commission finds that substitution for any customs duty of a fiscal nature meets with serious difficulties in a Member State, it shall authorise that State to retain the duty on condition that it shall abolish it not later than six years after the entry into force of this Treaty. Such authorisation must be applied for before the end of the first year after the entry into force of this Treaty.

SECTION 2: SETTING UP OF THE COMMON CUSTOMS TARIFF

ARTICLE 18

The Member States declare their readiness to contribute to the development of international trade and the lowering of barriers to trade by entering into agreements designed, on a basis of reciprocity and mutual advantage, to reduce customs duties below the general level of which they could avail themselves as a result of the establishment of a customs union between them.

ARTICLE 19

1. Subject to the conditions and within the limits provided for hereinafter, duties in the common customs tariff shall be at the level of the arithmetical average of the duties applied in the four customs territories comprised in the Community.

2. The duties taken as the basis for calculating this average shall be those applied by Member States on 1 January 1957.

In the case of the Italian tariff, however, the duty applied shall be that without the temporary 10 per cent reduction. Furthermore, with respect to items on which the Italian tariff contains a conventional duty, this duty shall be substituted for the duty applied as defined above, provided that it does not exceed the latter by more than 10 per cent. Where the conventional duty exceeds the duty applied as defined above by more than 10 per cent, the latter duty plus 10 per cent shall be taken as the basis for calculating the arithmetical average.

With regard to the tariff headings in List A, the duties shown in that List shall, for the purpose of calculating the arithmetical average, be substituted for the duties applied.

3. The duties in the common customs tariff shall not exceed:

(*a*) 3 per cent for products within the tariff headings in List B;

(*b*) 10 per cent for products within the tariff headings in List C;

(*c*) 15 per cent for products within the tariff headings in List D;

(*d*) 25 per cent for products within the tariff headings in List E; where, in respect of such products, the tariff of the Benelux countries contains a duty not exceeding 3 per cent, such duty shall, for the purpose of calculating the arithmetical average, be raised to 12 per cent.

4. List F prescribes the duties applicable to the products listed therein.

5. The Lists of tariff headings referred to in this Article and in Article 20 are set out in Annex I to this Treaty.

ARTICLE 20

The duties applicable to the products in List G shall be determined by negotiation between the Member States. Each Member State may add further products to this List to a value not exceeding 2 per cent of the total value of its imports from third countries in the course of the year 1956.

The Commission shall take all appropriate steps to ensure that such negotiations shall be undertaken before the end of the second year after the entry into force of this Treaty and be concluded before the end of the first stage.

If, for certain products, no agreement can be reached within these periods, the Council shall, on a proposal from the Commission, acting unanimously until the end of the second stage and by a qualified majority thereafter, determine the duties in the common customs tariff.

ARTICLE 21

1. Technical difficulties which may arise in applying Articles 19 and 20 shall be resolved, within two years of the entry into force of this Treaty, by directives issued by the Council acting by a qualified majority on a proposal from the Commission.

2. Before the end of the first stage, or at latest when the duties are determined, the Council shall, acting by a qualified majority on a proposal from the Commission, decide on any adjustments required in the interests of the internal consistency of the common customs tariff as a result of applying the rules set out in Articles 19 and 20, taking account in particular of the degree of processing undergone by the various goods to which the common tariff applies.

ARTICLE 22

The Commission shall, within two years of the entry into force of this Treaty, determine the extent to which the customs duties of a fiscal nature referred to in Article 17 (2) shall be taken into account in calculating the arithmetical average provided for in Article 19 (1). The Commission shall take account of any protective character which such duties may have.

Within six months of such determination, any Member State may request that the procedure provided for in Article 20 should be applied to the product in question, but in this event the percentage limit provided in that Article shall not be applicable to that State.

ARTICLE 23

1. For the purpose of the progressive introduction of the common customs

tariff, Member States shall amend their tariffs applicable to third countries as follows:

(*a*) in the case of tariff headings on which the duties applied in practice on 1 January 1957 do not differ by more than 15 per cent in either direction from the duties in the common customs tariff, the latter duties shall be applied at the end of the fourth year after the entry into force of this Treaty;

(*b*) in any other case, each Member State shall, as from the same date, apply a duty reducing by 30 per cent the difference between the duty applied in practice on 1 January 1957 and the duty in the common customs tariff;

(*c*) at the end of the second stage this difference shall again be reduced by 30 per cent;

(*d*) in the case of tariff headings for which the duties in the common customs tariff are not yet available at the end of the first stage, each Member State shall, within six months of the Council's action in accordance with Article 20, apply such duties as would result from application of the rules contained in this paragraph.

2. Where a Member State has been granted an authorisation under Article 17 (4), it need not, for as long as that authorisation remains valid, apply the preceding provisions to the tariff headings to which the authorisation applies. When such authorisation expires, the Member State concerned shall apply such duty as would have resulted from application of the rules contained in paragraph 1.

3. The common customs tariff shall be applied in its entirety by the end of the transitional period at the latest.

ARTICLE 24

Member States shall remain free to change their duties more rapidly than is provided for in Article 23 in order to bring them into line with the common customs tariff.

ARTICLE 25

1. If the Commission finds that the production in Member States of particular products contained in Lists B, C and D is insufficient to supply the demands of one of the Member States, and that such supply traditionally depends to a considerable extent on imports from third countries, the Council shall, acting by a qualified majority on a proposal from the Commission, grant the Member State concerned tariff quotas at a reduced rate of duty or duty free.

Such quotas may not exceed the limits beyond which the risk might arise of activities being transferred to the detriment of other Member States.

2. In the case of the products in List E, and of those in List G for which the rates of duty have been determined in accordance with the procedure provided for in the third paragraph of Article 20, the Commission shall, where a change in sources of supply or a shortage of supplies within the Community is such as to entail harmful consequences for the processing industries of a Member State, at the request of that Member State, grant it tariff quotas at a reduced rate of duty or duty free.

Such quotas may not exceed the limits beyond which the risk might arise of activities being transferred to the detriment of other Member States.

3. In the case of the products listed in Annex II to this Treaty, the Commission may authorise any Member State to suspend, in whole or in part, collection of the duties applicable or may grant such Member State tariff quotas at a reduced rate of duty or duty free, provided that no serious disturbance of the market of the products concerned results therefrom.

4. The Commission shall periodically examine tariff quotas granted pursuant to this Article.

ARTICLE 26

The Commission may authorise any Member State encountering special difficulties to postpone the lowering or raising of duties provided for in Article 23 in respect of particular headings in its tariff.

Such authorisation may only be granted for a limited period and in respect of tariff headings which, taken together, represent for such State not more than 5 per cent of the value of its imports from third countries in the course of the latest year for which statistical data are available.

ARTICLE 27

Before the end of the first stage, Member States shall, in so far as may be necessary, take steps to approximate their provisions laid down by law, regulation or administrative action in respect of customs matters. To this end, the Commission shall make all appropriate recommendations to Member States.

ARTICLE 28

Any autonomous alteration or suspension of duties in the common customs tariff shall be decided unanimously by the Council. After the transitional period has ended, however, the Council may, acting by a qualified majority on a proposal from the Commission, decide on alterations or suspensions which shall not exceed 20 per cent of the rate in the case of any one duty for a maximum period of six months. Such alterations or suspensions may only be extended, under the same conditions, for one further period of six months.

ARTICLE 29

In carrying out the tasks entrusted to it under this Section the Commission shall be guided by:

(a) the need to promote trade between Member States and third countries;

(b) developments in conditions of competition within the Community in so far as they lead to an improvement in the competitive capacity of undertakings;

(c) the requirements of the Community as regards the supply of raw materials and semi-finished goods; in this connection the Commission shall take care to avoid distorting conditions of competition between Member States in respect of finished goods;

(*d*) the need to avoid serious disturbances in the economies of Member States and to ensure rational development of production and an expansion of consumption within the Community.

Chapter 2: Elimination of Quantitative restrictions between Member States

ARTICLE 30

Quantitative restrictions on imports and all measures having equivalent effect shall, without prejudice to the following provisions, be prohibited between Member States.

ARTICLE 31

Member States shall refrain from introducing between themselves any new quantitative restrictions or measures having equivalent effect.

This obligation shall, however, relate only to the degree of liberalisation attained in pursuance of the decisions of the Council of the Organisation for European Economic Co-operation of 14 January 1955. Member States shall supply the Commission, not later than six months after the entry into force of this Treaty, with lists of the products liberalised by them in pursuance of these decisions. These lists shall be consolidated between Member States.

ARTICLE 32

In their trade with one another Member States shall refrain from making more restrictive the quotas and measures having equivalent effect existing at the date of the entry into force of this Treaty.

These quotas shall be abolished by the end of the transitional period at the latest. During that period, they shall be progressively abolished in accordance with the following provisions.

ARTICLE 33

1. One year after the entry into force of this Treaty, each Member State shall convert any bilateral quotas open to any other Member States into global quotas open without discrimination to all other Member States.

On the same date, Member States shall increase the aggregate of the global quotas so established in such a manner as to bring about an increase of not less than 20 per cent in their total value as compared with the preceding year. The global quota for each product, however, shall be increased by not less than 10 per cent.

The quotas shall be increased annually in accordance with the same rules and in the same proportions in relation to the preceding year.

The fourth increase shall take place at the end of the fourth year after the entry into force of this Treaty; the fifth, one year after the beginning of the second stage.

2. Where, in the case of a product which has not been liberalised, the global quota does not amount to 3 per cent of the national production of the State

M

concerned, a quota equal to not less than 3 per cent of such national production shall be introduced not later than one year after the entry into force of this Treaty. This quota shall be raised to 4 per cent at the end of the second year, and to 5 per cent at the end of the third. Thereafter, the Member State concerned shall increase the quota by not less than 15 per cent annually,

Where there is no such national production, the Commission shall take a decision establishing an appropriate quota.

3. At the end of the tenth year, each quota shall be equal to not less than 20 per cent of the national production.

4. If the Commission finds by means of a decision that during two successive years the imports of any product have been below the level of the quota opened, this global quota shall not be taken into account in calculating the total value of the global quotas. In such case, the Member State shall abolish quota restrictions on the product concerned.

5. In the case of quotas representing more than 20 per cent of the national production of the product concerned, the Council may, acting by a qualified majority on a proposal from the Commission, reduce the minimum percentage of 10 per cent laid down in paragraph 1. This alteration shall not, however, affect the obligation to increase the total value of global quotas by 20 per cent annually.

6. Member States which have exceeded their obligations as regards the degree of liberalisation attained in pursuance of the decisions of the Council of the Organisation for European Economic Co-operation of 14 January 1955 shall be entitled, when calculating the annual total increase of 20 per cent provided for in paragraph 1, to take into account the amount of imports liberalised by autonomous action. Such calculation shall be submitted to the Commission for its prior approval.

7. The Commission shall issue directives establishing the procedure and timetable in accordance with which Member States shall abolish, as between themselves, any measures in existence when this Treaty enters into force which have an effect equivalent to quotas.

8. If the Commission finds that the application of the provisions of this Article, and in particular of the provisions concerning percentages, makes it impossible to ensure that the abolition of quotas provided for in the second paragraph of Article 32 is carried out progressively, the Council may, on a proposal from the Commission, acting unanimously during the first stage and by a qualified majority thereafter, amend the procedure laid down in this Article and may, in particular, increase the percentages fixed.

ARTICLE 34

1. Quantitative restrictions on exports, and all measures having equivalent effect, shall be prohibited between Member States.

2. Member States shall, by the end of the first stage at the latest, abolish all quantitative restrictions on exports and any measures having equivalent effect which are in existence when this Treaty enters into force.

ARTICLE 35

The Member States declare their readiness to abolish quantitative restrictions on imports from and exports to other Member States more rapidly than is provided for in the preceding Articles, if their general economic situation and the situation of the economic sector concerned so permit.

To this end, the Commission shall make recommendations to the States concerned.

ARTICLE 36

The provisions of Articles 30 to 34 shall not preclude prohibitions or restrictions on imports, exports or goods in transit justified on grounds of public morality, public policy or public security; the protection of health and life of humans, animals or plants; the protection of national treasures possessing artistic, historic or archaeological value; or the protection of industrial and commercial property. Such prohibitions or restrictions shall not, however, constitute a means of arbitrary discrimination or a disguised restriction on trade between Member States.

ARTICLE 37

1. Member States shall progressively adjust any State monopolies of a commercial character so as to ensure that when the transitional period has ended no discrimination regarding the conditions under which goods are procured and marketed exists between nationals of Member States.

The provisions of this Article shall apply to any body through which a Member State, in law or in fact, either directly or indirectly supervises, determines or appreciably influences imports or exports between Member States. These provisions shall likewise apply to monopolies delegated by the State to others.

2. Member States shall refrain from introducing any new measure which is contrary to the principles laid down in paragraph 1 or which restricts the scope of the Articles dealing with the abolition of customs duties and quantitative restrictions between Member States.

3. The timetable for the measures referred to in paragraph 1 shall be harmonised with the abolition of quantitative restrictions on the same products provided for in Articles 30 to 34.

If a product is subject to a State monopoly of a commercial character in only one or some Member States, the Commission may authorise the other Member States to apply protective measures until the adjustment provided for in paragraph 1 has been effected; the Commission shall determine the conditions and details of such measures.

4. If a State monopoly of a commercial character has rules which are designed to make it easier to dispose of agricultural products or obtain for them the best return, steps should be taken in applying the rules contained in this Article to ensure equivalent safeguards for the employment and standard of living of the producers concerned, account being taken of the adjustments that will be possible and the specialisation that will be needed with the pasasge of time.

5. The obligations on Member States shall be binding only in so far as they are compatible with existing international agreements.

6. With effect from the first stage the Commission shall make recommendations as to the manner in which and the timetable according to which the adjustment provided for in this Article shall be carried out.

TITLE II: AGRICULTURE

ARTICLE 38

1. The common market shall extend to agriculture and trade in agricultural products. 'Agricultural products' means the products of the soil, of stock-farming and of fisheries and products of first-stage processing directly related to these products.

2. Save as otherwise provided in Articles 39 to 46, the rules laid down for the establishment of the common market shall apply to agricultural products.

3. The products subject to the provisions of Articles 39 to 46 are listed in Annex II to this Treaty. Within two years of the entry into force of this Treaty, however, the Council shall, acting by a qualified majority on a proposal from the Commission, decide what products are to be added to this list.

4. The operation and development of the common market for agricultural products must be accompanied by the establishment of a common agricultural policy among the Member States.

ARTICLE 39

1. The objectives of the common agricultural policy shall be:

(*a*) to increase agricultural productivity by promoting technical progress and by ensuring the rational development of agricultural production and the optimum utilisation of the factors of production, in particular labour;

(*b*) thus to ensure a fair standard of living for the agricultural community, in particular by increasing the individual earnings of persons engaged in agriculture;

(*c*) to stabilise markets;

(*d*) to assure the availability of supplies;

(*e*) to ensure that supplies reach consumers at reasonable prices.

2. In working out the common agricultural policy and the special methods for its application, account shall be taken of:

(*a*) the particular nature of agricultural activity, which results from the social structure of agriculture and from structural and natural disparities between the various agricultural regions;

(*b*) the need to effect the appropriate adjustments by degrees;

(*c*) the fact that in the Member States agriculture constitutes a sector closely linked with the economy as a whole.

ARTICLE 40

1. Member States shall develop the common agricultural policy by degrees during the transitional period and shall bring it into force by the end of that period at the latest.

2. In order to attain the objectives set out in Article 39 a common organisation of agricultural markets shall be established.

This organisation shall take one of the following forms, depending on the product concerned:

(*a*) common rules on competition;

(*b*) compulsory coordination of the various national market organisations;

(*c*) a European market organisation.

3. The common organisation established in accordance with paragraph 2 may include all measures required to attain the objectives set out in Article 39, in particular regulation of prices, aids for the production and marketing of the various products, storage and carry-over arrangements and common machinery for stabilising imports or exports.

The common organisation shall be limited to pursuit of the objectives set out in Article 39 and shall exclude any discrimination between producers or consumers within the Community.

Any common price policy shall be based on common criteria and uniform methods of calculation.

4. In order to enable the common organisation referred to in paragraph 2 to attain its objectives, one or more agricultural guidance and guarantee funds may be set up.

ARTICLE 41

To enable the objectives set out in Article 39 to be attained, provision may be made within the framework of the common agricultural policy for measures such as:

(*a*) an effective coordination of efforts in the spheres of vocational training, of research and of the dissemination of agricultural knowledge; this may include joint financing of projects or institutions;

(*b*) joint measures to promote consumption of certain products.

ARTICLE 42

The provisions of the Chapter relating to rules on competition shall apply to production of and trade in agricultural products only to the extent determined by the Council within the framework of Article 43 (2) and (3) and in accordance with the procedure laid down therein, account being taken of the objectives set out in Article 39.

The Council may, in particular, authorise the granting of aid:

(*a*) for the protection of enterprises handicapped by structural or natural conditions;

(*b*) within the framework of economic development programmes.

ARTICLE 43

1. In order to evolve the broad lines of a common agricultural policy, the Commission shall, immediately this Treaty enters into force, convene a conference of the Member States with a view to making a comparison of their agricultural policies, in particular by producing a statement of their resources and needs.

2. Having taken into account the work of the conference provided for in paragraph 1, after consulting the Economic and Social Committee and within two years of the entry into force of this Treaty, the Commission shall submit proposals for working out and implementing the common agricultural policy, including the replacement of the national organisations by one of the forms of common organisation provided for in Article 40 (2), and for implementing the measures specified in this Title.

These proposals shall take account of the interdependence of the agricultural matters mentioned in this Title.

The Council shall, on a proposal from the Commission and after consulting the Assembly, acting unanimously during the first two stages and by a qualified majority thereafter, make regulations, issue directives, or take decisions, without prejudice to any recommendations it may also make.

3. The Council may, acting by a qualified majority and in accordance with paragraph 2, replace the national market organisations by the common organisation provided for in Article 40 (2) if:

(*a*) the common organisation offers Member States which are opposed to this measure and which have an organisation of their own for the production in question equivalent safeguards for the employment and standard of living of the producers concerned, account being taken of the adjustments that will be possible and the specialisation that will be needed with the passage of time;

(*b*) such an organisation ensures conditions for trade within the Community similar to those existing in a national market.

4. If a common organisation for certain raw materials is established before a common organisation exists for the corresponding processed products, such raw materials as are used for processed products intended for export to third countries may be imported from outside the Community.

ARTICLE 44

1. In so far as progressive abolition of customs duties and quantitative restrictions between Member States may result in prices likely to jeopardise the attainment of the objectives set out in Article 39, each Member State shall, during the transitional period, be entitled to apply to particular products, in a non-discriminatory manner and in substitution for quotas and to such an extent as shall not impede the expansion of the volume of trade provided for in Article 45 (2), a system of minimum prices below which imports may be either:

– temporarily suspended or reduced; or

– allowed, but subjected to the condition that they are made at a price higher than the minimum price for the product concerned.

In the latter case the minimum prices shall not include customs duties.

2. Minimum prices shall neither cause a reduction of the trade existing between Member States when this Treaty enters into force nor form an obstacle to progressive expansion of this trade. Minimum prices shall not be applied so as to form an obstacle to the development of a natural preference between Member States.

3. As soon as this Treaty enters into force the Council shall, on a proposal from the Commission, determine objective criteria for the establishment of minimum price systems and for the fixing of such prices.

These criteria shall in particular take account of the average national production costs in the Member State applying the minimum price, of the position of the various undertakings concerned in relation to such average production costs, and of the need to promote both the progressive improvement of agricultural practice and the adjustments and specialisation needed within the common market.

The Commission shall further propose a procedure for revising these criteria in order to allow for and speed up technical progress and to approximate prices progressively within the common market.

These criteria and the procedure for revising them shall be determined by the Council acting unanimously within three years of the entry into force of this Treaty.

4. Until the decision of the Council takes effect, Member States may fix minimum prices on conditions that these are communicated beforehand to the Commission and to the other Member States so that they may submit their comments.

Once the Council has taken its decision, Member States shall fix minimum prices on the basis of the criteria determined as above.

The Council may, acting by a qualified majority on a proposal from the Commission, rectify any decisions taken by Member States which do not conform to the criteria defined above.

5. If it does not prove possible to determine the said objective criteria for certain products by the beginning of the third stage, the Council may, acting by a qualified majority on a proposal from the Commission, vary the minimum prices applied to these products.

6. At the end of the transitional period, a table of minimum prices still in force shall be drawn up. The Council shall, acting on a proposal from the Commission and by a majority of nine votes in accordance with the weighting laid down in the first subparagraph of Article 148 (2), determine the system to be applied within the framework of the common agricultural policy.

ARTICLE 45

1. Until national market organisations have been replaced by one of the forms of common organisation referred to in Article 40 (2), trade in products in respect of which certain Member States:

– have arrangements designed to guarantee national producers a market for their products; and

– are in need of imports,

shall be developed by the conclusion of long-term agreements or contracts between importing and exporting Member States.

These agreements or contracts shall be directed towards the progressive abolition of any discrimination in the application of these arrangements to the various producers within the Community.

Such agreements or contracts shall be concluded during the first stage; account shall be taken of the principle of reciprocity.

2. As regards quantities, these agreements or contracts shall be based on the average volume of trade between Member States in the products concerned during the three years before the entry into force of this Treaty, and shall provide for an increase in the volume of trade within the limits of existing requirements, account being taken of traditional patterns of trade.

As regards prices, these agreements or contracts shall enable producers to dispose of the agreed quantities at prices which shall be progressively approximated to those paid to national producers on the domestic market of the purchasing country.

This approximation shall proceed as steadily as possible and shall be completed by the end of the transitional period at the latest.

Prices shall be negotiated between the parties concerned within the framework of directives issued by the Commission for the purposes of implementing the two preceding subparagraphs.

If the first stage is extended, these agreements or contracts shall continue to be carried out in accordance with the conditions applicable at the end of the fourth year after the entry into force of this Treaty, the obligation to increase quantities and to approximate prices being suspended until the transition to the second stage.

Member States shall avail themselves of any opportunity open to them under their legislation, particularly in respect of import policy, to ensure the conclusion and carrying out of these agreements or contracts.

3. To the extent that Member States require raw materials for the manufacture of products to be exported outside the Community in competition with products of third countries, the above agreements or contracts shall not form an obstacle to the importation of raw materials for this purpose from third countries. This provision shall not, however, apply if the Council unanimously decides to make provision for payments required to compensate for the higher price paid on goods imported for this purpose on the basis of these agreements or contracts in relation to the delivered price of the same goods purchased on the world market.

ARTICLE 46

Where in a Member State a product is subject to a national market organisation or to internal rules having equivalent effect which affect the competitive position of similar production in another Member State, a countervailing charge shall be applied by Member States to imports of this product coming from the Member State where such organisation or rules exist, unless that State applies a countervailing charge on export.

The Commission shall fix the amount of these charges at the level required to redress the balance; it may also authorise other measures, the conditions and details of which it shall determine.

ARTICLE 47

As to the functions to be performed by the Economic and Social Committee in pursuance of this Title, its agricultural section shall hold itself at the disposal of the Commission to prepare, in accordance with the provisions of Articles 197 and 198, the deliberations of the Committee.

TITLE III: FREE MOVEMENT OF PERSONS, SERVICES AND CAPITAL

Chapter 1: Workers

ARTICLE 48

1. Freedom of movement for workers shall be secured within the Community by the end of the transitional period at the latest.

2. Such freedom of movement shall entail the abolition of any discrimination based on nationality between workers of the Member States as regards employment, remuneration and other conditions of work and employment.

3. It shall entail the right, subject to limitations justified on grounds of public policy, public security or public health:

(*a*) to accept offers of employment actually made;

(*b*) to move freely within the territory of Member States for this purpose;

(*c*) to stay in a Member State for the purpose of employment in accordance with the provisions governing the employment of nationals of that State laid down by law, regulation or administrative action;

(*d*) to remain in the territory of a Member State after having been employed in that State, subject to conditions which shall be ambodied in implementing regulations to be drawn up by the Commission.

4. The provisions of this Article shall not apply to employment in the public service.

ARTICLE 49

As soon as this Treaty enters into force, the Council shall, acting on a proposal from the Commission and after consulting the Economic and Social Committee, issue directives or make regulations setting out the measures required to bring about, by progressive stages, freedom of movement for workers, as defined in Article 48, in particular:

(*a*) by ensuring close cooperation between national employment services;

(*b*) by systematically and progressively abolishing those administrative procedures and practices and those qualifying periods in respect of eligibility for available employment, whether resulting from national legislation or from agreements previously concluded between Member States, the maintenance of which would form an obstacle to liberalisation of the movement of workers;

(*c*) by systematically and progressively abolishing all such qualifying periods and other restrictions provided for either under national legislation or under agreements previously concluded between Member States as imposed on workers of other Member States conditions regarding the free choice of employment other than those imposed on workers of the State concerned;

(*d*) by setting up appropriate machinery to bring offers of employment into touch with applications for employment and to facilitate the achievement of a balance between supply and demand in the employment market in such a way as to avoid serious threats to the standard of living and level of employment in the various regions and industries.

ARTICLE 50

Member States shall, within the framework of a joint programme, encourage the exchange of young workers.

ARTICLE 51

The Council shall, acting unanimously on a proposal from the Commission, adopt such measures in the field of social security as are necessary to provide freedom of movement for workers; to this end, it shall make arrangements to secure for migrant workers and their dependants:

(*a*) aggregation, for the purpose of acquiring and retaining the right to benefit and of calculating the amount of benefit, of all periods taken into account under the laws of the several countries;

(*b*) payment of benefits to persons resident in the territories of Member States.

Chapter 2: Right of establishment

ARTICLE 52

Within the framework of the provisions set out below, restrictions on the freedom of establishment of nationals of a Member State in the territory of another Member State shall be abolished by progressive stages in the course of the transitional period. Such progressive abolition shall also apply to restrictions on the setting up of agencies, branches or subsidiaries by nationals of any Member State established in the territory of any Member State.

Freedom of establishment shall include the right to take up and pursue activities as self-employed persons and to set up and manage undertakings, in particular companies or firms within the meaning of the second paragraph of Article 58, under the conditions laid down for its own nationals by the law of the country where such establishment is effected, subject to the provisions of the Chapter relating to capital.

ARTICLE 53

Member States shall not introduce any new restrictions on the right of establishment in their territories of nationals of other Member States, save as otherwise provided in this Treaty.

ARTICLE 54

1. Before the end of the first stage, the Council shall, acting unanimously on a proposal from the Commission and after consulting the Economic and Social Committee and the Assembly, draw up a general programme for the abolition of existing restrictions on freedom of establishment within the Community. The Commission shall submit its proposal to the Council during the first two years of the first stage.

The programme shall set out the general conditions under which freedom of establishment is to be attained in the case of each type of activity and in particular the stages by which it is to be attained.

2. In order to implement this general programme or, in the absence of such programme, in order to achieve a stage in attaining freedom of establishment as regards a particular activity, the Council shall, on a proposal from the Commission and after consulting the Economic and Social Committee and the Assembly, issue directives, acting unanimously until the end of the first stage and by a qualified majority thereafter.

3. The Council and the Commission shall carry out the duties devolving upon them under the preceding provisions, in particular:

(a) by according, as a general rule, priority treatment to activities where freedom of establishment makes a particularly valuable contribution to the development of production and trade;

(b) by ensuring close cooperation between the competent authorities in the Member States in order to ascertain the particular situation within the Community of the various activities concerned;

(c) by abolishing those administrative procedures and practices, whether resulting from national legislation or from agreements previously concluded between Member States, the maintenance of which would form an obstacle to freedom of establishment;

(d) by ensuring that workers of one Member State employed in the territory of another Member State may remain in that territory for the purpose of taking up activities therein as self-employed persons, where they satisfy the conditions which they would be required to satisfy if they were entering that State at the time when they intended to take up such activities;

(e) by enabling a national of one Member State to acquire and use land and buildings situated in the territory of another Member State, in so far as this does not conflict with the principles laid down in Article 39 (2);

(f) by effecting the progressive abolition of restrictions on freedom of establishment in every branch of activity under consideration, both as regards the conditions for setting up agencies, branches or subsidiaries in the territory of a Member State and as regards the conditions governing the entry of personnel belonging to the main establishment into managerial or supervisory posts in such agencies, branches or subsidiaries;

(g) by coordinating to the necessary extent the safeguards which, for the protection of the interests of members and others, are required by Member States of companies or firms within the meaning of the second paragraph of Article 58 with a view to making such safeguards equivalent throughout the Community;

(h) by satisfying themselves that the conditions of establishment are not distorted by aids granted by Member States.

ARTICLE 55

The provisions of this Chapter shall not apply, so far as any given Member State is concerned, to activities which in that State are connected, even occasionally, with the exercise of official authority.

The Council may, acting by a qualified majority on a proposal from the Commission, rule that the provisions of this Chapter shall not apply to certain activities.

ARTICLE 56

1. The provisions of this Chapter and measures taken in pursuance thereof shall not prejudice the applicability of provisions laid down by law, regulation or administrative action providing for special treatment for foreign nationals on grounds of public policy, public security or public health.

2. Before the end of the transitional period, the Council shall, acting unanimously on a proposal from the Commission and after consulting the Assembly, issue directives for the coordination of the aforementioned provisions laid down by law, regulation or administrative action. After the end of the second stage, however, the Council shall, acting by a qualified majority on a proposal from the Commission, issue directives for the coordination of such provisions as, in each Member State, are a matter for regulation or administrative action.

ARTICLE 57

1. In order to make it easier for persons to take up and pursue activities as self-employed persons, the Council shall, on a proposal from the Commission and after consulting the Assembly, acting unanimously during the first stage and by a qualified majority thereafter, issue directives for the mutual recognition of diplomas, certificates and other evidence of formal qualifications.

2. For the same purpose, the Council shall, before the end of the transitional period, acting on a proposal from the Commission and after consulting the Assembly, issue directives for the coordination of the provisions laid down by law, regulation or administrative action in Member States concerning the taking up and pursuit of activities as self-employed persons. Unanimity shall be required on matters which are the subject of legislation in at least one Member State and measures concerned with the protection of savings, in particular the granting of credit and the exercise of the banking profession,

and with the conditions governing the exercise of the medical and allied, and pharmaceutical professions in the various Member States. In other cases, the Council shall act unanimously during the first stage and by a qualified majority thereafter.

3. In the case of the medical and allied, and pharmaceutical professions, the progressive abolition of restrictions shall be dependent upon coordination of the conditions for their exercise in the various Member States.

ARTICLE 58

Companies or firms formed in accordance with the law of a Member State and having their registered office, central administration or principal place of business within the Community shall, for the purposes of this Chapter, be treated in the same way as natural persons who are nationals of Member States.

'Companies or firms' means companies or firms constituted under civil or commercial law, including cooperative societies, and other legal persons governed by public or private law, save for those which are non-profit-making.

Chapter 3: Services

ARTICLE 59

Within the framework of the provisions set out below, restrictions on freedom to provide services within the Community shall be progressively abolished during the transitional period in respect of nationals of Member States who are established in a State of the Community other than that of the person for whom the services are intended.

The Council may, acting unanimously on a proposal from the Commission, extend the provisions of this Chapter to nationals of a third country who provide services and who are established within the Community.

ARTICLE 60

Services shall be considered to be 'services' within the meaning of this Treaty where they are normally provided for remuneration, in so far as they are not governed by the provisions relating to freedom of movement for goods, capital and persons.

'Services' shall in particular include:

(*a*) activities of an industrial character;

(*b*) activities of a commercial character;

(*c*) activities of craftsmen;

(*d*) activities of the professions.

Without prejudice to the provisions of the Chapter relating to the right of establishment, the person providing a service may, in order to do so, temporarily pursue his activity in the State where the service is provided, under the same conditions as are imposed by that State on its own nationals.

ARTICLE 61

1. Freedom to provide services in the field of transport shall be governed by the provisions of the Title relating to transport.

2. The liberalisation of banking and insurance services connected with movements of capital shall be effected in step with the progressive liberalisation of movement of capital.

ARTICLE 62

Save as otherwise provided in this Treaty, Member States shall not introduce any new restrictions on the freedom to provide services which has in fact been attained at the date of the entry into force of this Treaty.

ARTICLE 63

1. Before the end of the first stage, the Council shall, acting unanimously on a proposal from the Commission and after consulting the Economic and Social Committee and the Assembly, draw up a general programme for the abolition of existing restrictions on freedom to provide services within the Community. The Commission shall submit its proposal to the Council during the first two years of the first stage.

The programme shall set out the general conditions under which and the stages by which each type of service is to be liberalised.

2. In order to implement this general programme or, in the absence of such programme, in order to achieve a stage in the liberalisation of a specific service, the Council shall, on a proposal from the Commission and after consulting the Economic and Social Committee and the Assembly, issue directives, acting unanimously until the end of the first stage and by a qualified majority thereafter.

3. As regards the proposals and decisions referred to in paragraphs 1 and 2, priority shall as a general rule be given to those services which directly affect production costs or the liberalisation of which helps to promote trade in goods.

ARTICLE 64

The Member States declare their readiness to undertake the liberalisation of services beyond the extent required by the directives issued pursuant to Article 63 (2), if their economic situation and the situation of the economic sector concerned so permit.

To this end, the Commission shall make recommendations to the Member States concerned.

ARTICLE 65

As long as restrictions on freedom to provide services have not been abolished, each Member State shall apply such restrictions without distinction on grounds of nationality or residence to all persons providing services within the meaning of the first paragraph of Article 59.

ARTICLE 66

The provisions of Articles 55 to 58 shall apply to the matters covered by this Chapter.

Chapter 4: Capital

ARTICLE 67

1. During the transitional period and to the extent necessary to ensure the proper functioning of the common market, Member States shall progressively abolish between themselves all restrictions on the movement of capital belonging to persons resident in Member States and any discrimination based on the nationality or on the place of residence of the parties or on the place where such capital is invested.

2. Current payments connected with the movement of capital between Member States shall be freed from all restrictions by the end of the first stage at the latest.

ARTICLE 68

1. Member States shall, as regards the matters dealt with in this Chapter, be as liberal as possible in granting such exchange authorisations as are still necessary after the entry into force of this Treaty.

2. Where a Member State applies to the movements of capital liberalised in accordance with the provisions of this Chapter the domestic rules governing the capital market and the credit system, it shall do so in a non-discriminatory manner.

3. Loans for the direct or indirect financing of a Member State or its regional or local authorities shall not be issued or placed in other Member States unless the States concerned have reached agreement thereon. This provision shall not preclude the application of Article 22 of the Protocol on the Statute of the European Investment Bank.

ARTICLE 69

The Council shall, on a proposal from the Commission, which for this purpose shall consult the Monetary Committee provided for in Article 105, issue the necessary directives for the progressive implementation of the provisions of Article 67, acting unanimously during the first two stages and by a qualified majority thereafter.

ARTICLE 70

1. The Commission shall propose to the Council measures for the progressive coordination of the exchange policies of Member States in respect of the movement of capital between those States and third countries. For this purpose the Council shall issue directives, acting unanimously. It shall endeavour to attain the highest possible degree of liberalisation.

2. Where the measures taken in accordance with paragraph 1 do not permit

the elimination of differences between the exchange rules of Member States and where such differences could lead persons resident in one of the Member States to use the freer transfer facilities within the Community which are provided for in Article 67 in order to evade the rules of one of the Member States concerning the movement of capital to or from third countries, that State may, after consulting the other Member States and the Commission, take appropriate measures to overcome these difficulties.

Should the Council find that these measures are restricting the free movement of capital within the Community to a greater extent than is required for the purpose of overcoming the difficulties, it may, acting by a qualified majority on a proposal from the Commission, decide that the State concerned shall amend or abolish these measures.

ARTICLE 71

Member States shall endeavour to avoid introducing within the Community any new exchange restrictions on the movement of capital and current payments connected with such movements, and shall endeavour not to make existing rules more restrictive.

They declare their readiness to go beyond the degree of liberalisation of capital movements provided for in the preceding Articles in so far as their economic situation, in particular the situation of their balance of payments, so permits.

The Commission may, after consulting the Monetary Committee, make recommendations to Member States on this subject.

ARTICLE 72

Member States shall keep the Commission informed of any movements of capital to and from third countries which come to their knowledge. The Commission may deliver to Member States any opinions which it considers appropriate on this subject.

ARTICLE 73

1. If movements of capital lead to disturbances in the functioning of the capital market in any Member State, the Commission shall, after consulting the Monetary Committee, authorise that State to take protective measures in the field of capital movements, the conditions and details of which the Commission shall determine.

The Council may, acting by a qualified majority, revoke this authorisation or amend the conditions or details thereof.

2. A Member State which is in difficulties may, however, on grounds of secrecy or urgency, take the measures mentioned above, where this proves necessary, on its own initiative. The Commission and the other Member States shall be informed of such measures by the date of their entry into force at the latest. In this event the Commission may, after consulting the Monetary Committee, decide that the State concerned shall amend or abolish the measures.

TITLE IV: TRANSPORT

ARTICLE 74

The objectives of this Treaty shall, in matters governed by this Title, be pursued by Member States within the framework of a common transport policy.

ARTICLE 75

1. For the purpose of implementing Article 74, and taking into account the distinctive features of transport, the Council shall, acting unanimously until the end of the second stage and by a qualified majority thereafter, lay down, on a proposal from the Commission and after consulting the Economic and Social Committee and the Assembly:

(*a*) common rules applicable to international transport to or from the territory of a Member State or passing across the territory of one or more Member States;

(*b*) the conditions under which non-resident carriers may operate transport services within a Member State;

(*c*) any other appropriate provisions.

2. The provisions referred to in (*a*) and (*b*) of paragraph 1 shall be laid down during the transitional period.

3. By way of derogation from the procedure provided for in paragraph 1, where the application of provisions concerning the principles of the regulatory system for transport would be liable to have a serious effect on the standard of living and on employment in certain areas and on the operation of transport facilities, they shall be laid down by the Council acting unanimously. In so doing, the Council shall take into account the need for adaptation to the economic development which will result from establishing the common market.

ARTICLE 76

Until the provisions referred to in Article 75 (1) have been laid down, no Member State may, without the unanimous approval of the Council, make the various provisions governing the subject when this Treaty enters into force less favourable in their direct or indirect effect on carriers of other Member States as compared with carriers who are nationals of that State.

ARTICLE 77

Aids shall be compatible with this Treaty if they meet the needs of coordination of transport or if they represent reimbursement for the discharge of certain obligations inherent in the concept of a public service.

ARTICLE 78

Any measures taken within the framework of this Treaty in respect of transport rates and conditions shall take account of the economic circumstances of carriers.

N

ARTICLE 79

1. In the case of transport within the Community, discrimination which takes the form of carriers charging different rates and imposing different conditions for the carriage of the same goods over the same transport links on grounds of the country of origin or of destination of the goods in question, shall be abolished, at the latest, before the end of the second stage.

2. Paragraph 1 shall not prevent the Council from adopting other measures in pursuance of Article 75 (1).

3. Within two years of the entry into force of this Treaty, the Council shall, acting by a qualified majority on a proposal from the Commission and after consulting the Economic and Social Committee, lay down rules for implementing the provisions of paragraph 1.

The Council may in particular lay down the provisions needed to enable the institutions of the Community to secure compliance with the rule laid down in paragraph 1 and to ensure that users benefit from it to the full.

4. The Commission shall, acting on its own initiative or on application by a Member State, investigate any cases of discrimination falling within paragraph 1, and, after consulting any Member State concerned, shall take the necessary decisions within the framework of the rules laid down in accordance with the provisions of paragraph 3.

ARTICLE 80

1. The imposition by a Member State, in respect of transport operations carried out within the Community, of rates and conditions involving any element of support or protection in the interest of one or more particular undertakings or industries shall be prohibited as from the beginning of the second stage, unless authorised by the Commission.

2. The Commission shall, acting on its own initiative or on application by a Member State, examine the rates and conditions referred to in paragraph 1, taking account in particular of the requirements of an appropriate regional economic policy, the needs of underdeveloped areas and the problems of areas seriously affected by political circumstances on the one hand, and of the effects of such rates and conditions on competition between the different modes of transport on the other.

After consulting each Member State concerned, the Commission shall take the necessary decisions.

3. The prohibition provided for in paragraph 1 shall not apply to tariffs fixed to meet competition.

ARTICLE 81

Charges or dues in respect of the crossing of frontiers which are charged by a carrier in addition to the transport rates shall not exceed a reasonable level after taking the costs actually incurred thereby into account.

Member States shall endeavour to reduce these costs progressively.

The Commission may make recommendations to Member States for the application of this Article.

ARTICLE 82

The provisions of this Title shall not form an obstacle to the application of measures taken in the Federal Republic of Germany to the extent that such measures are required in order to compensate for the economic disadvantages caused by the division of Germany to the economy of certain areas of the Federal Republic affected by that division.

ARTICLE 83

An Advisory Committee consisting of experts designated by the Governments of Member States, shall be attached to the Commission. The Commission, whenever it considers it desirable, shall consult the Committee on transport matters without prejudice to the powers of the transport section of the Economic and Social Committee.

ARTICLE 84

1. The provisions of this Title shall apply to transport by rail, road and inland waterway.

2. The Council may, acting unanimously, decide whether, to what extent and by what procedure appropriate provisions may be laid down for sea and air transport.

Part Three

Policy of the Community

TITLE I: COMMON RULES

Chapter 1: Rules on Competition

SECTION 1: RULES APPLYING TO UNDERTAKINGS

ARTICLE 85

1. The following shall be prohibited as incompatible with the common market: all agreements between undertakings, decisions by associations of undertakings and concerted practices which may affect trade between Member States and which have as their object or effect the prevention, restriction or distortion of competition within the common market, and in particular those which:

(*a*) directly or indirectly fix purchase or selling prices or any other trading conditions;

(*b*) limit or control production, markets, technical development, or investment;

(*c*) share markets or sources of supply;

(*d*) apply dissimilar conditions to equivalent transactions with other trading parties, thereby placing them at a competitive disadvantage;

(*e*) make the conclusion of contracts subject to acceptance by the other parties of supplementary obligations which, by their nature or according to commercial usage, have no connection with the subject of such contracts.

2. Any agreements or decisions prohibited pursuant to this Article shall be automatically void.

3. The provisions of paragraph 1 may, however, be declared inapplicable in the case of:

– any agreement or category of agreements between undertakings;
– any decision or category of decisions by associations of undertakings;
– any concerted practice or category of concerted practices;

which contributes to improving the production or distribution of goods or to promoting technical or economic progress, while allowing consumers a fair share of the resulting benefit, and which does not:

(*a*) impose on the undertakings concerned restrictions which are not indispensable to the attainment of these objectives;

(*b*) afford such undertakings the possibility of eliminating competition in respect of a substantial part of the products in question.

ARTICLE 86

Any abuse by one or more undertakings of a dominant position within the common market or in a substantial part of it shall be prohibited as incompatible with the common market in so far as it may affect trade between Member States. Such abuse may, in particular, consist in:

(*a*) directly or indirectly imposing unfair purchase or selling prices or other unfair trading conditions;

(*b*) limiting production, markets or technical development to the prejudice of consumers;

(*c*) applying dissimilar conditions to equivalent transactions with other trading parties, thereby placing them at a competitive disadvantage;

(*d*) making the conclusion of contracts subject to acceptance by the other parties of supplementary obligations which, by their nature or according to commercial usage, have no connection with the subject of such contracts.

ARTICLE 87

1. Within three years of the entry into force of this Treaty the Council shall, acting unanimously on a proposal from the Commission and after consulting the Assembly, adopt any appropriate regulations or directives to give effect to the principles set out in Articles 85 and 86.

If such provisions have not been adopted within the period mentioned, they shall be laid down by the Council, acting by a qualified majority on a proposal from the Commission and after consulting the Assembly.

2. The regulations or directives referred to in paragraph 1 shall be designed, in particular:

(*a*) to ensure compliance with the prohibitions laid down in Article 85 (1) and in Article 86 by making provision for fines and periodic penalty payments;

(*b*) to lay down detailed rules for the application of Article 85 (3), taking into account the need to ensure effective supervision on the one hand, and to simplify administration to the greatest possible extent on the other;

(*c*) to define, if need be, in the various branches of the economy, the scope of the provisions of Articles 85 and 86;

(*d*) to define the respective functions of the Commission and of the Court of Justice in applying the provisions laid down in this paragraph;

(*e*) to determine the relationship between national laws and the provisions contained in this Section or adopted pursuant to this Article.

ARTICLE 88

Until the entry into force of the provisions adopted in pursuance of Article 87, the authorities in Member States shall rule on the admissibility of agreements, decisions and concerted practices and on abuse of a dominant position in the common market in accordance with the law of their country and with the provisions of Article 85, in particular paragraph 3, and of Article 86.

ARTICLE 89

1. Without prejudice to Article 88, the Commission shall, as soon as it takes up its duties, ensure the application of the principles laid down in Articles 85 and 86. On application by a Member State or on its own initiative, and in co-operation with the competent authorities in the Member States, who shall give it their assistance, the Commission shall investigate cases of suspected infringement of these principles. If it finds that there has been an infringement, it shall propose appropriate measures to bring it to an end.

2. If the infringement is not brought to an end, the Commission shall record such infringement of the principles in a reasoned decision. The Commission may publish its decision and authorise Member States to take the measures, the conditions and details of which it shall determine, needed to remedy the situation.

ARTICLE 90

1. In the case of public undertakings and undertakings to which Member States grant special or exclusive rights, Member States shall neither enact nor maintain in force any measure contrary to the rules contained in this Treaty, in particular to those rules provided for in Article 7 and Articles 85 to 94.

2. Undertakings entrusted with the operation of services of general economic interest or having the character of a revenue-producing monopoly shall be subject to the rules contained in this Treaty, in particular to the rules on competition, in so far as the application of such rules does not obstruct the performance, in law or in fact, of the particular tasks assigned to them. The development of trade must not be affected to such an extent as would be contrary to the interests of the Community.

3. The Commission shall ensure the application of the provisions of this Article and shall, where necessary, address appropriate directives or decisions to Member States.

SECTION 2: DUMPING

ARTICLE 91

1. If, during the transitional period, the Commission, on application by a Member State or by any other interested party, finds that dumping is being practised within the common market, it shall address recommendations to the person or persons with whom such practices originate for the purpose of putting an end to them.

Should the practices continue, the Commission shall authorise the injured Member State to take protective measures, the conditions and details of which the Commission shall determine.

2. As soon as this treaty enters into force, products which originate in or are in free circulation in one Member State and which have been exported to another Member State shall, on reimportation, be admitted into the territory of the first-mentioned State free of all customs duties, quantitative restrictions

or measures having equivalent effect. The Commission shall lay down appropriate rules for the application of this paragraph.

SECTION 3: AIDS GRANTED BY STATES

ARTICLE 92

1. Save as otherwise provided in this Treaty, any aid granted by a Member State or through State resources in any form whatsoever which distorts or threatens to distort competition by favouring certain undertakings or the production of certain goods shall, in so far as it affects trade between Member States, be incompatible with the common market.

2. The following shall be compatible with the common market:

(*a*) aid having a social character, granted to individual consumers, provided that such aid is granted without discrimination related to the origin of the products concerned;

(*b*) aid to make good the damage caused by natural disasters or other exceptional occurrences;

(*c*) aid granted to the economy of certain areas of the Federal Republic of Germany affected by the division of Germany, in so far as such aid is required in order to compensate for the economic disadvantages caused by that division.

3. The following may be considered to be compatible with the common market:

(*a*) aid to promote the economic development of areas where the standard of living is abnormally low or where there is serious underemployment;

(*b*) aid to promote the execution of an important project of common European interest or to remedy a serious disturbance in the economy of a Member State;

(*c*) aid to facilitate the development of certain economic activities or of certain economic areas, where such aid does not adversely affect trading conditions to an extent contrary to the common interest. However, the aids granted to shipbuilding as of 1 January 1957 shall, in so far as they serve only to compensate for the absence of customs protection, be progressively reduced under the same conditions as apply to the elimination of customs duties, subject to the provisions of this Treaty concerning common commercial policy towards third countries;

(*d*) such other categories of aid as may be specified by decision of the Council acting by a qualified majority on a proposal from the Commission.

ARTICLE 93

1. The Commission shall, in cooperation with Member States, keep under constant review all systems of aid existing in those States. It shall propose to the latter any appropriate measures required by the progressive development or by the functioning of the common market.

2. If, after giving notice to the parties concerned to submit their comments,

the Commission finds that aid granted by a State or through State resources is not compatible with the common market having regard to Article 92, or that such aid is being misused, it shall decide that the State concerned shall abolish or alter such aid within a period of time to be determined by the Commission.

If the State concerned does not comply with this decision within the prescribed time, the Commission or any other interested State may, in derogation from the provisions of Articles 169 and 170, refer the matter to the Court of Justice direct.

On application by a Member State, the Council, may, acting unanimously, decide that aid which that State is granting or intends to grant shall be considered to be compatible with the common market, in derogation from the provisions of Article 92 or from the regulations provided for in Article 94, if such a decision is justified by exceptional circumstances. If, as regards the aid in question, the Commission has already initiated the procedure provided for in the first subparagraph of this paragraph, the fact that the State concerned has made its application to the Council shall have the effect of suspending that procedure until the Council has made its attitude known.

If, however, the Council has not made its attitude known within three months of the said application being made, the Commission shall give its decision on the case.

3. The Commission shall be informed, in sufficient time to enable it to submit its comments, of any plans to grant or alter aid. If it considers that any such plan is not compatible with the common market having regard to Article 92, it shall without delay initiate the procedure provided for in paragraph 2. The Member State concerned shall not put its proposed measures into effect until this procedure has resulted in a final decision.

ARTICLE 94

The Council may, acting by a qualified majority on a proposal from the Commission, make any appropriate regulations for the application of Articles 92 and 93 and may in particular determine the conditions in which Article 93 (3) shall apply and the categories of aid exempted from this procedure.

Chapter 2: Tax Provisions

ARTICLE 95

No Member State shall impose, directly or indirectly, on the products of other Member States any internal taxation of any kind in excess of that imposed directly or indirectly on similar domestic products.

Furthermore, no Member State shall impose on the products of other Member States any internal taxation of such a nature as to afford indirect protection to other products.

Member States shall, not later than at the beginning of the second stage, repeal or amend any provisions existing when this Treaty enters into force which conflict with the preceding rules.

ARTICLE 96

Where products are exported to the territory of any Member State, any repayment of internal taxation shall not exceed the internal taxation imposed on them, whether directly or indirectly.

ARTICLE 97

Member States which levy a turnover tax calculated on a cumulative multi-stage tax system may, in the case of internal taxation imposed by them on imported products or of repayments allowed by them on exported products, establish average rates for products or groups of products, provided that there is no infringement of the principles laid down in Articles 95 and 96.

Where the average rates established by a Member State do not conform to these principles, the Commission shall address appropriate directives or decisions to the State concerned.

ARTICLE 98

In the case of charges other than turnover taxes, excise duties and other forms of indirect taxation, remissions and repayments in respect of exports to other Member States may not be granted and countervailing charges in respect of imports from Member States may not be imposed unless the measures contemplated have been previously approved for a limited period by the Council acting by a qualified majority on a proposal from the Commission.

ARTICLE 99

The Commission shall consider how the legislation of the various Member States concerning turnover taxes, excise duties and other forms of indirect taxation, including countervailing measures applicable to trade between Member States can be harmonised in the interest of the common market.

The Commission shall submit proposals to the Council, which shall act unanimously without prejudice to the provisions of Articles 100 and 101.

Chapter 3: Approximation of laws

ARTICLE 100

The Council shall, acting unanimously on a proposal from the Commission, issue directives for the approximation of such provisions laid down by law, regulation or administrative action in Member States as directly affect the establishment or functioning of the common market.

The Assembly and the Economic and Social Committee shall be consulted in the case of directives whose implementation would, in one or more Member States, involve the amendment of legislation.

ARTICLE 101

Where the Commission finds that a difference between the provisions laid down by law, regulation or administrative action in Member States is distorting the conditions of competition in the common market and that the resultant

4. If need be, Member States shall consult each other on the measures to be taken to enable the payments and transfers mentioned in this Article to be effected; such measures shall not prejudice the attainment of the objectives set out in this Chapter.

ARTICLE 107

1. Each Member State shall treat its policy with regard to rates of exchange as a matter of common concern.

2. If a Member State makes an alteration in its rate of exchange which is inconsistent with the objectives set out in Article 104 and which seriously distorts conditions of competition, the Commission may, after consulting the Monetary Committee, authorise other Member States to take for a strictly limited period the necessary measures, the conditions and details of which it shall determine, in order to counter the consequences of such alteration.

ARTICLE 108

1. Where a Member State is in difficulties or is seriously threatened with difficulties as regards its balance of payments either as a result of an overall disequilibrium in its balance of payments, or as a result of the type of currency at its disposal, and where such difficulties are liable in particular to jeopardise the functioning of the common market or the progressive implementation of the common commercial policy, the Commission shall immediately investigate the position of the State in question and the action which, making use of all the means at its disposal, that State has taken or may take in accordance with the provisions of Article 104. The Commission shall state what measures it recommends the State concerned to take.

If the action taken by a Member State and the measures suggested by the Commission do not prove sufficient to overcome the difficulties which have arisen or which threaten, the Commission shall, after consulting the Monetary Committee, recommend to the Council the granting of mutual assistance and appropriate methods therefor.

The Commission shall keep the Council regularly informed of the situation and of how it is developing.

2. The Council, acting by a qualified majority, shall grant such mutual assistance; it shall adopt directives or decisions laying down the conditions and details of such assistance, which may take such forms as:

(*a*) a concerted approach to or within any other international organisations to which Member States may have recourse;

(*b*) measures needed to avoid deflection of trade where the State which is in difficulties maintains or reintroduces quantitative restrictions against third countries;

(*c*) the granting of limited credits by other Member States, subject to their agreement.

During the transitional period, mutual assistance may also take the form of special reductions in customs duties or enlargements of quotas in order to facilitate an increase in imports from the State which is in difficulties, subject to the agreement of the States by which such measures would have to be taken.

3. If the mutual assistance recommended by the Commission is not granted by the Council or if the mutual assistance granted and the measures taken are insufficient, the Commission shall authorise the State which is in difficulties to take protective measures, the conditions and details of which the Commission shall determine.

Such authorisation may be revoked and such conditions and details may be changed by the Council acting by a qualified majority.

ARTICLE 109

1. Where a sudden crisis in the balance of payments occurs and a decision within the meaning of Article 108 (2) is not immediately taken, the Member State concerned may, as a precaution, take the necessary protective measures. Such measures must cause the least possible disturbance in the functioning of the common market and must not be wider in scope than is strictly necessary to remedy the sudden difficulties which have arisen.

2. The Commission and the other Member States shall be informed of such protective measures not later than when they enter into force. The Commission may recommend to the Council the granting of mutual assistance under Article 108.

3. After the Commission has delivered an opinion and the Monetary Committee has been consulted, the Council may, acting by a qualified majority, decide that the State concerned shall amend, suspend or abolish the protective measures referred to above.

Chapter 3: Commercial policy

ARTICLE 110

By establishing a customs union between themselves Member States aim to contribute, in the common interest, to the harmonious development of world trade, the progressive abolition of restrictions on international trade and the lowering of customs barriers.

The common commercial policy shall take into account the favourable effect which the abolition of customs duties between Member States may have on the increase in the competitive strength of undertakings in those States.

ARTICLE 111

The following provisions shall, without prejudice to Articles 115 and 116, apply during the transitional period:

1. Member States shall coordinate their trade relations with third countries so as to bring about, by the end of the transitional period, the conditions needed for implementing a common policy in the field of external trade.

The Commission shall submit to the Council proposals regarding the procedure for common action to be followed during the transitional period and regarding the achievement of uniformity in their commercial policies.

2. The Commission shall submit to the Council recommendations for tariff negotiations with third countries in respect of the common customs tariff.

The Council shall authorise the Commission to open such negotiations.

The Commission shall conduct these negotiations in consultation with a special committee appointed by the Council to assist the Commission in this task and within the framework of such directives as the Council may issue to it.

3. In exercising the powers conferred upon it by this Article, the Council shall act unanimously during the first two stages and by a qualified majority thereafter.

4. Member States shall, in consultation with the Commission, take all necessary measures, particularly those designed to bring about an adjustment of tariff agreements in force with third countries, in order that the entry into force of the common customs tariff shall not be delayed.

5. Member States shall aim at securing as high a level of uniformity as possible between themselves as regards their liberalisation lists in relation to third countries or groups of third countries. To this end, the Commission shall make all appropriate recommendations to Member States.

If Member States abolish or reduce quantitative restrictions in relation to third countries, they shall inform the Commission beforehand and shall accord the same treatment to other Member States.

ARTICLE 112

1. Without prejudice to obligations undertaken by them within the framework of other international organisations, Member States shall, before the end of the transitional period, progressively harmonise the systems whereby they grant aid for exports to third countries, to the extent necessary to ensure that competition between undertakings of the Community is not distorted.

On a proposal from the Commission, the Council, shall, acting unanimously until the end of the second stage and by a qualified majority thereafter, issue any directives needed for this purpose.

2. The preceding provisions shall not apply to such drawback of customs duties or charges having equivalent effect nor to such repayment of indirect taxation including turnover taxes, excise duties and other indirect taxes as is allowed when goods are exported from a Member State to a third country, in so far as such drawback or repayment does not exceed the amount imposed, directly or indirectly, on the products exported.

ARTICLE 113

1. After the transitional period has ended, the common commercial policy shall be based on uniform principles, particularly in regard to changes in tariff rates, the conclusion of tariff and trade agreements, the achievement of uniformity in measures of liberalisation, export policy and measures to protect trade such as those to be taken in case of dumping or subsidies.

2. The Commission shall submit proposals to the Council for implementing the common commercial policy.

3. Where agreements with third countries need to be negotiated, the Commission shall make recommendations to the Council, which shall authorise the Commission to open the necessary negotiations.

The Commission shall conduct these negotiations in consultation with a special committee appointed by the Council to assist the Commission in this task and within the framework of such directives as the Council may issue to it.

4. In exercising the powers conferred upon it by this Article, the Council shall act by a qualified majority.

ARTICLE 114

The agreements referred to in Article 111 (2) and in Article 113 shall be concluded by the Council on behalf of the Community, acting unanimously during the first two stages and by a qualified majority thereafter.

ARTICLE 115

In order to ensure that the execution of measures of commercial policy taken in accordance with this Treaty by any Member State is not obstructed by deflection of trade, or where differences between such measures lead to economic difficulties in one or more of the Member States, the Commission shall recommend the methods for the requisite cooperation between Member States. Failing this, the Commission shall authorise Member States to take the necessary protective measures, the conditions and details of which it shall determine.

In case of urgency during the transitional period, Member States may themselves take the necessary measures and shall notify them to the other Member States and to the Commission, which may decide that the States concerned shall amend or abolish such measures.

In the selection of such measures, priority shall be given to those which cause the least disturbance to the functioning of the common market and which take into account the need to expedite, as far as possible, the introduction of the common customs tariff.

ARTICLE 116

From the end of the transitional period onwards, Member States shall, in respect of all matters of particular interest to the common market, proceed within the framework of international organisations of an economic character only by common action. To this end, the Commission shall submit to the Council, which shall act by a qualified majority, proposals concerning the scope and implementation of such common action.

During the transitional period, Member States shall consult each other for the purpose of concerting the action they take and adopting as far as possible a uniform attitude.

TITLE III: SOCIAL POLICY

Chapter 1: Social provisions

ARTICLE 117

Member States agree upon the need to promote improved working conditions and an improved standard of living for workers, so as to make possible their harmonisation while the improvement is being maintained.

They believe that such a development will ensue not only from the functioning of the common market, which will favour the harmonisation of social systems, but also from the procedures provided for in this Treaty and from the approximation of provisions laid down by law, regulation or administrative action.

ARTICLE 118

Without prejudice to the other provisions of this Treaty and in conformity with its general objectives, the Commission shall have the task of promoting close cooperation between Member States in the social field, particularly in matters relating to:

- employment;
- labour law and working conditions;
- basic and advanced vocational training;
- social security;
- prevention of occupational accidents and diseases;
- occupational hygiene;
- the right of association, and collective bargaining between employers and workers.

To this end, the Commission shall act in close contact with Member States by making studies, delivering opinions and arranging consultations both on problems arising at national level and on those of concern to international organisations.

Before delivering the opinions provided for in this Article, the Commission shall consult the Economic and Social Committee.

ARTICLE 119

Each Member State shall during the first stage ensure and subsequently maintain the application of the principle that men and women should receive equal pay for equal work.

For the purpose of this Article, 'pay' means the ordinary basic or minimum wage or salary and any other consideration, whether in cash or in kind, which the worker receives, directly or indirectly, in respect of his employment from his employer.

Equal pay without discrimination based on sex means:

(*a*) that pay for the same work at piece rates shall be calculated on the basis of the same unit of measurement;

(*b*) that pay for work at time rates shall be the same for the same job.

ARTICLE 120

Member States shall endeavour to maintain the existing equivalence between paid holiday schemes.

ARTICLE 121

The Council may, acting unanimously and after consulting the Economic and Social Committee, assign to the Commission tasks in connection with the implementation of common measures, particularly as regards social security for the migrant workers referred to in Articles 48 to 51.

ARTICLE 122

The Commission shall include a separate chapter on social developments within the Community in its annual report to the Assembly.

The Assembly may invite the Commission to draw up reports on any particular problems concerning social conditions.

Chapter 2: The European Social Fund

ARTICLE 123

In order to improve employment opportunities for workers in the common market and to contribute thereby to raising the standard of living, a European Social Fund is hereby established in accordance with the provisions set out below; it shall have the task of rendering the employment of workers easier and of increasing their geographical and occupational mobility within the Community.

ARTICLE 124

The Fund shall be administered by the Commission.

The Commission shall be assisted in this task by a Committee presided over by a member of the Commission and composed of representatives of Governments, trade unions and employers' organisations.

ARTICLE 125

1. On application by a Member State the Fund shall, within the framework of the rules provided for in Article 127, meet 50 per cent of the expenditure incurred after the entry into force of this Treaty by that State or by a body governed by public law for the purposes of:

(*a*) ensuring productive re-employment of workers by means of:
    vocational retraining;
    resettlement allowances;

(*b*) granting aid for the benefit of workers whose employment is reduced or temporarily suspended, in whole or in part, as a result of the conversion of an undertaking to other production, in order that they may retain the same wage level pending their full re-employment.

2. Assistance granted by the Fund towards the cost of vocational retraining shall be granted only if the unemployed workers could not be found employment except in a new occupation and only if they have been in productive employment for at least six months in the occupation for which they have been retrained.

Assistance towards resettlement allowances shall be granted only if the

o

unemployed workers have been caused to change their home within the Community and have been in productive employment for at least six months in their new place of residence.

Assistance for workers in the case of the conversion of an undertaking shall be granted only if:

(*a*) the workers concerned have again been fully employed in that undertaking for at least six months;

(*b*) the Government concerned has submitted a plan beforehand, drawn up by the undertaking in question, for that particular conversion and for financing it;

(*c*) the Commission has given its prior approval to the conversion plan.

ARTICLE 126

When the transitional period has ended, the Council, after receiving the opinion of the Commission and after consulting the Economic and Social Committee and the Assembly, may:

(*a*) rule, by a qualified majority, that all or part of the assistance referred to in Article 125 shall no longer be granted; or

(*b*) unanimously determine what new tasks may be entrusted to the Fund within the framework of its terms of reference as laid down in Article 123.

ARTICLE 127

The Council shall, acting by a qualified majority on a proposal from the Commission and after consulting the Economic and Social Committee and the Assembly, lay down the provisions required to implement Articles 124 to 126; in particular it shall determine in detail the conditions under which assistance shall be granted by the Fund in accordance with Article 125 and the classes of undertakings whose workers shall benefit from the assistance provided for in Article 125 (1) (*b*).

ARTICLE 128

The Council shall, acting on a proposal from the Commission and after consulting the Economic and Social Committee, lay down general principles for implementing a common vocational training policy capable of contributing to the harmonious development both of the national economies and of the common market.

TITLE IV: THE EUROPEAN INVESTMENT BANK

ARTICLE 129

A European Investment Bank is hereby established; it shall have legal personality.

The members of the European Investment Bank shall be the Member States.

The Statute of the European Investment Bank is laid down in a Protocol annexed to this Treaty.

ARTICLE 130

The task of the European Investment Bank shall be to contribute, by having recourse to the capital market and utilising its own resources, to the balanced and steady development of the common market in the interest of the Community. For this purpose the Bank shall, operating on a non-profit-making basis, grant loans and give guarantees which facilitate the financing of the following projects in all sectors of the economy:

(*a*) projects for developing less developed regions;

(*b*) projects for modernising or converting undertakings or for developing fresh activities called for by the progressive establishment of the common market, where these projects are of such a size or nature that they cannot be entirely financed by the various means available in the individual Member States;

(*c*) projects of common interest to several Member States which are of such a size or nature that they cannot be entirely financed by the various means available in the individual Member States.

Part Four

Association of the overseas countries and territories

The Member States agree to associate with the Community the non-European countries and territories which have special relations with Belgium, France, Italy, the Netherlands, Norway and the United Kingdom. These countries and territories (hereinafter called the 'countries and territories') are listed in Annex IV to this Treaty.

The purpose of association shall be to promote the economic and social development of the countries and territories and to establish close economic relations between them and the Community as a whole.

In accordance with the principles set out in the Preamble to this Treaty, association shall serve primarily to further the interests and prosperity of the inhabitants of these countries and territories in order to lead them to the economic, social and cultural development to which they aspire.

ARTICLE 132

Association shall have the following objectives:

1. Member States shall apply to their trade with the countries and territories the same treatment as they accord each other pursuant to this Treaty.

2. Each country or territory shall apply to its trade with Member States and with the other countries and territories the same treatment as that which it applies to the European State with which it has special relations.

3. The Member States shall contribute to the investments required for the progressive development of these countries and territories.

4. For investments financed by the Community, participation in tenders and supplies shall be open on equal terms to all natural and legal persons who are nationals of a Member State or of one of the countries and territories.

5. In relations between Member States and the countries and territories the right of establishment of nationals and companies or firms shall be regulated in accordance with the provisions and procedures laid down in the Chapter relating to the right of establishment and on a non-discriminatory basis, subject to any special provisions laid down pursuant to Article 136.

ARTICLE 133

1. Customs duties on imports into the Member States of goods originating in the countries and territories shall be completely abolished in conformity

[1]As amended by Article 24 of the Act of Accession of 1972. See Note II on page 150, on the consequences of the Norwegian decision not to accede to the European Communities.

with the progressive abolition of customs duties between Member States in accordance with the provisions of this Treaty.

2. Customs duties on imports into each country or territory from Member States or from the other countries or territories shall be progressively abolished in accordance with the provisions of Articles 12, 13, 14, 15 and 17.

3. The countries and territories may, however, levy customs duties which meet the needs of their development and industrialisation or produce revenue for their budgets.

The duties referred to in the preceding subparagraph shall nevertheless be progressively reduced to the level of those imposed on imports of products from the Member State with which each country or territory has special relations. The percentages and the timetable of the reductions provided for under this Treaty shall apply to the difference between the duty imposed on a product coming from the Member State which has special relations with the country or territory concerned and the duty imposed on the same product coming from within the Community on entry into the importing country or territory.

4. Paragraph 2 shall not apply to countries and territories which, by reason of the particular international obligations by which they are bound, already apply a non-discriminatory customs tariff when this Treaty enters into force.

5. The introduction of or any change in customs duties imposed on goods imported into the countries and territories shall not, either in law or in fact, give rise to any direct or indirect discrimination between imports from the various Member States.

ARTICLE 134

If the level of the duties applicable to goods from a third country on entry into a country or territory is liable, when the provisions of Article 133 (1) have been applied, to cause deflections of trade to the detriment of any Member State, the latter may request the Commission to propose to the other Member States the measures needed to remedy the situation.

ARTICLE 135

Subject to the provisions relating to public health, public security or public policy, freedom of movement within Member States for workers from the countries and territories, and within the countries and territories for workers from Member States, shall be governed by agreements to be concluded subsequently with the unanimous approval of Member States.

ARTICLE 136

For an initial period of five years after the entry into force of this Treaty, the details of and procedure for the association of the countries and territories with the Community shall be determined by an Implementing Convention annexed to this Treaty.

Before the Convention referred to in the preceding paragraph expires, the Council shall, acting unanimously, lay down provisions for a further period, on the basis of the experience acquired and of the principles set out in this Treaty.

Part Five

Institutions of the Community

TITLE I: PROVISIONS GOVERNING THE INSTITUTIONS

Chapter 1: The Institutions

SECTION 1: THE ASSEMBLY

ARTICLE 137

The Assembly, which shall consist of representatives of the peoples of the States brought together in the Community, shall exercise the advisory and supervisory powers which are conferred upon it by this Treaty.

ARTICLE 138[1]

1. The Assembly shall consist of delegates who shall be designated by the respective Parliaments from among their members in accordance with the procedure laid down by each Member State.

2. The number of these delegates shall be as follows:

Belgium	14
Denmark	10
Germany	36
France	36
Ireland	10
Italy	36
Luxembourg	6
Netherlands	14
Norway[2]	10
United Kingdom	36

3. The Assembly shall draw up proposals for elections by direct universal suffrage in accordance with a uniform procedure in all Member States.

The Council shall, acting unanimously, lay down the appropriate provisions which it shall recommend to Member States for adoption in accordance with their respective constitutional requirements.

ARTICLE 139[3]

The Assembly shall hold an annual session. It shall meet, without requiring to be convened, on the second Tuesday in March.

[1]As amended by Article 10 of the Act of Accession of 1972.
[2]See Note II on page 150, on the consequences of the decision of Norway not to accede to the European Communities.
[3]As amended by Article 27 (1) of the Merger Treaty of 1965.

The Assembly may meet in extraordinary session at the request of a majority of its members or at the request of the Council or of the Commission.

ARTICLE 140

The Assembly shall elect its President and its officers from among its members.

Members of the Commission may attend all meetings and shall, at their request, be heard on behalf of the Commission.

The Commission shall reply orally or in writing to questions put to it by the Assembly or by its members.

The Council shall be heard by the Assembly in accordance with the conditions laid down by the Council in its rules of procedure.

ARTICLE 141

Save as otherwise provided in this Treaty, the Assembly shall act by an absolute majority of the votes cast.

The rules of procedure shall determine the quorum.

ARTICLE 142

The Assembly shall adopt its rules of procedure, acting by a majority of its members.

The proceedings of the Assembly shall be published in the manner laid down in its rules of procedure.

ARTICLE 143

The Assembly shall discuss in open session the annual general report submitted to it by the Commission.

ARTICLE 144

If a motion of censure on the activities of the Commission is tabled before it, the Assembly shall not vote thereon until at least three days after the motion has been tabled and only by open vote.

If the motion of censure is carried by a two-thirds majority of the votes cast, representing a majority of the members of the Assembly, the members of the Commission shall resign as a body. They shall continue to deal with current business until they are replaced in accordance with Article 158.

SECTION 2: THE COUNCIL[1]

ARTICLE 145

To ensure that the objectives set out in this Treaty are attained, the Council shall, in accordance with the provisions of this Treaty:

– ensure co-ordination of the general economic policies of the Member States;
– have power to take decisions.

[1]Article 1 of the Merger Treaty of 1965 provides for the establishment of a single Council of the European Communities to replace the Special Council of Ministers of ECSC and the Councils of EEC and Euraton, and to exercise the powers and jurisdiction of the former Councils.

ARTICLE 146[1]

[*This Article was repealed by Article 7 of the Merger Treaty of 1965, and its provisions replaced by those of Article 2 of the Merger Treaty (as amended by Article 11 of the Act of Accession of 1972) which now reads as follows:*

'Article 2: The Council shall consist of representatives of the Member States. Each Government shall delegate to it one of its members.

'The office of President shall be held for a term of six months by each member of the Council in turn, in the following order of Member States: Belgium, Denmark, Germany, France, Ireland, Italy, Luxembourg, Netherlands, Norway, United Kingdom.']

ARTICLE 147

[*This Article was repealed by Article 7 of the Merger Treaty of 1965, and its provisions replaced by those of Article 3 of the Merger Treaty which reads as follows:*

'Article 3: The Council shall meet when convened by its President on his own initiative or at the request of one of its members or of the Commission.']

ARTICLE 148[2]

1. Save as otherwise provided in this Treaty, the Council shall act by a majority of its members.

2. Where the Council is required to act by a qualified majority, the votes of its members shall be weighted as follows:

Belgium	5
Denmark	3
Germany	10
France	10
Ireland	3
Italy	10
Luxembourg	2
Netherlands	5
Norway[3]	3
United Kingdom	10

For their adoption, acts of the Council shall require at least:

– forty-three votes in favour where this Treaty requires them to be adopted on a proposal from the Commission;

– forty-three votes in favour, cast by at least six members, in other cases.

3. Abstentions by members present in person or represented shall not prevent the adoption by the Council of acts which require unanimity.

ARTICLE 149

Where, in pursuance of this Treaty, the Council acts on a proposal from the Commission, unanimity shall be required for an act constituting an amendment to that proposal.

[1]See Note II on page 150, on the consequences of the decision of Norway not to accede to the European Communities.
[2]As amended by Article 14 of the Act of Accession of 1972.
[3]See Note II on page 150, on the consequences of the decision of Norway not to accede to the European Communities.

As long as the Council has not acted, the Commission may alter its original proposal, in particular where the Assembly has been consulted on that proposal.

ARTICLE 150

Where a vote is taken, any member of the Council may also act on behalf of not more than one other member.

ARTICLE 151

[*This Article was repealed by Article 7 of the Merger Treaty of 1965, and its provisions replaced by those of Articles 4 and 5 of the Merger Treaty, which read as follows:*
'Article 4: A committee consisting of the Permanent Representatives of the Member States shall be responsible for preparing the work of the Council and for carrying out the tasks assigned to it by the Council.
'Article 5: The Council shall adopt its rules of procedure.']

ARTICLE 152

The Council may request the Commission to undertake any studies which the Council considers desirable for the attainment of the common objectives, and to submit to it any appropriate proposals.

ARTICLE 153

The Council shall, after receiving an opinion from the Commission, determine the rules governing the committees provided for in this Treaty.

ARTICLE 154

[*This Article was repealed by Article 7 of the Merger Treaty of 1965, and its provisions replaced by those of Article 6 of the Merger Treaty, which reads as follows:*
'Article 6: The Council shall, acting by a qualified majority, determine the salaries, allowances and pensions of the President and members of the Commission, and of the President, Judges, Advocates-General and Registrar of the Court of Justice. It shall also, again by a qualified majority, determine any payment to be made instead of remuneration.']

SECTION 3: THE COMMISSION[1]

ARTICLE 155

In order to ensure the proper functioning and development of the common market, the Commission shall:
  – ensure that the provisions of this Treaty and the measures taken by the institutions pursuant thereto are applied;

[1]Article 9 of the Merger Treaty of 1965 provides for the establishment of a single Commission of the European Communities to replace the High Authority of ECSC, and the Commissions of EEC and Euratom, and to exercise the powers and jurisdiction of the former bodies.

– formulate recommendations or deliver opinions on matters dealt with in this Treaty, if it expressly so provides or if the Commission considers it necessary;
– have its own power of decision and participate in the shaping of measures taken by the Council and by the Assembly in the manner provided for in this Treaty;
– exercise the powers conferred on it by the Council for the implementation of the rules laid down by the latter.

ARTICLE 156

[*This Article was repealed by Article 19 of the Merger Treaty of 1965, and its provisions replaced by those of Article 18 of the Merger Treaty, which reads as follows:*

'Article 18: The Commission shall publish annually, not later than one month before the opening of the session of the Assembly, a general report on the activities of the Communities.']

ARTICLE 157[1]

[*This Article was repealed by Article 19 of the Merger Treaty of 1965 and its provisions replaced by those of Article 10 of the Merger Treaty (as amended by Article 15 of the Act of Accession of 1972) which now reads as follows:*

'Article 10: 1. The Commission shall consist of fourteen[1] members, who shall be chosen on the grounds of their general competence and whose independence is beyond doubt.

The number of members of the Commission may be altered by the Council, acting unanimously.

Only nationals of Member States may be members of the Commission.

The Commission must include at least one national of each of the Member States, but may not include more than two members having the nationality of the same State.

2. The Members of the Commission shall, in the general interest of the Communities, be completely independent in the performance of their duties.

In the performance of these duties, they shall neither seek nor take instructions from any Government or from any other body. They shall refrain from any action incompatible with their duties. Each Member State undertakes to respect this principle and not to seek to influence the members of the Commission in the performance of their tasks.

The members of the Commission may not, during their term of office, engage in any other occupation, whether gainful or not. When entering upon their duties they shall give a solemn undertaking that, both during and after their term of office, they will respect the obligations arising therefrom and in particular their duty to behave with integrity and discretion as regards the acceptance, after they have ceased to hold office, of certain appointments or benefits. In the event of any breach of these obligations, the Court of Justice may, on application by the Council or the Commission, rule that the member concerned be, according to the circumstances, either compulsorily retired

[1]See Note II on page 150, on the consequences of the decision of Norway not to accede to the European Communities.

in accordance with the provisions of Article 13 or deprived of his right to a pension or other benefits in its stead.']

ARTICLE 158

[*This Article was repealed by Article 19 of the Merger Treaty of 1965 and its provisions replaced by those of Article 11 of the Merger Treaty, which reads as follows:*

'Article 11: The members of the Commission shall be appointed by common accord of the Governments of the Member States.

Their term of office shall be four years. It shall be renewable.']

ARTICLE 159

[*This article was repealed by Article 19 of the Merger Treaty of 1965 and its provisions replaced by those of Article 12 of the Merger Treaty, which reads as follows:*

'Article 12: Apart from normal replacement, or death, the duties of a member of the Commission shall end when he resigns or is compulsorily retired.

The vacancy thus caused shall be filled for the remainder of the member's term of office. The Council may, acting unanimously, decide that such a vacancy need not be filled.

Save in the case of compulsory retirement under the provisions of Article 13[1], members of the Commission shall remain in office until they have been replaced.']

ARTICLE 160

[*This Article was repealed by Article 19 of the Merger Treaty of 1965 and its provisions replaced by those of Article 13 of the Merger Treaty, which reads as follows:*

'Article 13: If any member of the Commission no longer fulfils the conditions required for the performance of his duties or if he has been guilty of serious misconduct, the Court of Justice may, on application by the Council or the Commission, compulsorily retire him.']

ARTICLE 161[2]

[*This Article was repealed by Article 19 of the Merger Treaty of 1965 and its provisions replaced by those of Article 14 of the Merger Treaty (as amended by Article 16 of the Act of Accession of 1972), which now reads as follows:*

'Article 14: The President and the five Vice-Presidents of the Commission shall be appointed from among its members for a term of two years in accordance with the same procedure as that laid down for the appointment of members of the Commission. Their appointments may be renewed.

Save where the entire Commission is replaced, such appointments shall be made after the Commission has been consulted.

In the event of retirement or death, the President and the Vice-Presidents shall be replaced for the remainder of their term of office in accordance with the preceding provisions.']

[1]Of the Merger Treaty of 1965 (see Article 160 below).
[2]See Note II on page 150, on the consequences of the decision of Norway not to accede to the European Communities.

ARTICLE 162

[*This Article was repealed by Article 19 of the Merger Treaty of 1965 and its provisions replaced by those of Articles 15 and 16 of the Merger Treaty, which read as follows:*

'Article 15: The Council and the Commission shall consult each other and shall settle by common accord their methods of cooperation.

'Article 16: The Commission shall adopt its rules of procedure so as to ensure that both it and its departments operate in accordance with the provisions of the Treaties establishing the European Coal and Steel Community, the European Economic Community and the European Atomic Energy Community, and of this Treaty. It shall ensure that these rules are published.']

ARTICLE 163

[*This Article was repealed by Article 19 of the Merger Treaty of 1965 and its provisions replaced by those of Article 17 of the Merger Treaty, which reads as follows:*

'Article 17: The Commission shall act by a majority of the number of members provided for in Article 10[1].

A meeting of the Commission shall be valid only if the number of members laid down in its rules of procedure is present.']

SECTION 4: THE COURT OF JUSTICE

ARTICLE 164

The Court of Justice shall ensure that in the interpretation and application of this Treaty the law is observed.

ARTICLE 165[2]

The Court of Justice shall consist of eleven Judges.

The Court of Justice shall sit in plenary session. It may, however, form chambers, each consisting of three or five Judges, either to undertake certain preparatory inquiries or to adjudicate on particular categories of cases in accordance with rules laid down for these purposes.

Whenever the Court of Justice hears cases brought before it by a Member State or by one of the institutions of the Community or has to give preliminary rulings on questions submitted to it pursuant to Article 177, it shall sit in plenary session.

Should the Court of Justice so request, the Council may, acting unanimously, increase the number of Judges and make the necessary adjustments to the second and third paragraphs of this Article and to the second paragraph of Article 167.

ARTICLE 166[3]

The Court of Justice shall be assisted by three Advocates-General.

[1]Of the Merger Treaty of 1965 (see Article 157 above).
[2]As amended by Article 17 of the Act of Accession of 1972. See Note II on page 150, on the consequences of the decision of Norway not to accede to the European Communities.
[3]As amended by Article 18 of the Act of Accession of 1972. See Note II on page 150, on the consequences of the decision of Norway not to accede to the European Communities.

It shall be the duty of the Advocate-General, acting with complete impartiality and independence, to make, in open court, reasoned submissions on cases brought before the Court of Justice, in order to assist the Court in the performance of the task assigned to it in Article 164.

Should the Court of Justice so request, the Council may, acting unanimously, increase the number of Advocates-General and make the necessary adjustments to the third paragraph of Article 167.

ARTICLE 167[1]

The Judges and Advocates-General shall be chosen from persons whose independence is beyond doubt and who possess the qualifications required for appointment to the highest judicial offices in their respective countries or who are jurisconsults of recognised competence; they shall be appointed by common accord of the Governments of the Member States for a term of six years.

Every three years there shall be a partial replacement of the Judges. Six and five Judges shall be replaced alternately.

Every three years there shall be a partial replacement of the Advocates-General. One and two Advocates-General shall be replaced alternately.

Retiring Judges and Advocates-General shall be eligible for reappointment.

The Judges shall elect the President of the Court of Justice from among their number for a term of three years. He may be re-elected.

ARTICLE 168

The Court of Justice shall appoint its Registrar and lay down the rules governing his service.

ARTICLE 169

If the Commission considers that a Member State has failed to fulfil an obligation under this Treaty, it shall deliver a reasoned opinion on the matter after giving the State concerned the opportunity to submit its observations.

If the State concerned does not comply with the opinion within the period laid down by the Commission, the latter may bring the matter before the Court of Justice.

ARTICLE 170

A Member State which considers that another Member State has failed to fulfil an obligation under this Treaty may bring the matter before the Court of Justice.

Before a Member State brings an action against another Member State for an alleged infringement of an obligation under this Treaty, it shall bring the matter before the Commission.

The Commission shall deliver a reasoned opinion after each of the States concerned has been given the opportunity to submit its own case and its observations on the other party's case both orally and in writing.

[1]As amended by Article 19 of the Act of Accession of 1972. See Note II on page 150, on the consequences of the decision of Norway not to accede to the European Communities.

If the Commission has not delivered an opinion within three months of the date on which the matter was brought before it, the absence of such opinion shall not prevent the matter from being brought before the Court of Justice.

ARTICLE 171

If the Court of Justice finds that a Member State has failed to fulfil an obligation under this Treaty, the State shall be required to take the necessary measures to comply with the judgment of the Court of Justice.

ARTICLE 172

Regulations made by the Council pursuant to the provisions of this Treaty may give the Court of Justice unlimited jurisdiction in regard to the penalties provided for in such regulations.

ARTICLE 173

The Court of Justice shall review the legality of acts of the Council and the Commission other than recommendations or opinions. It shall for this purpose have jurisdiction in actions brought by a Member State, the Council or the Commission on grounds of lack of competence, infringement of an essential procedural requirement, infringement of this Treaty or of any rule of law relating to its application, or misuse of powers.

Any natural or legal person may, under the same conditions, institute proceedings against a decision addressed to that person or against a decision which, although in the form of a regulation or a decision addressed to another person, is of direct and individual concern to the former.

The proceedings provided for in this Article shall be instituted within two months of the publication of the measure, or of its notification to the plaintiff, or, in the absence thereof, of the day on which it came to the knowledge of the latter, as the case may be.

ARTICLE 174

If the action is well founded, the Court of Justice shall declare the act concerned to be void.

In the case of a regulation, however, the Court of Justice shall, if it considers this necessary, state which of the effects of the regulation which it has declared void shall be considered as definitive.

ARTICLE 175

Should the Council or the Commission, in infringement of this Treaty, fail to act, the Member States and the other institutions of the Community may bring an action before the Court of Justice to have the infringement established.

The action shall be admissible only if the institution concerned has first been called upon to act. If, within two months of being so called upon, the institution concerned has not defined its position, the action may be brought within a further period of two months.

Any natural or legal person may, under the conditions laid down in the preceding paragraphs, complain to the Court of Justice that an institution of the Company has failed to address to that person any act other than a recommendation or an opinion.

ARTICLE 176

The institution whose act has been declared void or whose failure to act has been declared contrary to this Treaty shall be required to take the necessary measures to comply with the judgment of the Court of Justice.

This obligation shall not affect any obligation which may result from the application of the second paragraph of Article 215.

ARTICLE 177

The Court of Justice shall have jurisdiction to give preliminary rulings concerning:

(a) the interpretation of this Treaty;

(b) the validity and interpretation of acts of the institutions of the Community;

(c) the interpretation of the statutes of bodies established by an act of the Council, where those statutes so provide.

Where such a question is raised before any court or tribunal of a Member State, that court or tribunal may, if it considers that a decision on the question is necessary to enable it to give judgment, request the Court of Justice to give a ruling thereon.

Where any such question is raised in a case pending before a court or tribunal of a Member State, against whose decisions there is no judicial remedy under national law, that court or tribunal shall bring the matter before the Court of Justice.

ARTICLE 178

The Court of Justice shall have jurisdiction in disputes relating to the compensation for damage provided for in the second paragraph of Article 215.

ARTICLE 179

The Court of Justice shall have jurisdiction in any dispute between the Community and its servants within the limits and under the conditions laid down in the Staff Regulations or the Conditions of Employment.

ARTICLE 180

The Court of Justice shall, within the limits hereinafter laid down, have jurisdiction in disputes concerning:

(a) the fulfilment by Member States of obligations under the Statute of the European Investment Bank. In this connection, the Board of Directors of the Bank shall enjoy the powers conferred upon the Commission by Article 169;

(b) measures adopted by the Board of Governors of the Bank. In this connection, any Member State, the Commission or the Board of Directors of the Bank may institute proceedings under the conditions laid down in Article 173;

(*c*) measures adopted by the Board of Directors of the Bank. Proceedings against such measures may be instituted only by Member States or by the Commission, under the conditions laid down in Article 173, and solely on the grounds of non-compliance with the procedure provided for in Article 21 (2), (5), (6) and (7) of the Statute of the Bank.

ARTICLE 181

The Court of Justice shall have jurisdiction to give judgment pursuant to any arbitration clause contained in a contract concluded by or on behalf of the Community, whether that contract be governed by public or private law.

ARTICLE 182

The Court of Justice shall have jurisdiction in any dispute between Member States which relates to the subject matter of this Treaty if the dispute is submitted to it under a special agreement between the parties.

ARTICLE 183

Save where jurisdiction is conferred on the Court by this Treaty, disputes to which the Community is a party shall not on that ground be excluded from the jurisdiction of the courts or tribunals of the Member States.

ARTICLE 184

Notwithstanding the expiry of the period laid down in the third paragraph of Article 173, any party may, in proceedings in which a regulation of the Council or of the Commission is in issue, plead the grounds specified in the first paragraph of Article 173, in order to invoke before the Court of Justice the inapplicability of that regulation.

ARTICLE 185

Actions brought before the Court of Justice shall not have suspensory effect. The Court of Justice may, however, if it considers that circumstances so require, order that application of the contested act be suspended.

ARTICLE 186

The Court of Justice may in any cases before it prescribe any necessary interim measures.

ARTICLE 187

The judgments of the Court of Justice shall be enforceable under the conditions laid down in Article 192.

ARTICLE 188

The Statute of the Court of Justice is laid down in a separate Protocol.

The Court of Justice shall adopt its rules of procedure. These shall require the unanimous approval of the Council.

Chapter 2: Provisions common to several institutions

ARTICLE 189

In order to carry out their task the Council and the Commission shall, in accordance with the provisions of this Treaty, make regulations, issue directives, take decisions, make recommendations or deliver opinions.

A regulation shall have general application. It shall be binding in its entirety and directly applicable in all Member States.

A directive shall be binding, as to the result to be achieved, upon each Member State to which it is addressed, but shall leave to the national authorities the choice of form and methods.

A decision shall be binding in its entirety upon those to whom it is addressed.

Recommendations and opinions shall have no binding force.

ARTICLE 190

Regulations, directives and decisions of the Council and of the Commission shall state the reasons on which they are based and shall refer to any proposals or opinions which were required to be obtained pursuant to this Treaty.

ARTICLE 191

Regulations shall be published in the Official Journal of the Community. They shall enter into force on the date specified in them or, in the absence thereof, on the twentieth day following their publication.

Directives and decisions shall be notified to those to whom they are addressed and shall take effect upon such notification.

ARTICLE 192

Decisions of the Council or of the Commission which impose a pecuniary obligation on persons other than States shall be enforceable.

Enforcement shall be governed by the rules of civil procedure in force in the State in the territory of which it is carried out. The order for its enforcement shall be appended to the decision, without other formality than verification of the authenticity of the decision, by the national authority which the Government of each Member State shall designate for this purpose and shall make known to the Commission and to the Court of Justice.

When these formalities have been completed on application by the party concerned, the latter may proceed to enforcement in accordance with the national law, by bringing the matter directly before the competent authority.

Enforcement may be suspended only by a decision of the Court of Justice. However, the courts of the country concerned shall have jurisdiction over complaints that enforcement is being carried out in an irregular manner.

Chapter 3: The Economic and Social Committee

ARTICLE 193

An Economic and Social Committee is hereby established. It shall have advisory status.

P

The Committee shall consist of representatives of the various categories of economic and social activity, in particular, representatives of producers, farmers, carriers, workers, dealers, craftsmen, professional occupations and representatives of the general public.

ARTICLE 194[1]

The number of members of the Committee shall be as follows:

Belgium	12
Denmark	9
Germany	24
France	24
Ireland	9
Italy	24
Luxembourg	6
Netherlands	12
Norway[2]	9
United Kingdom	24

The members of the Committee shall be appointed by the Council, acting unanimously, for four years. Their appointments shall be renewable.

The members of the Committee shall be appointed in their personal capacity and may not be bound by any mandatory instructions.

ARTICLE 195

1. For the appointment of the members of the Committee, each Member State shall provide the Council with a list containing twice as many candidates as there are seats allotted to its nationals.

The composition of the Committee shall take account of the need to ensure adequate representation of the various categories of economic and social activity.

2. The Council shall consult the Commission. It may obtain the opinion of European bodies which are representative of the various economic and social sectors to which the activities of the Community are of concern.

ARTICLE 196

The Committee shall elect its chairman and officers from among its members for a term of two years.

It shall adopt its rules of procedure and shall submit them to the Council for its approval, which must be unanimous.

The Committee shall be convened by its chairman at the request of the Council or of the Commission.

ARTICLE 197

The Committee shall include specialised sections for the principal fields covered by this Treaty.

[1]As amended by Article 21 of the Act of Accession of 1972.
[2]See Note II on page 150, on the consequences of the decision of Norway not to accede to the European Communities.

In particular, it shall contain an agricultural section and a transport section, which are the subject of special provisions in the Titles relating to agriculture and transport.

These specialised sections shall operate within the general terms of reference of the Committee. They may not be consulted independently of the Committee.

Sub-committees may also be established within the Committee to prepare, on specific questions or in specific fields, draft opinions to be submitted to the Committee for its consideration.

The rules of procedure shall lay down the methods of composition and the terms of reference of the specialised sections and of the sub-committees.

ARTICLE 198

The Committee must be consulted by the Council or by the Commission where this Treaty so provides. The Committee may be consulted by these institutions in all cases in which they consider it appropriate.

The Council or the Commission shall, if it considers it necessary, set the Committee, for the submission of its opinion, a time limit which may not be less than ten days from the date on which the chairman receives notification to this effect. Upon expiry of the time limit, the absence of an opinion shall not prevent further action.

The opinion of the Committee and that of the specialised section, together with a record of the proceedings, shall be forwarded to the Council and to the Commission.

TITLE II: FINANCIAL PROVISIONS[1]

ARTICLE 199

All items of revenue and expenditure of the Community, including those relating to the European Social Fund, shall be included in estimates to be drawn up for each financial year and shall be shown in the budget.

The revenue and expenditure shown in the budget shall be in balance.

ARTICLE 200

1. The budget revenue shall include, irrespective of any other revenue, financial contributions of Member States on the following scale:

Belgium	7·9
Germany	28
France	28
Italy	28
Luxembourg	0·2
Netherlands	7·9

[1]The financial contributions of Member States to the budget of the Communities, and the rules governing their use, have been altered (a) by a Decision of the Council of 21 April 1970 (Official Journal (L) No. 94 of 28 April 1970) and (b) by Article 129 of the Act of Accession annexed to the Treaty of Accession of 1972. They will require further adjustment by the Council as a result of the withdrawal of Norway from the Communities.

2. The financial contributions of Member States to cover the expenditure of the European Social Fund, however, shall be determined on the following scale:

Belgium	8·8
Germany	32
France	32
Italy	20
Luxembourg	0·2
Netherlands	7

3. The scales may be modified by the Council, acting unanimously.

ARTICLE 201[1]

The Commission shall examine the conditions under which the financial contributions of Member States provided for in Article 200 could be replaced by the Community's own resources, in particular by revenue accruing from the common customs tariff when it has been finally introduced.

To this end, the Commission shall submit proposals to the Council.

After consulting the Assembly on these proposals the Council may, acting unanimously, lay down the appropriate provisions, which it shall recommend to the Member States for adoption in accordance with their respective constitutional requirements.

ARTICLE 202

The expenditure shown in the budget shall be authorised for one financial year, unless the regulations made pursuant to Article 209 provide otherwise.

In accordance with conditions to be laid down pursuant to Article 209, any appropriations, other than those relating to staff expenditure, that are unexpended at the end of the financial year may be carried forward to the next financial year only.

Appropriations shall be classified under different chapters grouping items of expenditure according to their nature or purpose and subdivided, as far as may be necessary, in accordance with the regulations made pursuant to Article 209.

The expenditure of the Assembly, the Council, the Commission and the Court of Justice shall be set out in separate parts of the budget, without prejudice to special arrangements for certain common items of expenditure.

ARTICLE 203[2]

1. The financial year shall run from 1 January to 31 December.

2. Each institution of the Community shall, before 1 July, draw up estimates of its expenditure. The Commission shall consolidate these estimates in a preliminary draft budget. It shall attach thereto an opinion which may contain different estimates.

[1]The financial contributions of Member States to the budget of the Communities, and the rules governing their use, have been altered (a) by a Decision of the Council of 21 April 1970 (Official Journal (L) No. 94 of 28 April 1970) and (b) by Article 129 of the Act of Accession annexed to the Treaty of Accession of 1972. They will require further adjustment by the Council as a result of the withdrawal of Norway from the Communities.
[2]As amended by Article 4 of the Luxembourg Treaty of 1970.

The preliminary draft budget shall contain an estimate of revenue and an estimate of expenditure.

3. The Commission shall place the preliminary draft budget before the Council not later than 1 September of the year preceding that in which the budget is to be implemented.

The Council shall consult the Commission and, where appropriate, the other institutions concerned whenever it intends to depart from the preliminary draft budget.

The Council shall, acting by a qualified majority, establish the draft budget and forward it to the Assembly.

4. The draft budget shall be placed before the Assembly not later than 5 October of the year preceding that in which the budget is to be implemented.

The Assembly shall have the right to amend the draft budget, acting by a majority of its members, and to propose to the Council, acting by an absolute majority of the votes cast, modifications to the draft budget relating to expenditure necessarily resulting from this Treaty or from acts adopted in accordance therewith.

If, within forty-five days of the draft budget being placed before it, the Assembly has given its approval, the budget shall stand as finally adopted. If within this period the Assembly has not amended the draft budget nor proposed any modifications thereto, the budget shall be deemed to be finally adopted.

If within this period the Assembly has adopted amendments or proposed modifications, the draft budget together with the amendments or proposed modifications shall be forwarded to the Council.

5. After discussing the draft budget with the Commission and, where appropriate, with the other institutions concerned, the Council may, acting by a qualified majority, modify any of the amendments adopted by the Assembly and shall pronounce, also by a qualified majority, on the modifications proposed by the latter. The draft budget shall be modified on the basis of the proposed modifications accepted by the Council.

If, within fifteen days of the draft budget being placed before it, the Council has not modified any of the amendments adopted by the Assembly and has accepted the modifications proposed by the latter, the budget shall be deemed to be finally adopted. The Council shall inform the Assembly that it has not modified any of the amendments and has accepted the proposed modifications.

If within this period the Council has modified one or more of the amendments adopted by the Assembly or has not accepted the modifications proposed by the latter, the draft budget shall again be forwarded to the Assembly. The Council shall inform the Assembly of the results of its deliberations.

6. Within fifteen days of the draft budget being placed before it, the Assembly, which shall have been notified of the action taken on its proposed modifications, shall act, by a majority of its members and three fifths of the votes cast, on the modifications to its amendments made by the Council and shall adopt the budget accordingly. If within this period the Assembly has not acted, the budget shall be deemed to be finally adopted.

7. When the procedure provided for in this Article has been completed, the President of the Assembly shall declare that the budget has been finally adopted.

8. A maximum rate of increase in relation to the expenditure of the same type to be incurred during the current year shall be fixed annually for the total expenditure other than that necessarily resulting from this Treaty or from acts adopted in accordance therewith.

The Commission shall, after consulting the Conjunctural Policy Committee and the Budgetary Policy Committee, declare what this maximum rate is as it results from:

- the trend in terms of volume, of the gross national product within the Community;
- the average variation in the budgets of the Member States; and
- the trend of the cost of living during the preceding financial year.

The maximum rate shall be communicated, before 1 May, to all the institutions of the Community. The latter shall be required to conform to this during the budgetary procedure, subject to the provisions of the fourth and fifth subparagraphs of this paragraph.

If, in respect of expenditure other than that necessarily resulting from this Treaty or from the acts adopted in accordance therewith, the actual rate of increase in the draft budget established by the Council is over half of the maximum rate, the Assembly may, exercising its right of amendment, further increase the total amount of that expenditure to a limit not exceeding half of the maximum rate.

Where, in exceptional cases, the Assembly, the Council or the Commission considers that the activities of the Communities require that the rate determined according to the procedure laid down in this paragraph should be exceeded, another rate may be fixed by agreement between the Council, acting by a qualified majority, and the Assembly, acting by a majority of its members and three fifths of the votes cast.

9. Each institution shall exercise the powers conferred upon it by this Article, with due regard for the provisions of this Treaty and for acts adopted in accordance therewith, in particular those relating to the Communities' own resources and to the balance between revenue and expenditure.

ARTICLE 203a[1]

By way of derogation from the provisions of Article 203, the following provisions shall apply to budgets for financial years preceding the financial year 1975:

1. The financial year shall run from 1 January to 31 December.

2. Each institution of the Community shall, before 1 July, draw up estimates of its expenditure. The Commission shall consolidate these estimates in a preliminary draft budget. It shall attach thereto an opinion which may contain different estimates.

The preliminary draft budget shall contain an estimate of revenue and an estimate of expenditure.

[1]Added by Article 5 of the Luxembourg Treaty of 1970.

3. The Commission shall place the preliminary draft budget before the Council not later than 1 September of the year preceding that in which the budget is to be implemented.

The Council shall consult the Commission and, where appropriate, the other institutions concerned whenever it intends to depart from the preliminary draft budget.

The Council shall, acting by a qualified majority, establish the draft budget and forward it to the Assembly.

4. The draft budget shall be placed before the Assembly not later than 5 October of the year preceding that in which the budget is to be implemented.

The Assembly shall have the right to propose to the Council modifications to the draft budget.

If, within forty-five days of the draft budget being placed before it, the Assembly has given its approval or has not proposed any modifications to the draft budget, the budget shall be deemed to be finally adopted.

If within this period the Assembly has proposed modifications, the draft budget together with the proposed modifications shall be forwarded to the Council.

5. The Council shall, after discussing the draft budget with the Commission and, where appropriate, with the other institutions concerned, adopt the budget, within thirty days of the draft budget being placed before it, under the following conditions.

Where a modification proposed by the Assembly does not have the effect of increasing the total amount of the expenditure of an institution, owing in particular to the fact that the increase in expenditure which it would involve would be expressly compensated by one or more proposed modifications correspondingly reducing expenditure, the Council may, acting by a qualified majority, reject the proposed modification. In the absence of a decision to reject it, the proposed modification shall stand as accepted.

Where a modification proposed by the Assembly has the effect of increasing the total amount of the expenditure of an institution, the Council must act by a qualified majority in accepting the proposed modification.

Where, in pursuance of the second or third subparagraph of this paragraph, the Council has rejected or has not accepted a proposed modification, it may, acting by a qualified majority, either retain the amount shown in the draft budget or fix another amount.

6. When the procedure provided for in this Article has been completed, the President of the Council shall declare that the budget has been finally adopted.

7. Each institution shall exercise the powers conferred upon it by this Article, with due regard for the provisions of this Treaty and for acts adopted in accordance therewith, in particular those relating to the Communities' own resources and to the balance between revenue and expenditure.

ARTICLE 204

If, at the beginning of a financial year, the budget has not yet been voted, a sum equivalent to not more than one twelfth of the budget appropriations for the preceding financial year may be spent each month in respect of any chapter or other subdivision of the budget in accordance with the provisions of the regulations made pursuant to Article 209; this arrangement shall not, however, have the effect of placing at the disposal of the Commission appropriations in excess of one twelfth of those provided for in the draft budget in course of preparation.

The Council may, acting by a qualified majority, provided that the other conditions laid down in the first paragraph are observed, authorise expenditure in excess of one twelfth.

Member States shall pay every month, on a provisional basis and in accordance with the scales laid down for the preceding financial year, the amounts necessary to ensure application of this Article.

ARTICLE 205

The Commission shall implement the budget, in accordance with the provisions of the regulations made pursuant to Article 209, on its own responsibility and within the limits of the appropriations.

The regulations shall lay down detailed rules for each institution concerning its part in effecting its own expenditure.

Within the budget, the Commission may, subject to the limits and conditions laid down in the regulations made pursuant to Article 209, transfer appropriations from one chapter to another or from one sub-division to another.

ARTICLE 206[1]

The accounts of all revenue and expenditure shown in the budget shall be examined by an Audit Board consisting of auditors whose independence is beyond doubt, one of whom shall be chairman. The Council shall, acting unanimously, determine the number of the auditors. The auditors and the chairman of the Audit Board shall be appointed by the Council, acting unanimously, for a period of five years. Their remuneration shall be determined by the Council, acting by a qualified majority.

The purpose of the audit, which shall be based on records and, if necessary, performed on the spot, shall be to establish that all revenue has been received and all expenditure incurred in a lawful and regular manner and that the financial management has been sound. After the close of each financial year, the Audit Board shall draw up a report, which shall be adopted by a majority of its members.

The Commission shall submit annually to the Council and to the Assembly the accounts of the preceding financial year relating to the implementation of the budget, together with the report of the Audit Board. The Commission shall also forward to them a financial statement of the assets and liabilities of the Community.

The Council and the Assembly shall give a discharge to the Commission in respect of the implementation of the budget. To this end, the report of the Audit Board shall be examined in turn by the Council, which shall act by a qualified majority and by the Assembly. The Commission shall stand discharged only after the Council and the Assembly have acted.

[1]As amended by Article 6 of the Luxembourg Treaty of 1970.

ARTICLE 207

The budget shall be drawn up in the unit of account determined in accordance with the provisions of the regulations made pursuant to Article 209.

The financial contributions provided for in Article 200 (1) shall be placed at the disposal of the Community by the Member States in their national currencies.

The available balances of these contributions shall be deposited with the Treasuries of Member States or with bodies designed by them. While on deposit, such funds shall retain the value corresponding to the parity, at the date of deposit, in relation to the unit of account referred to in the first paragraph.

The balances may be invested on terms to be agreed between the Commission and the Member State concerned.

The regulations made pursuant to Article 209 shall lay down the technical conditions under which financial operations relating to the European Social Fund shall be carried out.

ARTICLE 208

The Commission may, provided it notifies the competent authorities of the Member States concerned, transfer into the currency of one of the Member States its holdings in the currency of another Member State, to the extent necessary to enable them to be used for purposes which come within the scope of this Treaty. The Commission shall as far as possible avoid making such transfers if it possesses cash or liquid assets in the currencies which it needs.

The Commission shall deal with each Member State through the authority designated by the State concerned. In carrying out financial operations the Commission shall employ the services of the bank of issue of the Member State concerned or of any other financial institution approved by that State.

ARTICLE 209

The Council shall, acting unanimously on a proposal from the Commission:

(a) make financial regulations specifying in particular the procedure to be adopted for establishing and implementing the budget and for presenting and auditing accounts;

(b) determine the methods and procedure whereby the contributions of Member States shall be made available to the Commission;

(c) lay down rules concerning the responsibility of authorising officers and accounting officers and concerning appropriate arrangements for inspection.

Part Six

General and Final Provisions

ARTICLE 210

The Community shall have legal personality.

ARTICLE 211

In each of the Member States, the Community shall enjoy the most extensive legal capacity accorded to legal persons under their laws; it may, in particular, acquire or dispose of movable and immovable property and may be a party to legal proceedings. To this end, the Community shall be represented by the Commission.

ARTICLE 212[1]

[*This Article was repealed by Article 24 (2) of the Merger Treaty of 1965, and its provisions replaced by those of the second sub paragraph of Article 24 (1) of the Merger Treaty, which reads as follows:*
'The Council shall, acting by a qualified majority on a proposal from the Commission and after consulting the other institutions concerned, lay down the Staff Regulations of officials of the European Communities and the Conditions of Employment of other servants of those Communities.']

ARTICLE 213

The Commission may, within the limits and under the conditions laid down by the Council in accordance with the provisions of this Treaty, collect any information and carry out any checks required for the performance of the tasks entrusted to it.

ARTICLE 214

The members of the institutions of the Community, the members of committees, and the officials and other servants of the Community shall be required, even after their duties have ceased, not to disclose information of the kind covered by the obligation of professional secrecy, in particular information about undertakings, their business relations or their cost components.

ARTICLE 215

The contractual liability of the Community shall be governed by the law applicable to the contract in question.

---

[1]The first sub paragraph of Article 24 (1) of the Merger Treaty of 1965 provides for the formation of a single administration of the European Communities on the date of entry into force of the Treaty.

In the case of non-contractual liability, the Community shall, in accordance with the general principles common to the laws of the Member States, make good any damage caused by its institutions or by its servants in the performance of their duties.

The personal liability of its servants towards the Community shall be governed by the provisions laid down in their Staff Regulations or in the Conditions of Employment applicable to them.

ARTICLE 216

The seat of the institutions of the Community shall be determined by common accord of the Governments of the Member States.

ARTICLE 217

The rules governing the languages of the institutions of the Community shall, without prejudice to the provisions contained in the rules of procedure of the Court of Justice, be determined by the Council, acting unanimously.

ARTICLE 218

[*This Article was repealed by the second paragraph of Article 28 of the Merger Treaty of 1965, and its provisions replaced by the first paragraph of Article 28 of the Merger Treaty, which reads as follows:*

'Article 28: The European Communities shall enjoy in the territories of the Member States such privileges and immunities as are necessary for the performance of their tasks, under the conditions laid down in the Protocol annexed to this Treaty. The same shall apply to the European Investment Bank.']

ARTICLE 219

Member States undertake not to submit a dispute concerning the interpretation or application of this Treaty to any method of settlement other than those provided for therein.

ARTICLE 220

Member States shall, so far as is necessary, enter into negotiations with each other with a view to securing for the benefit of their nationals:

– the protection of persons and the enjoyment and protection of rights under the same conditions as those accorded by each State to its own nationals;

– the abolition of double taxation within the Community;

– the mutual recognition of companies or firms within the meaning of the second paragraph of Article 58, the retention of legal personality in the event of transfer of their seat from one country to another, and the possibility of mergers between companies or firms governed by the laws of different countries;

– the simplification of formalities governing the reciprocal recognition and enforcement of judgments of courts or tribunals and of arbitration awards.

ARTICLE 221

Within three years of the entry into force of this Treaty, Member States shall accord nationals of the other Member States the same treatment as their own nationals as regards participation in the capital of companies or firms within the meaning of Article 58, without prejudice to the application of the other provisions of this Treaty.

ARTICLE 222

This Treaty shall in no way prejudice the rules in Member States governing the system of property ownership.

ARTICLE 223

1. The provisions of this Treaty shall not preclude the application of the following rules:

(*a*) No Member State shall be obliged to supply information the disclosure of which it considers contrary to the essential interests of its security;

(*b*) Any Member State may take such measures as it considers necessary for the protection of the essential interests of its security which are connected with the production of or trade in arms, munitions and war material; such measures shall not, however, adversely affect the conditions of competition in the common market regarding products which are not intended for specifically military purposes.

2. During the first year after the entry into force of this Treaty, the Council shall, acting unanimously, draw up a list of products to which the provisions of paragraph 1 (*b*) shall apply.

3. The Council may, acting unanimously on a proposal from the Commission, make changes in this list.

ARTICLE 224

Member States shall consult each other with a view to taking together the steps needed to prevent the functioning of the common market being affected by measures which a Member State may be called upon to take in the event of serious internal disturbances affecting the maintenance of law and order, in the event of war or serious international tension constituting a threat of war, or in order to carry out obligations it has accepted for the purpose of maintaining peace and international security.

ARTICLE 225

If measures taken in the circumstances referred to in Articles 223 and 224 have the effect of distorting the conditions of competition in the common market, the Commission shall, together with the State concerned, examine how these measures can be adjusted to the rules laid down in this Treaty.

By way of derogation from the procedure laid down in Articles 169 and 170, the Commission or any Member State may bring the matter directly before the Court of Justice if it considers that another Member State is making improper use of the powers provided for in Articles 223 and 224. The Court of Justice shall give its ruling *in camera*.

ARTICLE 226

1. If, during the transitional period, difficulties arise which are serious and liable to persist in any sector of the economy or which could bring about serious deterioration in the economic situation of a given area, a Member State may apply for authorisation to take protective measures in order to rectify the situation and adjust the sector concerned to the economy of the common market.

2. On application by the State concerned, the Commission shall, by emergency procedure, determine without delay the protective measures which it considers necessary, specifying the circumstances and the manner in which they are to be put into effect.

3. The measures authorised under paragraph 2 may involve derogations from the rules of this Treaty, to such an extent and for such periods as are strictly necessary in order to attain the objectives referred to in paragraph 1. Priority shall be given to such measures as will least disturb the functioning of the common market.

ARTICLE 227[1]

1. This Treaty shall apply to the Kingdom of Belgium, the Kingdom of Denmark, the Federal Republic of Germany, the French Republic, Ireland, the Italian Republic, the Grand Duchy of Luxembourg, the Kingdom of the Netherlands, the Kingdom of Norway[1] and the United Kingdom of Great Britain and Northern Ireland.

2. With regard to Algeria and the French overseas departments, the general and particular provisions of this Treaty relating to:

– the free movement of goods;
– the agriculture, save for Article 40 (4);
– the liberalisation of services;
– the rules on competition;
– the protective measures provided for in Articles 108, 109 and 226;
– the institutions;

shall apply as soon as this Treaty enters into force.

The conditions under which the other provisions of this Treaty are to apply shall be determined, within two years of the entry into force of this Treaty, by decisions of the Council, acting unanimously on a proposal from the Commission.

The institutions of the Community will, within the framework of the procedures provided for in this Treaty, in particular Article 226, take care that the economic and social development of these areas is made possible.

---

[1]As amended by Article 26 of the Act of Accession of 1972. See Note II on page 150, on the consequences of the decision of Norway not to accede to the European Communities.

3. The special arrangements for association set out in Part Four of this Treaty shall apply to the overseas countries and territories listed in Annex IV to this Treaty.

This Treaty shall not apply to those overseas countries and territories having special relations with the United Kingdom of Great Britain and Northern Ireland which are not included in the aforementioned list.

4. The provisions of this Treaty shall apply to the European territories for whose external relations a Member State is responsible.

5. Notwithstanding the preceding paragraphs:

(*a*) This Treaty shall not apply to the Faroe Islands. The Government of the Kingdom of Denmark may, however, give notice, by a declaration deposited by 31 December 1975 at the latest with the Government of the Italian Republic, which shall transmit a certified copy thereof to each of the Governments of the other Member States, that this Treaty shall apply to those Islands. In that event, this Treaty shall apply to those Islands from the first day of the second month following the deposit of the declaration.

(*b*) This Treaty shall not apply to the Sovereign Base Areas of the United Kingdom of Great Britain and Northern Ireland in Cyprus.

(*c*) This Treaty shall apply to the Channel Islands and the Isle of Man only to the extent necessary to ensure the implementation of the arrangements for those islands set out in the Treaty concerning the accession of the Kingdom of Denmark, Ireland, the Kingdom of Norway and the United Kingdom of Great Britain and Northern Ireland to the European Economic Community and to the European Atomic Energy Community.

ARTICLE 228

1. Where this Treaty provides for the conclusion of agreements between the Community and one or more States or an international organisation, such agreements shall be negotiated by the Commission. Subject to the powers vested in the Commission in this field, such agreements shall be concluded by the Council, after consulting the Assembly where required by this Treaty.

The Council, the Commission or a Member State may obtain beforehand the opinion of the Court of Justice as to whether an agreement envisaged is compatible with the provisions of this Treaty. Where the opinion of the Court of Justice is adverse, the agreement may enter into force only in accordance with Article 236.

2. Agreements concluded under these conditions shall be binding on the institutions of the Community and on Member States.

ARTICLE 229

It shall be for the Commission to ensure the maintenance of all appropriate relations with the organs of the United Nations, of its specialised agencies and of the General Agreement on Tariffs and Trade.

The Commission shall also maintain such relations as are appropriate with all international organisations.

ARTICLE 230

The Community shall establish all appropriate forms of co-operation with the Council of Europe.

ARTICLE 231

The Community shall establish close co-operation with the Organisation for European Economic Co-operation, the details to be determined by common accord.

ARTICLE 232

1. The provisions of this Treaty shall not affect the provisions of the Treaty establishing the European Coal and Steel Community, in particular as regards the rights and obligations of Member States, the powers of the institutions of that Community and the rules laid down by that Treaty for the functioning of the common market in coal and steel.

2. The provisions of this Treaty shall not derogate from those of the Treaty establishing the European Atomic Energy Community.

ARTICLE 233

The provisions of this Treaty shall not preclude the existence or completion of regional unions between Belgium and Luxembourg, or between Belgium, Luxembourg and the Netherlands, to the extent that the objectives of these regional unions are not attained by application of this Treaty.

ARTICLE 234

The rights and obligations arising from agreements concluded before the entry into force of this Treaty between one or more Member States on the one hand, and one or more third countries on the other, shall not be affected by the provisions of this Treaty.

To the extent that such agreements are not compatible with this Treaty, the Member State or States concerned shall take all appropriate steps to eliminate the incompatibilities established. Member States shall, where necessary, assist each other to this end and shall, where appropriate, adopt a common attitude.

In applying the agreements referred to in the first paragraph, Member States shall take into account the fact that the advantages accorded under this Treaty by each Member State form an integral part of the establishment of the Community and are thereby inseparably linked with the creation of common institutions, the conferring of powers upon them and the granting of the same advantages by all the other Member States.

ARTICLE 235

If action by the Community should prove necessary to attain, in the course of the operation of the common market, one of the objectives of the Community and this Treaty has not provided the necessary powers, the Council shall, acting unanimously on a proposal from the Commission and after consulting the Assembly, take the appropriate measures.

ARTICLE 236

The Government of any Member State or the Commission may submit to the Council proposals for the amendment of this Treaty.

If the Council, after consulting the Assembly and, where appropriate, the Commission, delivers an opinion in favour of calling a conference of representatives of the Governments of the Member States, the conference shall be convened by the President of the Council for the purpose of determining by common accord the amendments to be made to this Treaty.

The amendments shall enter into force after being ratified by all the Member States in accordance with their respective constitutional requirements.

ARTICLE 237

Any European State may apply to become a member of the Community. It shall address its application to the Council, which shall act unanimously after obtaining the opinion of the Commission.

The conditions of admission and the adjustments to this Treaty necessitated thereby shall be the subject of an agreement between the Member States and the applicant State. This agreement shall be submitted for ratification by all the contracting States in accordance with their respective constitutional requirements.

ARTICLE 238

The Community may conclude with a third State, a union of States or an international organisation agreements establishing an association involving reciprocal rights and obligations, common action and special procedures.

These agreements shall be concluded by the Council, acting unanimously after consulting the Assembly.

Where such agreements call for amendments to this Treaty, these amendments shall first be adopted in accordance with the procedure laid down in Article 236.

ARTICLE 239

The Protocols annexed to this Treaty by common accord of the Member States shall form an integral part thereof.

ARTICLE 240

This Treaty is concluded for an unlimited period.

Setting up of the Institutions

ARTICLE 241

The Council shall meet within one month of the entry into force of this Treaty.

ARTICLE 242

The Council shall, within three months of its first meeting, take all appropriate measures to constitute the Economic and Social Committee.

ARTICLE 243

The Assembly shall meet within two months of the first meeting of the Council, having been convened by the President of the Council, in order to elect its officers and draw up its rules of procedure. Pending the election of its officers, the oldest member shall take the chair.

ARTICLE 244

The Court of Justice shall take up its duties as soon as its members have been appointed. Its first President shall be appointed for three years in the same manner as its members.

The Court of Justice shall adopt its rules of procedure within three months of taking up its duties.

No matter may be brought before the Court of Justice until its rules of procedure have been published. The time within which an action must be brought shall run only from the date of this publication.

Upon his appointment, the President of the Court of Justice shall exercise the powers conferred upon him by this Treaty.

ARTICLE 245

The Commission shall take up its duties and assume the responsibilities conferred upon it by this Treaty as soon as its members have been appointed.

Upon taking up its duties, the Commission shall undertake the studies and arrange the contacts needed for making an overall survey of the economic situation of the Community.

ARTICLE 246

1. The first financial year shall run from the date on which this Treaty enters into force until 31 December following. Should this Treaty, however, enter into force during the second half of the year, the first financial year shall run until 31 December of the following year.

2. Until the budget for the first financial year has been established, Member States shall make the Community interest-free advances which shall be deducted from their financial contributions to the implementation of the budget.

3. Until the Staff Regulations of officials and the Conditions of Employment of other servants of the Community provided for in Article 212 have been laid down, each institution shall recruit the staff it needs and to this end conclude contracts of limited duration.

Each institution shall examine together with the Council any question concerning the number, remuneration and distribution of posts.

Final Provisions

ARTICLE 247

This Treaty shall be ratified by the High Contracting Parties in accordance

Q

with their respective constitutional requirements. The instruments of ratification shall be deposited with the Government of the Italian Republic.

This Treaty shall enter into force on the first day of the month following the deposit of the instrument of ratification by the last signatory State to take this step. If, however, such deposit is made less than fifteen days before the beginning of the following month, this Treaty shall not enter into force until the first day of the second month after the date of such deposit.

ARTICLE 248

This Treaty, drawn up in a single original in the Dutch, French, German and Italian languages, all four texts being equally authentic, shall be deposited in the archives of the Government of the Italian Republic, which shall transmit a certified copy to each of the Governments of the other signatory States.

IN WITNESS WHEREOF, the undersigned Plenipotentiaries have signed this Treaty.

DONE at Rome this twenty-fifth day of March in the year one thousand nine hundred and fifty-seven.

P.H. SPAAK	J. CH. SNOY et d'OPPUERS
ADENAUER	HALLSTEIN
PINEAU	M. FAURE
Antonio SEGNI	Gaetano MARTINO
BECH	Lambert SCHAUS
J. LUNS	J. LINTHORST HOMAN

Appendix B

Rules of procedure
of the
European Parliament

NOTE

The Rules of Procedure of the European Parliament were extensively revised on 19 October 1967, and further amendments were made to Rules 23 and 50 on 17 May 1971. (See Chapter XVI on Revision of the Treaties and of the Rules of Procedure of the Parliament.) The English text of the Rules printed here is, with minor alterations, an unofficial translation prepared by the English translation section of the Secretariat of the European Parliament in October 1972. It is expected that amendments will be made to the Rules of Procedure soon after the enlargement of the Communities on 1 January 1973.

CONTENTS OF THE RULES OF PROCEDURE OF THE EUROPEAN PARLIAMENT

Rules of Procedure of the European Parliament

Chapter I: Session of Parliament

RULE 1

1. Parliament shall hold an annual session.

2. It shall meet, without requiring to be convened, on the second Tuesday in March each year and shall itself determine the duration of breaks in the session.

3. The enlarged Bureau may alter the duration of such breaks by a reasoned decision of a majority of its members taken at least two weeks before the date previously fixed by Parliament for resuming the session; the date of resumption shall not, however, be postponed for more than two weeks.

4. Exceptionally, the President may, on behalf of the enlarged Bureau, convene Parliament at the request of a majority of its current members or at the request of the Commission or the Council of the Communities.*

RULE 2

1. Parliament shall hold its plenary sittings and its committees shall meet at the place fixed as its seat under the provisions of the Treaties.

2. Exceptionally, however, on a resolution adopted by a majority of its current members, Parliament may decide to hold one or more plenary sittings elsewhere than at its seat.

3. Any committee may decide to ask that one or more meetings be held away from the said seat. Its request, with the reasons therefor, shall be made to the President, who shall lay it before the Bureau. If the matter is urgent, the President may take the decision himself. Should the decision taken by the Bureau or the President be unfavourable, the reasons shall be stated.

Chapter II: Verification of Credentials

RULE 3

1. Parliament shall verify the credentials of its members. This shall be done on the basis of a report by the Bureau, which shall check whether appointments comply with the provisions of the Treaties.

2. Any dispute shall be referred to the appropriate committee, which shall report to Parliament as soon as possible.

*hereinafter referred to as 'the Commission' and 'the Council'.

3. Any Representative whose credentials have not yet been verified may provisionally take his seat in Parliament or on its committees, and shall have the same rights as other members of Parliament.

RULE 4

1. A Representative's term of office shall end on expiry of the appointment conferred on him by his national parliament, on death, on resignation notified by him to the President of the European Parliament, on unseating by the European Parliament or on loss of his seat in his national parliament.

2. Should he lose his seat in his national parliament, a Representative may continue to sit until the appointment of his successor has been notified to the European Parliament; subject however to a maximum period of six months and to the appointment conferred on him by his national parliament not having expired.

3. Any dispute concerning the validity of the appointment of a Representative whose credentials have been verified shall be referred to the appropriate committee, which shall report to Parliament not later than at the beginning of the next part-session.

Chapter III: Bureau of Parliament

RULE 5

1. The Bureau shall consist of the President and the eight Vice-Presidents of Parliament.

2. No Representative who is a member of a national government shall be a member of the Bureau.

3. The enlarged Bureau shall consist of the Bureau and the chairmen of the political groups.
   The chairman of a political group may arrange to be represented by a member of his group.

4. Should voting on a decision of the Bureau or enlarged Bureau result in a tie, the President shall have a casting vote.

RULE 6

1. At the sitting held on the second Tuesday in March each year, the oldest Representative shall take the chair until the President has been declared elected.

2. No business shall be transacted while the oldest Representative is in the chair unless it is concerned with the election of the President or the verification of credentials.

RULE 7

1. The President and Vice-Presidents shall be elected by secret ballot. Four tellers chosen by lot shall count the votes cast.

2. The President shall be elected first. Nominations shall be handed before each ballot to the oldest Representative, who shall announce them to Parliament. If after three ballots no candidate has obtained an absolute majority of the votes cast, the fourth ballot shall be confined to the two Representatives who have obtained the highest number of votes in the third ballot. In the event of a tie, the elder candidate shall be declared elected.

3. As soon as the President has been elected, the oldest Representative shall vacate the chair.

4. The eight Vice-Presidents shall then be elected on a single ballot paper. Those who on the first ballot obtain an absolute majority of the votes cast shall be declared elected. Should the number of candidates elected be less than the number of seats to be filled, a second ballot shall be held under the same conditions among candidates not yet elected. Should a third ballot be necessary, a relative majority shall suffice for election to the remaining seats, and in the event of a tie, the oldest candidates shall be declared elected.

5. The Vice-Presidents shall take precedence in the order in which they were elected, and in the event of a tie, by age.

6. Should it be necessary for the President or a Vice-President to be replaced, his successor shall be elected in accordance with the above provisions.

7. Should the seat become vacant during a break in the session, the group to which the Representative whose seat has become vacant belonged shall nominate a candidate for interim membership of the Bureau pending the election referred to in the foregoing paragraph.

The nomination shall be submitted to the enlarged Bureau for ratification.

An interim member of the Bureau shall enjoy the same rights as a Vice-President.

Should the President's seat become vacant, the first Vice-President shall act as President.

Chapter IV: Presidency

RULE 8

1. The President shall direct all the activities of Parliament and of its organs, under the conditions laid down in these Rules. He shall enjoy all the powers necessary to preside over the proceedings of Parliament and to ensure that they are properly conducted.

2. The duties of the President shall be to open, adjourn and close sittings; to ensure observance of these Rules, maintain order, call upon speakers, close debates, put questions to the vote and announce the results of votes; and to refer to committees any communications within their competence.

3. The President may speak in a debate only to sum up or to call speakers to order. Should he wish to take part in a debate, he shall vacate the chair and shall not resume it until that debate is over.

RULE 9

Should the President be absent or unable to discharge his duties, or should he speak in a debate in accordance with Rule 8 (3), he shall be replaced by one of the Vice-Presidents in accordance with Rule 7 (5).

RULE 10

1. The President shall call to order any Representative who creates a disturbance during proceedings.

2. Should the offence be repeated, the President shall again call the Representative to order, and the fact shall be recorded in the minutes of proceedings.

3. In the event of a further offence, the President may exclude the offender from the Chamber for the remainder of the sitting.

4. In serious cases, the President may move that Parliament pass a vote of censure which shall automatically involve immediate exclusion from the Chamber and suspension for two to five days. Any Representative against whom such disciplinary action is requested shall be entitled to be heard.

5. The vote of censure shall be taken without debate by sitting and standing.

RULE 11

1. No person shall enter the Chamber except Representatives, members of the Commission or Council, the Secretary-General of Parliament, members of the staff whose duties require their presence there, and experts or officials of the Communities.

2. Only holders of an admission card duly issued by the President or Secretary-General of Parliament shall be admitted to the galleries.

3. Members of the public admitted to the galleries shall remain seated and keep silent. Any person expressing approval or disapproval shall immediately be ejected by the ushers.

Chapter V: Agenda of Sittings

RULE 12

1. The enlarged Bureau shall prepare the draft agenda for sittings of Parliament on the basis of information passed to it by the Presidential Committee.

This committee shall consist of the members of the enlarged Bureau together with the chairman or one of the vice-chairmen of each of the parliamentary committees.

The Commission and Council may attend meetings of the Presidential Committee at the invitation of the President.

2. The President shall lay before Parliament, for its approval, the draft agenda for sittings, which Parliament may amend.

3. Before Parliament rises, the President shall announce the date, time and agenda of the next sitting.

RULE 13

Except in the cases of urgency referred to in Rule 14, a debate may not be opened on a report unless it has been distributed at least twenty-four hours previously.

RULE 14

1. A proposal that a debate be treated as urgent may be made to Parliament by the President, by at least ten Representatives, or by the Commission or Council.

2. Urgent procedure shall be adopted where it has been requested in writing by one-third of the current members of Parliament.

3. Questions to be dealt with by urgent procedure shall be given absolute priority over other items on the agenda.

4. Where the adoption of urgent procedure has been decided upon by Parliament, discussion may take place without a report or on the basis of an oral report by the appropriate committee.

Chapter VI: Official Languages

RULE 15

1. The official languages of Parliament shall be Dutch, French, German and Italian.

2. All documents of Parliament shall be drawn up in these official languages.

3. Speeches delivered in one of the official languages shall be simultaneously interpreted into each of the other official languages and into any other language the Bureau may consider necessary.

Chapter VII: Publicity of proceedings

RULE 16

Debates in Parliament shall be public unless Parliament decides otherwise.

RULE 17

1. The minutes of proceedings of each sitting, containing the decisions of Parliament and the names of speakers, shall be distributed at least half-an-hour before the opening of the following sitting.

2. At the beginning of each sitting the President shall lay before Parliament, for its approval, the minutes of proceedings of the previous sitting.

The minutes of proceedings of the last sitting of a part-session shall be laid before Parliament for its approval before the sitting is closed, and if no objection is raised they shall be declared adopted.

3. If the minutes of proceedings are challenged, Parliament shall, if necessary, decide whether the changes requested are to be considered.

4. The minutes of proceedings shall be signed by the President and the Secretary-General and preserved in the archives of Parliament. They shall be published within one month in the Official Journal of the European Communities.

RULE 18

A summary report of debates of each sitting shall be drawn up and distributed in the official languages.

RULE 19

1. A verbatim report of debates of each sitting shall be drawn up in the official languages.

2. Speakers shall be required to return typescripts of their speeches to the Secretariat not later than the day following that on which they were handed to them.

3. The verbatim report shall be published as an annex to the Official Journal of the European Communities.

Chapter VIII: Conduct of sittings

RULE 20

1. The annual general report of the Commission on the activities of the Communities shall be printed and distributed as soon as it is brought out.

2. The various parts of the report shall be forwarded to the appropriate committees.

RULE 21

1. Any Representative may hand to the President of Parliament a motion of censure on the Commission.

2. The motion shall be presented in writing, labelled 'motion of censure' and supported by reasons. It shall be printed and distributed in the official languages as soon as it is received, and be brought to the notice of the Commission.

3. The President shall announce that a motion of censure has been tabled immediately he receives it, if Parliament is sitting, or else at the beginning of the next suitable sitting. The debate on the motion shall not be opened earlier than twenty-four hours after its receipt is announced. The vote shall not be taken on the motion until at least three clear days after such announcement. Voting shall be by open ballot by way of roll call.

4. The motion of censure shall be adopted only if it secures a two-thirds majority of the votes cast representing a majority of the members of Parliament. The result of the vote shall be notified to the President of the Commission and the President of the Council.

RULE 22

1. Requests from the Commission or Council for an opinion or for advice shall be printed, distributed and referred to the appropriate committee.

2. Any resolution adopted by Parliament following a request from an institution for an opinion or for advice shall be forwarded immediately to the President of that institution. Should the request have come from the President of the Council, the resolution shall also be forwarded to the Commission.

RULE 23[1]

1. The following documents shall be printed and distributed:

- the draft budget of the European Communities;
- the documents drawn up by the Commission in pursuance of Articles 49 and 50 of the ECSC Treaty, and in particular the report of the Commission to the Council on the basis of which the latter adapts the portion of expenditure covered by the ECSC levies to the budget of the Communities;
- any request for advice made by the Council before the draft budget is finally adopted;
- the report of the board of auditors of the Communities;
- the report of the ECSC auditor.

2. These documents shall be referred to the appropriate committee, which shall report to Parliament.

3. Where other committees have been asked for their opinions, the President shall fix the time-limit within which these shall be communicated to the committee responsible.

RULE 23a[2]

1. Subject to the conditions set out below, any Representative may propose and speak in support of modifications to the draft budget of the Communities.

2. Such proposals shall be admissible only if they are presented in writing, bear the signatures of at least five Representatives, and specify the budget head to which they refer.

3. The President shall fix a time-limit for the tabling of proposed modifications.

4. The appropriate committee shall deliver its opinion on the proposals for proposed modifications before they are discussed in plenary sitting.

5. Proposed modifications to the section of the draft budget relating to Parliament which are similar to those already rejected by Parliament at the time the estimates were drawn up shall be discussed only where the appropriate committee has delivered a favourable opinion.

---

[1]Rule amended in accordance with resolution adopted on 17 May 1971 (Official Journal of the European Communities No. C55, 3 June 1971, p. 6).
[2]New Rule inserted in accordance with resolution adopted on 17 May 1971 (Official Journal of the European Communities No. C55, 3 June 1971, p. 6).

6. Notwithstanding the provisions of Rule 26 (1), Parliament shall take separate and successive votes on:
– each proposed modification,
– each section of the draft budget,
– the draft budget as a whole,
– any motion for a resolution concerning the draft budget.

7. If Parliament adopts the draft budget as submitted to it by the Council, the President shall declare it to have been finally adopted.

8. The President shall forward to the Council and Commission the minutes of proceedings of the sitting at which Parliament reached a decision on the draft budget.

9. Where Parliament has adopted modifications, the draft budget, modified accordingly, shall be annexed to the minutes of proceedings and printed. The President shall forward it to the Council and notify the Commission.

10. The procedure laid down in Rules 23 and 23a shall also apply to draft supplementary budgets.

RULE 24

1. Amendments proposed by the Commission and Council under Article 95 of the ECSC Treaty shall be printed at the same time as the assenting opinion thereon delivered by the Court of Justice.
    These documents shall be distributed and referred to the appropriate committee. In its report the committee shall recommend either adoption or rejection of the proposed amendment as a whole.

2. No amendment thereto shall be admissible, and voting item by item shall not be permitted. The proposed amendment as a whole shall require for adoption a three-quarters majority of the votes cast representing a two-thirds majority of the members of Parliament.

3. Any Representative may table a motion for a resolution proposing to the Commission and Council amendments to the ECSC Treaty under Article 95 of that treaty.
    Such a motion shall be printed, distributed and referred to the appropriate committee. It shall be adopted only if it secures the votes of a majority of the current members of Parliament.

RULE 25

Any Representative may table a motion for a resolution on a matter falling within the sphere of activities of the Communities.
    Such a motion shall be printed, distributed and, without prejudice to Rule 14, referred to the appropriate committee, which shall include the text of the motion in its report.

RULE 26

1. The debate shall be based on the report of the appropriate committee. Parliament shall vote only on the motion for a resolution.

2. Reference back to committee may be requested at any time. Such a request shall always be granted if it is made by the committee responsible. Parliament may fix a time-limit within which the committee shall report its conclusions.

3. Once the general debate and consideration of the texts have been concluded, only explanations of vote shall be permitted before the matter as a whole is put to the vote.

RULE 27

1. Committees may, in agreement with the Commission, ask that motions for resolutions contained in their reports be put to the vote without further discussion.

2. The political groups shall be notified of any such request.

3. At the first sitting of each part-session, or at the latest on the day before the sitting on whose agenda they appear, the President shall announce any texts that can be voted on without debate.

4. If no request to speak has been entered when these texts come up for attention, the President shall put them to the vote immediately.

RULE 28

1. The President may, in agreement with the chairmen of the political groups, propose to Parliament that speaking time be apportioned for a particular debate.

2. If Parliament decides to organize a debate in this way, the President shall convene the chairmen of the political groups, of the committees responsible and of the committees asked for their opinions.

3. They shall apportion speaking time among the political groups, with the proviso that neither the number nor the length of the sittings shown on the agenda shall be exceeded; they shall fix the time by which a vote is to be taken.

RULE 29

1. Any Representative may propose and speak in support of amendments.

2. Amendments shall relate to the text it is sought to alter. They shall be submitted in writing. The President shall decide whether they are admissible. Unless Parliament decides otherwise, they shall not be put to the vote until they have been printed and distributed in the official languages.

3. Amendments shall have priority over the text to which they relate and shall be put to the vote before that text.

4. If two or more mutually exclusive amendments are moved to the same part of a text, the amendment that departs furthest from the text submitted by the committee shall have priority and shall be put to the vote first. If it is adopted, the other amendments shall stand rejected. If it is rejected, the amendment

next in priority shall be put to the vote and similarly for each of the remaining amendments. In case of doubt as to priority, the President shall decide.

5. Reference to committee may be requested at any time. Such a request shall always be granted if it is made by the committee responsible. Parliament may fix a time-limit within which the committee shall report its conclusions on the amendments referred to it. Reference of an amendment to committee shall not necessarily interrupt the debate.

RULE 30

1. No Representative may speak unless called upon to do so by the President. Representatives shall speak from their places and shall address the chair; the President may invite them to come to the rostrum.

2. If a speaker departs from the subject, the President shall call him to order. If a speaker has already been called to order twice in the same debate, the President may, on the third occasion, forbid him to speak for the remainder of the debate on the same subject.

3. Without prejudice to his other disciplinary powers, the President may cause to be deleted from the reports of sittings the speeches of Representatives who have not been called upon to speak by him or who continue to speak beyond the time allotted to them.

4. A speaker may not be interrupted. He may, however, by leave of the President, give way during his speech to allow another Representative, the Commission or the Council to put to him a question on a particular point in his speech.

RULE 31

1. The names of Representatives who ask leave to speak shall be entered in the speakers' list in the order in which their requests are received.

2. The President shall call upon Representatives to speak, ensuring as far as possible that speakers of different political views and using different languages are heard in turn.

On request, however, priority may be given to the chairman of a political group who wishes to speak on its behalf or to a speaker deputizing for him for the same purpose.

No Representative shall speak more than twice on the same subject, except by leave of the President. The chairman and the rapporteur of the committees concerned shall, however, be allowed to speak at their request.

A Representative who wishes to make a personal statement shall be heard, but only at the end of a sitting.

3. The Commission and Council shall be heard at their request.

4. On a proposal from the President, Parliament may decide to limit speaking time.

5. No Representative shall speak for more than five minutes on any of the following: the minutes of proceedings, explanations of vote, procedural motions and personal statements.

RULE 32

1. A Representative who asks leave to speak for a procedural motion, in particular:

(*a*) to raise a point of order,

(*b*) to move reference to committee,

(*c*) to move the closure of a debate,

(*d*) to move the adjournment of a debate,

(*e*) to move the previous question,

shall have a prior right to do so,

2. The above matters shall take precedence over the main question, the discussion of which shall be suspended while they are being considered.

3. Without prejudice to Rule 31 (5), only the following shall be heard in debates on the above matters: the proposer of the motion, one speaker for and one against the motion, the chairman or the rapporteur of the committees concerned.

Chapter IX: Voting

RULE 33

1. The Parliament may deliberate, settle its agenda and approve the minutes of proceedings, whatever the number of Representatives present.

2. A quorum shall exist when a majority of the current members of Parliament is present.

3. All votes other than votes by roll call shall be valid whatever the number of Representatives voting, unless, before the voting has begun, the President has been requested by at least ten Representatives to ascertain the number of those present.

4. A vote by roll call shall be valid only if a majority of the current members of Parliament have taken part in it.

5. Should this not be the case, the vote shall be placed on the agenda of the next sitting.

RULE 34

The right to vote is a personal right. Voting by proxy is prohibited.

RULE 35

1. Normally Parliament shall vote by show of hands.

2. If the result of the show of hands is doubtful, a fresh vote shall be taken by sitting and standing.

3. If the result of this second vote is doubtful or whenever ten or more Representatives so desire, or should a qualified majority be required, the vote shall be taken by roll call.

R

4. The roll shall be called in alphabetical order, beginning with the name of a Representative drawn by lot. The President shall be the last to be called to vote.

Voting shall be by word of mouth and shall be expressed by 'Yes', 'No', or 'I abstain'. In calculating whether a motion has been adopted or rejected, account shall be taken only of votes cast for and against. The President shall establish the result of the vote and announce it.

Votes shall be recorded in the minutes of proceedings of the sitting in the alphabetical order of Representatives' names.

5. Without prejudice to Rules 2 (2), 7 (2, 4), 21 (4), 24 (2, 3), 41 (5) and 54, motions put to the vote shall be declared adopted only if they have secured a majority of the votes cast.

In the event of a tie the motion shall stand rejected.

6. In the case of appointments, voting shall be by secret ballot. Only ballot papers bearing the names of persons who have been entered as candidates shall be taken into account in calculating the number of votes cast.

Chapter X: Groups and committees

RULE 36

1. Representatives may form themselves into groups according to their political affinities.

2. A political group shall be considered to have been set up after the President has been handed a statement to that effect containing the name of the group, the signatures of its members and the composition of its Bureau.

3. This statement shall be published in the Official Journal of the European Communities.

4. No Representative may be a member of more than one group.

5. A group shall consist of not less than fourteen members.

RULE 37

1. Parliament shall set up standing or temporary, general or special committees, and shall define their powers and duties. The Bureau of each committee shall consist of a chairman and one or two vice-chairmen. No Representative who is a member of a national government may be a member of the Bureau of a committee.

2. Committee members shall be elected at the beginning of the session which opens each year on the second Tuesday in March. Nominations shall be addressed to the Bureau of Parliament, which shall lay before Parliament proposals designed to ensure fair representation of Member States and of political views.

3. Should any dispute arise, Parliament shall decide thereon by secret ballot.

4. The Bureau of Parliament may provisionally decide to fill any vacancy on a

committee with the agreement of the persons concerned and having regard t o the provisions of paragraph 2 above.

5. Any such changes shall be laid before Parliament for ratification at its next sitting.

RULE 38

1. Committees shall examine questions referred to them by Parliament or, during a break in the session, by the President on behalf of the Bureau.

2. Should a committee declare itself incompetent to consider a question, or should a conflict arise over the competence of two or more committees, the question of competence shall be placed on Parliament's agenda on a proposal from the Bureau or at the request of one of the committees concerned.

3. Should two or more committees be competent to deal with a question, one committee shall be named as the committee responsible and the others as committees asked for their opinions.

A question may not, however, be referred simultaneously to more than three committees, unless it is decided for sound reasons to depart from this rule under the conditions laid down in paragraph 1 above.

RULE 39

1. A committee shall meet when convened by its chairman or at the request of the President.

2. A committee may, in the interest of its work, appoint one or more sub-committees, of which it shall at the same time determine the composition and competence. Sub-committees shall report to the committee which set them up.

3. Any two or more committees or sub-committees may jointly consider matters coming within their competence but may not take a joint decision.

4. Any committee may, with the agreement of the Bureau of Parliament, instruct one or more of its members to proceed on a study or fact-finding mission.

RULE 40

1. Committee meetings shall not be held in public unless a committee decides otherwise.

2. The Commission and Council may take part in committee meetings if invited to do so on behalf of a committee by its chairman.

By special decision of a committee, any other person may be invited to attend and to speak at a meeting.

3. Any member of a committee may arrange for his place to be taken at meetings by another Representative of his choice. The name of the substitute shall be notified in advance to the chairman of the committee.

4. Substitutes shall be allowed to sit on sub-committees under the same conditions.

5. Without prejudice to Rule 44 (6) and unless a committee decides otherwise, Representatives may attend meetings of committees of which they are not members but may not take part in their deliberations.

Such Representatives may, however, be allowed by the committee to take part in its proceedings in an advisory capacity.

RULE 41

1. Rules 7 (2), 29, 30, 31, 32 and 35 (4, 5, 6) shall apply, as appropriate, to committee meetings.

2. A committee may validly deliberate and vote when one-third of its members are present. However, if so requested by one-sixth of its members before voting begins, the vote shall be valid only if the number of voters represents an absolute majority of the committee members.

3. Voting in committee shall be by show of hands, unless any Representative demands a vote by roll call.

4. The chairman may take part in discussions and may vote, but without having a casting vote.

5. The Bureau shall be elected by secret ballot without discussion. Its election shall require an absolute majority of the votes cast. If, however, a second ballot is necessary, a relative majority shall suffice.

6. The procedure for sub-committees shall be the same as for committees.

7. The minutes of each meeting of a committee shall be distributed to all its members and submitted to the committee for its approval at its next meeting.

8. In addition, a summary report of the proceedings shall be drawn up. Unless the committee decides otherwise, however, such report shall not be distributed but shall be kept available to all Representatives.

9. Unless the committee decides otherwise, the only texts that shall be made public shall be reports adopted and statements that have been prepared on the responsibility of the chairman.

RULE 42

1. Committees shall appoint for each subject a rapporteur who shall be responsible for preparing the committee's report and for introducing it in Parliament.

The final report of the committee shall include a motion for a resolution and an explanatory statement.

2. The report shall state the result of the vote taken on the report as a whole. If the committee is not unanimous, the report shall also state the views of the minority.

RULE 43

1. On a proposal from its Bureau, a committee may fix a time-limit within which the rapporteur shall submit his draft report. This time-limit may be extended.

2. Once the time-limit has elapsed, the committee may instruct its chairman to ask for the matter referred to it to be placed on the agenda of one of the next sittings of Parliament. The debates may then be conducted on the basis of an oral report by the committee concerned.

RULE 44

1 Should the committee to which a question was first referred wish to hear the views of another committee, or should another committee wish to make known its views on the report of the committee to which a question was first referred, such committees may request the President that, in accordance with Rule 38 (3), one committee be named as the committee responsible and the other as the committee asked for its opinion.

2 The committee asked for its opinion may communicate the opinion to the committee responsible either orally, through its chairman or rapporteur, or in writing. Its opinion shall relate to the text referred to it.

3 In its report the committee responsible shall set out the views of the committee asked for its opinion, in so far as these differ from its own.

4. If the committee asked for its opinion is unable to deliver the opinion before the report of the committee responsible is finally adopted, it may instruct its chairman or rapporteur to lay the opinion before Parliament during the debate on the report, provided that it notifies the President of this intention before the debate is opened.

5. The opinion may include amendments to the text referred to the committee and suggestions for parts of the motion for a resolution submitted by the committee responsible, but shall not include any distinct motion for a resolution.

6. The chairman and rapporteur of the committee asked for its opinion may take part in an advisory capacity in meetings of the committee responsible, in so far as these relate to the matter of common concern. In special cases, the committee asked for its opinion may nominate up to five other members who, with the agreement of the chairman of the committee responsible, may take part in an advisory capacity in the meetings of that committee, in so far as these deal with the matter of common concern.

Chapter XI: Questions

RULE 45

1. Questions for written answer may be put to the Commission or Council by any Representative.

These questions shall be brief and relate to specific points, and shall be passed in writing to the President who shall communicate them to the institution concerned.

2. Questions to which answers have been given shall be published, together with the answers, in the Official Journal of the European Communities.

3. Questions to which no answer has been given within one month by the Commission, or within two months by the Council, shall also be published in the Official Journal of the European Communities.

RULE 46

1. Any Representative may put questions to the Commission or Council and ask that they be placed on the agenda of Parliament and dealt with by oral procedure without debate.

Such questions shall be passed in writing to the President, who shall lay them before the enlarged Bureau at the next sitting held for the purpose of drafting the agenda.

The enlarged Bureau shall decide whether the question is to be converted into a question for written answer or dealt with by oral procedure without debate under the conditions laid down below.

The decision of the enlarged Bureau shall be notified immediately to the questioner and to the institutions concerned. If the question is addressed to the Commission such notification shall be made at least one week and if to the Council at least six weeks before the opening of the sitting on whose agenda it is to appear.

2. Questions shall be brief and relate to specific points, not to problems of a general nature. Parliament shall set aside not more than half a day during each part-session for oral answers to these questions. Questions which remain unanswered during that period shall be carried forward to the next part-session or converted into questions for written answer, as the questioner may choose.

3. The questioner shall read his question out. He may speak to it for not more than ten minutes. A member of the institution concerned shall give a brief answer. Where the question is addressed to the Commission, the questioner may ask one or two supplementary questions, to which the member of the institution concerned shall give a brief reply.

RULE 47

1. Questions may be put to the Commission or Council by a committee, a political group or five or more Representatives for placing on the agenda of Parliament in order that they may be dealt with by oral procedure with debate.

Such questions, which may also relate to problems of a general nature, shall be passed in writing to the President, who shall lay them before the enlarged Bureau at the next meeting held for the purpose of drafting the agenda.

2. The enlarged Bureau shall decide whether the Commission or Council is to be consulted. It shall decide whether the question is to be converted into a question for written answer, dealt with by oral procedure without debate in accordance with Rule 46, or dealt with by the procedure with debate under the conditions laid down below.

Any question put by a political group shall be automatically dealt with by the procedure with debate.

The decision of the enlarged Bureau shall be notified immediately to the questioner and to the institutions concerned.

The procedure for oral questions with debate shall be proposed only where notice of the question can be given within the following time-limits: if the question is addressed to the Commission at least one week and if to the Council at least six weeks before the opening of the sitting on whose agenda it is to appear.

In urgent cases, the President may propose direct to Parliament that a question which could not be laid before the enlarged Bureau under the foregoing conditions be placed on the agenda. Such questions, together with any that could not be notified within the time-limits specified above, may be placed on the agenda only with the agreement of the institutions to which they are addressed.

3. One of the questioners may speak to the question for up to twenty minutes. One member of the institution concerned shall answer. Representatives who wish to speak may do so for not more than ten minutes and may speak only once.

One of the questioners may, at his request, briefly comment on the answer given.

4. In order to wind up the debate on a question put to the Commission, any committee or political group, or five or more Representatives, may lay before the President a motion for a resolution with a request that a vote be taken on it immediately.

As soon as the motion for a resolution has been distributed, Parliament shall first decide, if necessary after hearing one of the movers, whether a vote is to be taken immediately. Thereafter only explanations of vote shall be permitted.

Should an immediate vote be decided upon, the motion for a resolution shall be put to the vote without reference to committee. Only explanations of vote shall be permitted.

Chapter XII: Petitions

RULE 48

1. Petitions to Parliament shall show the name, occupation, nationality and permanent address of each petitioner.

2. Petitions that comply with the conditions laid down in paragraph 1 above shall be entered in a register in the order in which they are received.

3. They shall be referred by the President to one of the committees set up under Rule 37 (1) which shall first ascertain whether they fall within the sphere of activities of the Communities.

4. At the request of the appropriate committee, the President shall forward petitions declared admissible, together with the committee's opinion, to the Commission or Council.

The committee consulted may report to Parliament.

5. Notice shall be given in open sitting of the petitions referred to in paragraph 2 above, and of the decision to forward or report on them.

Such announcements shall be entered in the minutes of proceedings. The petitioner shall be notified of them.

6. The texts of petitions entered in the register, together with the texts of committee opinions forwarded with them, shall be preserved in the archives of Parliament where they shall be available for inspection by any Representative.

Chapter XIII: Secretariat of Parliament: Accounting

RULE 49

1. Parliament shall be assisted by a Secretary-General appointed by the Bureau.

The Secretary-General shall give a solemn undertaking before the Bureau to perform his duties conscientiously and with absolute impartiality.

2. The Secretary-General shall head a Secretariat the composition and organization of which shall be determined by the Bureau.

3. The Bureau, after consulting the appropriate committee of Parliament, shall decide the number of staff and lay down regulations relating to their administrative and financial situation.

The Bureau shall also decide to what categories of officials and servants Articles 12 to 14 of the Protocol on the Privileges and Immunities of the European Communities shall apply in whole or in part.

The President of Parliament shall inform the appropriate institutions of the European Communities accordingly.

RULE 50 [1]

1. The Bureau shall draw up a first preliminary draft of the estimates of Parliament on the basis of a report prepared by the Secretary-General, and shall consult the appropriate committee on the subject.

2. After receiving the opinion of that committee, the enlarged Bureau shall adopt the preliminary draft estimates.

3. The President shall forward the preliminary draft estimates to the appropriate committee, which shall draw up the draft estimates and report to Parliament.

4. The President shall fix a time-limit for the tabling of amendments to the draft estimates.

The appropriate committee shall give its opinion on these amendments.

5. Parliament shall adopt the estimates.

6. The President shall forward the estimates to the Commission and Council.

7. The foregoing provisions shall also apply to supplementary estimates.

---

[1]Rule amended in accordance with resolution adopted on 17 May 1971 (Official Journal of the European Communities No. C55, 3 June 1971, p. 6).

RULE 50a[1]

1. The President shall incur and settle, or cause to be incurred and settled, the expenditure covered by the internal financial regulations issued by the Bureau after consulting the appropriate committee.

2. The President shall forward the draft annual accounts to the appropriate committee.

3. On the basis of a report by its appropriate committee, Parliament shall pass its accounts and decide on the giving of a discharge.

Chapter XIV: Miscellaneous provisions

RULE 51

1. Passes to allow Representatives to circulate freely in the Member States shall be issued by the President as soon as their appointment has been notified to him.

2. Any request addressed to the President by the appropriate authority of a Member State that the immunity of a Representative be waived shall be communicated to Parliament and referred to the appropriate committee.

3. Should a Representative be arrested or prosecuted after having been found in the act of committing an offence, any member of Parliament may request that the proceedings be suspended or that he be released.

4. The appropriate committee shall consider such a request without delay but shall not go into the merits of the case. It shall hear the Representative concerned, should he so wish. If he is in custody, he may have himself represented by another member of Parliament.

5. The report of the committee shall be placed at the head of the agenda of the first sitting following the day on which it was laid upon the Table.
   Discussion shall be confined to the reasons for or against the waiver of immunity.

6. The President shall immediately communicate Parliament's decision to the appropriate authority of the Member State concerned.

RULE 52

1. At the beginning of the session which opens on the second Tuesday in March each year, the Presidential Committee shall appoint a rapporteur to prepare a report to the Consultative Assembly of the Council of Europe on the activities of Parliament.

2. After this report has been approved by the Presidential Committee and by Parliament, it shall be forwarded direct by the President of Parliament to the President of the Consultative Assembly of the Council of Europe.

[1]New Rule inserted in accordance with resolution adopted on 17 May 1971 (Official Journal of the European Communities No. C55, 3 June 1971, p. 6).

RULE 53

Parliament shall be represented in international relations, on ceremonial occasions, and in administrative, legal or financial matters by the President, who may delegate his powers.

RULE 54

1. Motions for resolutions for amendment of these Rules shall be printed and referred to the appropriate committee.

2. Such motions shall be adopted only if they secure the votes of a majority of the members of Parliament.

Appendix C

Principal Debates, Reports and Resolutions of the Parliament 1958–1972

Official Report of Debates

The Official Report of Debates of the European Parliament is published in the official languages of the Communities as an annex to the Official Journal of the European Communities. The Reports and indices are numbered in continuous series.

PRINCIPAL DEBATES, REPORTS AND RESOLUTIONS OF THE PARLIAMENT 1958-1972

SESSION 1958

Date	Subject of Debate	Official Report of Debates No.
		No. 1
19 March	Debate on statements of the President of the Councils of the Communities and of the Commissions and the High Authority.	pp. 20–30
20 March	Debate on the communications of the Presidents of the Commissions.	34–47 and 50–86
	Number, constitution and powers of committees (Res.).	48–49
	Name of the Assembly (Res.).	87–88
21 March	Composition of the Economic and Social Committee (Res.).	95–106 and 108
	Division of members of the Assembly in the chamber (Res.).	106
		No. 3
13 May	Statement of the President of the High Authority.	pp. 7–17
	Debate on Sixth General Report on the Activities of the European Coal and Steel Community.	17–31
14 May	Debate on the seat of the European institutions.	34–47
21 June	Seat of the European institutions (Res.).	56–98
23 June	Rules of Procedure of the European Parliamentary Assembly (Rep.-Res.).	103–111, 112–119, and 120–131
	Seat of the European institutions.	111–112 119–120 and 138–139
	Statement of the President of the Commission of Euratom (Res.).	131–138 and 139–141
	Scientific and technical research (Rep.).	141–159
	Co-ordination of the three Communities (Rep.).	159–162
24 June	Co-ordination of the three Communities (Rep.).	164–177

Date	*Subject of Debate*	*Official Report of Debates No.*
	Safety and hygiene at work (Rep.).	177–200
	Social policy of the ECSC (Rep.).	200–230
25 June	Internal market of the Community (Rep.).	234–262
	Closure of the Accounts of the Common Assembly (Rep.-Res.).	262–263
	Free exchange area (Rep.).	264–317
26 June	Internal market of the Community (Rep.).	322–341
	Budget of the Assembly (Rep.-Res.).	342–350
	Administrative expenses of the ECSC (Rep.-Res.).	351–354
	Budget of the ECSC (Rep.-Res.).	354–361
	Commercial policy and external relations (Rep.-Res.).	361–366
	Investment, financial questions and long-term policy (Rep.).	366–389
	Energy policy of the High Authority (Rep.).	390–406
	Transport (Rep.).	406–422
27 June	Free-exchange area (Rep.-Res.).	427–433 and 444–449
	Safety and hygiene at work (Rep.-Res.).	434–435
	Scientific and technical research (Rep.-Res.).	436
	Social policy of the ECSC (Rep.-Res.).	437–439
	Internal market of the Community (Rep.-Res.).	439–444
	Co-ordination of the three Communities (Rep.-Res.).	449–450
	Transport (Rep.-Res.).	450–451
	Investment, financial questions and long-term policy (Rep.-Res.).	452–453
	Energy policy of the High Authority (Rep.-Res.).	453–454
		No. 4
21 October	Statement by President of the Commission of the EEC.	pp. 9–20
	Statements by members of the Commission of Euratom.	20–32
	Communication on behalf of the President of the Council of the EEC.	32–35
22 October	Debate on the statements of the Council and Commission of the EEC and on the General Report of the Commission.	38–91

Date	Subject of Debate	Official Report of Debates No.
	Debate on the statement of the Commission of Euratom and the General Report.	91–97
23 October	Debate on the statement of the Commission of Euratom and the General Report.	106–109
	Statement of President of the High Authority and debate on Common Market in coal.	109–144
24 October	Debate on Common Market in coal.	149
		No. 6
15 December	Budget (Rep.).	pp. 8–55
16 December	Common Market in coal (Res.).	58–67
	Scientific and technical research (Res.).	67–89
	Research and Investment Budget of Euratom (Rep.).	89–91
	Health protection against radiation (Rep.).	91–105
17 December	Health protection against radiation (Rep.-Res.).	108–123
	Report to the Consultative Assembly of the Council of Europe (Rep.).	124–126
	Budgetary problems (Rep.-Res.).	126–134

SESSION 1959–60

Date	Subject of Debate	Official Report of Debates No.
		No. 9
7 January	Opening of the Common Market (Rep.).	pp. 11–29
8 January	European energy policy and long-term economic policy of Euratom (Rep.).	32–81
	Safety and hygiene at work and health protection (Rep.).	81–97
9 January	Social policy of the EEC (Rep.).	100–126
10 January	Reduction of length of work in the coal industry (Rep.).	128–147
12 January	Transport problems in the EEC (Rep.).	151–180
	Long-term economic policy of the EEC and Euratom (Rep.).	180–221
13 January	Free exchange area (Res.).	223–280
14 January	Agricultural problems (Rep.).	282–308

Date	*Subject of Debate*	*Official Report of Debates No.*
15 January	Daily subsistence of Members of the Assembly (Rep.-Res.).	313–314
	Association of overseas countries and territories (Rep.-Res.).	314–328 and 343–344
	Seat of European institutions (Res.).	328–330
	Safety and hygiene at work and health protection (Rep.-Res.).	330–332
	Reduction of the length of work in the coal industry (Rep.-Res.).	332–336
	Opening of the Common Market (Rep.-Res.).	336–337
	Long-term economic policy of the EEC and Euratom (Rep.-Res.).	338–339
	Social policy of the EEC (Rep.-Res.).	339–341
	European energy policy (Rep.-Res.).	342–343
		No. 11
9 April	Statements by the President of the High Authority, the President of the Commission of Euratom and a Vice-President of the Commission of the EEC	pp. 12–31
10 April	Budget of the EEC and Euratom (Rep.).	36–98
11 April	Budget of the EEC and Euratom (Rep.-Res.).	102–114 and 122–125
	Financial consequences of the dispersal of the institutions (Rep.-Res.).	114–121
13 April	Agricultural problems (Rep.).	127–168
14 April	The situation of the coal market (Rep.).	165–222
15 April	The situation of the coal market (Rep.).	227–246 and 261–274
	Agricultural problems (Rep.-Res.).	247–253
	Social aspects of the coal problem (Rep.-Res.).	253–260
	Assistance to Madagascar (Res.).	260–261
16 April	The situation of the coal market (Rep.-Res.).	276–284
		No. 13
12 May	European University (Rep.).	pp. 9–38
13 May	Debate on the activities of the ECSC.	40–56
	Safety in the mines (Rep.).	57–73
	Economic and technical research in the ECSC (Rep.).	76–91
14 May	Safety in the mines (Rep.-Res.).	95–98

Date	Subject of Debate	Official Report of Debates No.
	Closure of Accounts of the European Parliamentary Assembly for 1958 (Rep.-Res.).	99–100
	Economic and technical research in the ECSC (Rep.-Res.).	100–102
	Seat of the institutions of the European Communities (Rep.-Res.).	102–118
	European University (Rep.-Res.).	119–125
		No. 15
22 June	Budget of the Assembly (Rep.-Res.).	pp.7–11
	Budgetary and financial questions of the ECSC (Rep.-Res.).	11–41
23 June	Scientific and technical research in Euratom (Rep.).	46–61
	Agricultural problems (Rep.).	62–105
24 June	Agricultural problems (Rep.).	109–211
25 June	Statement by President of the Commission of the general situation in the EEC.	213–227
	Energy policy (Rep.-Res.).	227–260
26 June	Statement of the President of the High Authority.	262–275
	Agricultural problems (Rep.-Res.).	281–284
		No. 17
22 September	Labour and employment problems in the ECSC (Rep.).	pp. 16–43
	Health protection and job security in the EEC and Euratom (Rep.).	43–64
23 September	The opening of the markets (Rep.).	66–100
	Statement of the President of the High Authority.	100–113
24 September	European Economic Association (Rep.).	122–129
	Statement of the President of the EEC Commission.	129–138
	Reply to the statement of the President of the High Authority.	145–169
25 September	European Economic Association (Rep.).	184–220
	Supplementary Budget of the Court of Justice (Rep.-Res.).	220–221
	Amendment of Rule 32 of the Rules of Procedure (Rep.-Res.).	222–223

S

Date	*Subject of Debate*	*Official Report of Debates No.*
	Reply to statement of the President of the High Authority (Res.).	223
	Health protection and job security in the EEC and Euratom (Rep.-Res.).	223–225
	The opening of the markets (Rep.-Res.).	225–226
	Labour and employment problems in the ECSC (Rep.-Res.).	226–228
		No. 21
20 November	Budgets of the EEC and Euratom (Rep.).	pp.11–39
21 November	Budgets of the EEC and Euratom (Rep.).	42–79
	Amendment of the Rules of Procedure (Rep.-Res.).	79
23 November	Association of overseas countries and territories (Rep.).	82–104
24 November	Budgets of the EEC and Euratom (Rep.-Res.).	106–116
	Association of overseas countries and territories (Rep.).	116–124
	Exchange of views between the Assembly, the Councils and the Executives of the Communities.	124–162
25 November	Exchange of views (continued).	166–268
26 November	Relations between the Assembly and the Councils of the Communities (Rep.).	272–273
	Association of overseas countries and territories (Rep.).	273–303
27 November	Relations between the Assembly and the Councils of the Community (Rep.-Res.).	306–307
	Association of overseas countries and territories (Rep.-Res.).	307–133
		No. 23
11 January	European Social Fund (Rep.).	pp. 10–37
12 January	European Social Fund (Rep.).	39–79
13 January	Problem of the evolution of the ECSC— Debate on a statement by the High Authority.	84–115
	Social problems of the EEC (Rep.).	115–144
14 January	Seat of the European institutions (Rep.).	146–164 and 179–198
	Problems of the evolution of the ECSC (Rep.-Res.).	165–166
	European Social Fund (Rep.-Res.).	166–179

Date	Subject of Debate	*Official Report of Debates No.*
15 January	Seat of the European Institutions (Rep.-Res.).	213–228
	Association of Tunisia, Morocco, Greece and Turkey (Rep.).	200–210

SESSION 1960–61

		No. 26
28 March	Statement by the President of the Council of the EEC.	pp. 14–20
	Debate on acceleration of the implementation of the Common Market Treaty.	20–53
29 March	Debate on the amendment of Article 56 of the ECSC Treaty (Res.).	56–70
	Debate on acceleration of the implementation of the Common Market Treaty.	71–101
30 March	Common agricultural policy (Rep.).	107–160
31 March	Accounts of the Assembly for 1959 (Rep.-Res.).	163–164
	Amendment of Rules of Procedure of the Assembly (Rep.-Res.).	164–170
	Problems common to Africa and Europe (Rep.-Res.).	170–176
	Parliamentary conference between the associated states and the Community (Rep.-Res.).	177–180
	Acceleration of the implementation of the Common Market Treaty (Rep.-Res.).	180–213
	Common agricultural policy (Rep.).	213–263
1 April	Common agricultural policy (Rep.).	266–297
	Presentation of the Eighth Report of the High Authority of ECSC.	299–319
		No. 28
10 May	Direct election of the European Parliamentary Assembly (Rep.).	pp. 19–30
11 May	Direct election of the European Parliamentary Assembly (Rep.).	31–101
12 May	Economic policy (Rep.).	103–156

Date	*Subject of Debate*	*Official Report of Debates No.*
13 May	Economic policy (Rep.).	160–219
16 May	Report to the Consultative Assembly of the Council of Europe (Rep.-Res.).	222–227
	Statement by President of the Council of Ministers of EEC on decisions of the Council.	227–233
	Statement by the President of the Commission of EEC on acceleration of implementation of the Treaty.	233–238
	Debate on Third General Report of the Commission of Euratom.	238–245
17 May	Direct election of the European Parliamentary Assembly (Rep.-Res.).	251–270 and 276–328
	Economic policy (Rep.-Res.).	270–276
18 May	Supplementary budget for press and information service (Rep.-Res.).	334–335
	Debate on Third General Report of the Commission of Euratom.	335–362
		No. 30
27 June	Current problems of the Coal and Steel Community (Rep.).	pp. 12–37
	Social problems in the coal industry (Rep.).	38–43
28 June	Social problems in the coal industry (Rep.).	46–55
	Current problems of the Coal and Steel Community (Rep.).	55–62
	Debate on the Third General Report of the EEC.	62–70
	Problems of scrap-iron (Rep.).	76–81
	Safety in mines (Rep.).	81–86
	Scientific research on safety at work (Rep.-Res.).	86–96
29 June	Budget of the European Parliamentary Assembly (Rep.-Res.).	96–101
	Accounts of the European Parliamentary Assembly for 1958 (Res.).	103
	Amendment of the Rules of Procedure (Rep.-Res.).	104
	Functions of the Committee on Scientific and Technical Research (Rep.-Res.).	105–106
29 June	Energy policy (Rep.).	108–157
30 June	Budgetary and financial questions of ECSC (Rep.-Res.).	160

Date	Subject of Debate	Official Report of Debates No.
	Energy policy (Rep.-Res.).	166–172
	Debate on Third General Report of the EEC.	172–187
	Seat of the Assembly (Rep.-Res.).	187–198
1 July	European University (Rep.-Res.).	200–225
	Current problems of the Coal and Steel Community (Rep.-Res.).	225–227
	Social problems in the coal industry (Res.).	227–229
1 July	Safety in mines (Res.).	229
	Scientific research on safety at work (Res.).	231–232
		No. 32
12 October	Common agricultural policy (Rep.).	pp.39–53
13 October	Common agricultural policy (Rep.).	82–108
	European University (Rep.-Res.).	108–116
	Free movement of labour (Rep.).	117–126
14 October	Common agricultural policy (Rep.-Res.).	129–156
	Petrol and natural gas (Rep.).	157–174
15 October	Free movement of labour (Rep.-Res.).	182–225
17 October	Commercial policy of the EEC (Rep.-Res.).	228–247
18 October	Free circulation of industrial products (Rep.-Res.).	249–269
		No. 34
17 November	Association of the Community with overseas countries (Rep.).	pp.10–24
18 November	Association of the Community with overseas countries (Rep.).	25–60
	European transport (Rep.-Res.).	60–72
19 November	Safety at work (Rep.).	74–85
	Right of Community representation abroad (Rep.-Res.).	85–96
	Information policy in the Communities (Rep.).	96–98
21 and 22 November	Foreign policies of member states	111–145 and 148–228
23 November	Budgets of EEC and Euratom (Rep.).	230–289
	Statute of personnel of EEC and Euratom (Rep.).	245–249

Date	Subject of Debate	Official Report of Debates No.
24 November	Statute of personnel of EEC and Euratom (Rep.-Res.).	292–303
	Association of the Community with overseas countries (Rep.-Res.).	303–306
	Safety at work (Res.).	309
	Merger of the executives of the European communities (Rep.-Res.).	310–313
	Information policy in the Communities (Rep.-Res.).	313–318
	Scientific and technical research in Euratom (Rep.-Res.).	318–319
	Budgets of EEC and Euratom (Rep.-Res.).	319–321
		No. 36
16 and 17 January	Debate on the activities of the Councils of EEC and Euratom.	pp.9–18 and 20–49
18 January	Agricultural problems (Rep.).	51–102
19 January	Economic situation in the Communities.	104–111
	Agricultural workers (Rep.).	111–132
20 January	Agricultural problems (Rep.-Res.).	134–144

SESSION 1961–62

		No. 38
7 March	Freedom of establishment and provision of services (Rep.).	pp. 17–32
8 March	Freedom of establishment and provision of services (Rep.).	35–59
	Tax on the importation of certain agricultural products (Rep.-Res.).	59–65
	Agricultural wages (Rep.-Res.).	65–73
9 March	Debate on the results of the inter-governmental conference of 10 and 11 February 1961.	76–118
10 March	Development aid (Rep.-Res.).	122–123
	Closure of Accounts of the Assembly for 1960 (Rep.-Res.).	123–124
	Economic situation in the Community.	124–144
	Freedom of establishment and provision of services (Rep.-Res.).	144–148

Date	Subject of Debate	Official Report of Debates No.
		No. 40
8 May	Debate on the annual report of the activities of the ECSC.	pp. 7–26
9 May	Association with overseas countries (Rep.).	27–61
10 May	Political co-operation in the six member states (Rep.).	63–66
	Association with overseas countries (Rep.-Res.).	66–67
		No. 42
26 June	Budget of the Assembly (Rep.-Res.).	pp.9–10
	Composition of the Agriculture Committee (Rep.-Res.).	12–13
	Conditions of voting in Committee (Rep.-Res.).	14–15
27 June	Coal and steel market (Rep.-Res.).	18–36
	Safety in the mines (Rep.-Res.).	37–63
	Economic and technical Research (Rep.).	64–71
	Financial and budgetary affairs (Rep.-Res.).	71–85
28 June	Debate on the Annual Report on the activities of the EEC.	88–102
	Planning in the EEC (Rep.-Res.).	102–104
	Economic policy of the Community (Rep.).	104–111
	Political co-operation between member states (Rep.).	112–141
29 June	Recommendation of the Conference with the Parliaments of African States and Madagascar.	145–150
	Acceleration of the Common Market (Res.).	150–151
	Report to the Consultative Assembly of the Council of Europe (Rep.).	151–152
	Debate on the annual report on the activities of Euratom.	152–160 and 168–173
29 June	Political co-operation between member states (Rep.-Res.).	161–168
	European University (Rep.-Res.).	173–177
	Exploitation of agricultural families (Rep.).	178–196
		No. 44
18 September	Association of Greece with the Common Market (Rep.).	pp. 10–31

Date	Subject of Debate	Official Report of Debates No.
19 September	Association of Greece with the Common Market (Rep.-Res.).	34–60
	Political co-operation between member states of the European Communities (Rep.-Res.).	63–65
	Supplementary Budget of Euratom (Rep.-Res.).	65–71
		No. 46
16 October	Statute of Personnel and Community tax (Rep.).	pp. 8–26
17 October	Problems of Euratom (Rep.).	24–47
	Organisation of agricultural markets (Rep.).	48–61
18 October	Organisation of agricultural markets (Rep.-Res.).	79–119 and 128–157
	Minimum price systems (Rep.-Res.).	119–124
	Problems of Euratom (Rep.-Res.)	124–127
19 October	Debate on the situation in Berlin.	162–168
	Application of Articles 85 and 86 of the EEC Treaty (Rep.-Res.).	169–201 and 221–256
	Statute of Personnel and Community tax (Rep.-Res.).	210–221
20 October	Equal pay for men and women (Rep.-Res.).	258–265
	Merger of the Executives of the Communities (Rep.-Res.).	265–282
	Conclusion of agreements of accession (Rep.-Res.).	284–289
	Transport problems (Rep.-Res.).	289–291
		No. 48
20 and 21 November	Exchange of views between the Assembly, the Councils and the Executives of the Communities.	pp. 6–44 and 45–98
22 November	Safety, hygiene at work and health protection (Rep.-Res.).	104–112 and 151
	Free movement of labour (Rep.-Res.).	114–118 and 152–153
	Harmonisation of social policy (Rep.-Res.).	118–151
23 November	Collaboration between the Assembly and the governments of member states (Rep.-Res.).	156–157
	Composition and powers of committees (Res.).	157–158

Date	Subject of Debate	*Official Report of Debates No.*
	Budgets of the EEC and Euratom (Rep.-Res.).	158–200
24 November	Association of overseas states and territories (Rep.-Res.).	202–203
	Passing from the first to the second stage of Common Market (Rep.-Res.).	203–205
	The fruit and vegetable market (Rep.-Res.).	205–234
	The wine market (Rep.-Res.).	234–245
	Tobacco problems (Rep.-Res.)	245–250
		No. 50
19 December	European University (Rep.-Res.).	pp. 10–30
	Problems of scrap iron (Rep.).	30–65
20 December	Transport policy (Rep.-Res.).	69–113
	Help to the Republic of Somalia (Rep.-Res.).	113–115
	Agricultural policy (Rep.-Res.).	115–117
	Proposal for a Union of European peoples (Rep.).	117–137
21 December	Proposal for a Union of European peoples (Rep.-Res.).	140–172
	Problem of scrap iron (Rep.-Res.).	172–173
		No. 52
22 January	Debate on the moving to the second stage of the Common Market.	pp. 7–15
22 January	Statement from the Commission on the Economic Situation of the Community.	16–30
	Accounts of the EEC and Euratom for 1958 and 1959 (Rep.-Res.).	30–39
	Use of colouring agents in food (Rep.-Res.).	39–49
23 January	Political and institutional aspects of accession or association to the Community (Rep.).	54–96
	Accession of the United Kingdom to the EEC (Rep.-Res.).	96–116
24 January	Co-ordination of energy policy (Rep.).	119–171
25 January	Health protection (Rep.-Res.).	177–156
	Problems of the market and equalisation of tariffs (Rep.-Res.).	182–188
	Political and institutional aspects of accession or association to the Community (Rep.-Res.).	186–187

Date	Subject of Debate	Official Report of Debates No.
		No. 54
20 February	Policy statement from the Commission of Euratom.	pp. 9–15
	Economic situation of the EEC (Rep.-Res.).	15–34
	Co-ordination of energy policy (Rep.-Res.).	34–76
21 February	The catastrophe at Völlingen and problems of safety (Rep.-Res.).	83–84
22 February	The catastrophe in North Germany (Res.).	85–87
	International transport of goods by road (Rep.-Res.).	87–97
	European Identity Card (Rep.-Res.).	97–99
	Recommendation adopted by the Permanent Joint Committee at Abidjan (Rep.-Res.).	99–109
	Social situation in the Community in 1960 (Rep.).	109–111
	Common policy for rice (Rep.-Res.).	111–115

SESSION 1962-63

Date	Subject of Debate	Official Report of Debates No.
		No. 56
27 March	Social security of frontier and seasonal labour (Rep.-Res.).	pp.14–38
28 March	Road traffic (Rep.-Res.).	39–52
29 March	Statements by the Councils on their activities.	64–78
	The catastrophe in North Germany (Rep.-Res.).	78–84
	Professional education (Rep.).	84–112
30 March	Professional education (Rep.-Res.).	114–122
	Accounting Regulations of the Assembly for 1961 (Rep.-Res.).	122–123
	Structure for agriculture (Rep.-Res.).	123–133
	Free movement of labour (Rep.-Res.).	133–134
	Name of the Assembly (Res.).	136–139
		No. 57
7 May	Statement by the High Authority of the ECSC.	pp.6–13
8 May	Common transport policy (Rep.-Res.).	16–48
9 May	European Political Union (Rep.-Res.).	52–74

Date	Subject of Debate	*Official Report of Debates No.*
10 May	Co-ordination of budgetary and financial policy (Rep.).	80–89
	Co-ordination of monetary policy (Rep.).	89–97
11 May	European list of industrial sickness (Rep.-Res.).	99–104
	Medical care at work (Rep.-Res.).	104–113
		No. 58
25 June	Milk, beef and rice markets (Rep.).	pp. 10–37
26 June	Agriculture – Rate of exchange and units of account (Rep.-Res.).	41–45
	Common policy for fat products (Rep.).	45–60, 92–104 and 142
	Accession of the United Kingdom and Denmark to the Communities (Rep.-Res.).	61–81
	Relations between the EEC and GATT (Rep.-Res.).	81–91
	Milk, beef and rice markets (Rep.-Res.).	104–142
	Agricultural policy (Rep.-Res.).	143–144
	Potatoes (Rep.-Res.).	144–146
27 June	The Activities of the ECSC (Rep.-Res.).	149–214
	European Statute for Minors (Res.).	215–216
	Amendment of the Rules of Procedure of the Parliament (Rep.-Res.).	216–225
	Report to the Consultative Assembly of the Council of Europe (Rep.).	226–229
28 June	Association of African States and Madagascar (Rep.-Res.).	232–256
	Arbitration in the field of fruit and vegetables (Rep.-Res.).	257–258
	Application of Articles 85 and 86 of the EEC Treaty (Rep.-Res.).	258–263
	Equal pay for men and women (Rep.-Res.).	264–268
	Free movement of frontier and seasonal labour (Rep.).	268–274
29 June	Free movement of frontier and seasonal labour (Rep.-Res.).	276–298
	Budget of the Parliament (Rep.-Res.).	298–301
	Budgetary affairs in the ECSC (Rep.-Res.).	305–312
	Supplementary Budgets of the EEC and Euratom (Rep.-Res.).	312–327

Date	Subject of Debate	*Official Report of Debates No.*
		No. 59
15 October	Activities of Euratom (Rep.).	pp.13–21
16 October	Activities of Euratom (Rep.-Res.).	23–43
	Association of the Netherlands with EEC (Rep.).	44–60
	Interpretation of Article 136 of the EEC Treaty (Rep.).	60–67
17 October	Co-ordination of monetary, budgetary and financial policy (Rep.-Res.).	70–105
	Activities of the EEC (Rep.).	105–135
18 October	Activities of the EEC (Rep.-Res.).	143–170
19 October	Statute of Personnel (Rep.-Res.).	172–173
	Association of the Netherlands Antilles to the EEC (Rep.-Res.).	173–174
	Interpretation of Article 136 of the EEC Treaty (Rep.-Res.).	174–179
	Parliamentary Committee on Association with Greece (Rep.-Res.).	179–184
	Importing mixed cereals (Rep.-Res.).	185–186
	Agriculture – Rates of exchange and units of account (Rep.-Res.).	186–189
		No. 60
19 November	Transport problems (Rep.-Res.).	pp. 10–42
20 November	Exchange of views between the Parliament, the Councils and the Executives	43–79
21 November	Exchange of views between the Parliament, the Council and the Executives	82–136
	Budgets of the EEC and Euratom for 1963 (Rep.-Res.).	136–156
	Statute of Personnel (Rep.-Res.).	156–158
	Recommendation of the Standing Joint Committee with Associated States (Rep.).	158–162
22 November	Transport problems in the ECSC (Rep.-Res.).	164–178
	Movement and residence of foreigners (Rep.-Res.).	178–184
	Freedom of establishment in agriculture (Rep.-Res.).	184–196
23 November	Health supervision regarding meat (Rep.-Res.).	197–200
	Information services of the Communities (Rep.-Res.).	200–209

Date	Subject of Debate	Official Report of Debates No.
		No. 61
4 February	Statement by the Commission on the economic situation of the Community	pp.16–24
5 February	Debate on the close of the negotiations of Brussels	25–66
6 February	Close of negotiations of Brussels (Res.).	69–116
	Administration Accounts of the EEC and ECSC (Rep.-Res.).	116–121
	Statute of Personnel (Rep.-Res.).	123–124
	Common transport policy (Rep.).	125–136
7 February	Common transport policy (Rep.-Res.).	139–145
	Production of hatching eggs (Rep.-Res.).	146–149
	Agricultural prices (Rep.-Res.).	149–164 and 174–184
	European Gas Industry (Rep.-Res.).	164–174
	European Social Fund (Rep.-Res.).	185–199
	Free supply of services (Rep.-Res.).	199–201
8 February	Association of the African States and Madagascar (Rep.-Res.).	210–212
	Payments for exchange of services (Rep.-Res).	212
	Cinema industry (Rep.-Res.).	213–223
	Free movement in the Community (Rep.-Res.).	223–228
	Reinsurance and reconveyance (Rep.-Res.).	228–230

SESSION 1963–1964

		No. 62
26 March	Movement of cattle and pigs (Rep.-Res.).	pp. 19–39
	Economic situation in the Community (Rep.-Res.).	39–55
	Commercial transactions concerning invisibles (Rep.-Res.).	56–57
27 March	Negotiations with the United Kingdom (Rep.)	60–103
	Commercial policy (Rep.-Res.).	104–120
28 March	Association Agreement with African states and Madagascar (Rep.-Res.).	125–138

Date	*Subject of Debate*	*Official Report of Debates No.*
	Cereal prices for 1963–64 (Rep.-Res.).	139–156
	Oil pipe-lines (Rep.-Res.).	157–182
	Social security for seasonal workers (Rep.-Res.).	186–188
	Social situation in the Community in 1961 Rep.-Res.).	188–200
	Free movement of labour (Rep.-Res.).	201–224
29 March	Negotiations with the United Kingdom (Res.)	225–226
	Sicilian sulphur industry (Rep.-Res.).	226–234
	Supplementary budget for EEC in 1963 (Rep.-Res.).	235–236
		No. 63
13 May	Sixth Report of the Commission of Euratom.	pp. 7–13
	Pharmaceutical products (Rep.-Res.).	13–19
14 May	Eleventh Report of the High Authority of ECSC.	22–29
	European Social Charter (Rep.-Res.).	29–36
	Wholesaling (Rep.-Res.).	36–40
	Convention with African states and Madagascar (Rep.-Res.).	40–44
		No. 64
24 June	Budgetary and administrative problems of ECSC (Rep.Res.).	pp. 10–18
	Budget of the Parliament (Rep.-Res.).	18–25
	Cultural cooperation (Rep.-Res.).	25–38
25 June	Activities of the Councils of the EEC and Euratom.	39–62
26 June	Activities of the EEC.	66–73
	Activities of the ECSC (Rep.).	73–113
27 June	Debate on the Sixth General Report of Euratom (Rep.-Res.).	117–155
	Competence and powers of the European Parliament (Rep.-Res.).	156–185
28 June	Equal pay (Rep.-Res.).	191–196
	Immunities and privileges of Community officials (Rep.-Res.).	196–200
	Preservatives in foodstuffs (Rep.-Res.).	200–210
	Relations with Latin America (Rep.-Res.).	210–219
	Tariff negotiations in GATT (Rep.-Res.).	219–223
	Survey of wine industry (Rep.-Res.).	223–224

Date	Subject of Debate	Official Report of Debates No.
		No. 65
16 September	Convention with African states and Madagascar (Rep.-Res.).	pp. 10–43
	Supplementary budgets (Rep.-Res.).	43–46
		No. 66
14 October	Budget of the European Parliament (Rep.-Res.).	pp. 5–10
15 October	Association between the EEC and Greece (Rep.-Res.).	12–13
	Road transport vehicles (Rep.).	13–24
	Concerted practices and agreements (Rep.-Res.).	24–27
16 October	Debate on the Sixth General Report of EEC (Rep.-Res.).	29–61
17 October	Road transport vehicles (Res.).	64–65
	Turnover taxes (Rep.-Res.).	67–87
	Energy policy (Rep.-Res.).	87–127
	European agricultural fund (Rep.).	127–138
18 October	Budget of the Parliament (Res.).	140–141
	Statute of Personnel (Rep.-Res.).	141–145
	European agricultural fund (Rep.-Res.).	145–168
	Agricultural accounting (Rep.-Res.).	168–172
		No. 67
26 November	Colloquy between the Parliament, the Councils and the Executives of the Communities.	pp. 20–48
27 November	Cereal prices (Rep.-Res.).	50–74
	Freedom of establishment and of provision of services (Rep.-Res.).	74–94
	Budgets of the EEC and Euratom (Rep.-Res.).	95–125
28 November	Conclusion of colloquy with the Councils and the Executives of the Communities.	136–144
	Association between the EEC and Turkey (Rep.-Res.).	144–162
	Young workers' exchanges (Rep.-Res.).	162–170
	Social aspects of Community energy policy (Rep.-Res.).	171–184
	Students' vacation employment (Rep.-Res.).	184–192

Date	Subject of Debate	Official Report of Debates No.
		No. 68
7 January	Brussels agreements on agricultural policy.	pp. 6–18
	Agricultural problems (Rep.).	18–26
8 January	Agricultural problems (Rep.-Res.).	28–73
		No. 69
20 January	Tariff negotiations in GATT (Rep.).	pp. 3–12
21 January	Economic situation of the Communities.	13–25
	Mid-term economic policies (Rep.-Res.).	25–40
	Monetary and financial cooperation within the EEC (Rep.-Res.).	41–48
22 January	Social situation in the Communities (Rep.-Res.).	50–73
	Relations between the EEC and Israel (Rep.-Res.).	75–82
	Regional policy (Rep.-Res.).	82–105
	Energy policy (Rep.-Res.).	105–116
23 January	Free movement of labour (Rep.-Res.).	118–138
	External relations of Euratom (Rep.-Res.).	138–150
	Enquiry into transport costs (Rep.-Res.).	150–159
	European road policy (Rep.-Res.).	159–165
	Association of overseas countries with the Communities (Rep.-Res.).	165–173
24 January	Debate on reports of a visit to the West Indies (Rep.-Res.).	175–192

SESSION 1964–65

Date	Subject of Debate	Official Report of Debates No.
		No. 70
21 March	Procedure for consideration of the general reports on the activities of the Communities (Res.).	pp. 12–13
23 March	Economic situation in the Community (Rep.-Res.).	17–34 and 43–63
	Statement on the activities of the Councils of the Communities.	34–43
24 March	Debate on the activities of the Councils of the Communities.	68–93
	Safety in the coal mines (Rep.-Res.).	94–110

Date	Subject of Debate	*Official Report of Debates No.*
	Accounts of the European Parliament for 1963 and supplementary Budget of the EEC for 1964 (Rep.-Res.).	111–112
	Social policy in agriculture (Rep.-Res.).	113–133
	Objectives in agricultural regulations (Rep.-Res.).	133–136
	Rice and rice products (Rep.).	137–143
25 March	Rice and rice products (Rep.-Res.).	146–157
	Commercial agreement with Iran (Rep.-Res.).	154–158
	UNCTAD (Rep.-Res.).	159–170
	Nuclear energy (Rep.-Res.).	170–184
		No. 71
11 May	Request for waiver of parliamentary immunity of two Members (Rep.).	pp. 5–7
	Commercial agreement between the EEC and Israel (Rep.).	7
	Equal pay for men and women (Rep.-Res.).	8–19
12 May	Statement of the High Authority on the 12th General Report of the ECSC.	22–27
	Budgetary powers of the European Parliament (Rep.-Res.).	28–41
	Social aspects of the decennial report of the ECSC (Rep.-Res.).	43–54
13 May	Commercial agreements between the EEC and Israel.	58–62
	Fruit and vegetable markets (Rep.-Res.).	63–69
	Creation of a European University (Rep.-Res.).	69–86
	Agreements, decisions and restrictive practices (Rep.-Res.).	91–100
14 May	Energy policy (Rep.-Res.).	106–120
	Report to the Consultative Assembly of the Council of Europe (Rep.).	121–122
	Competition in transport (Rep.-Res.).	122–137
		No. 72
15 June	Request for waiver of parliamentary immunity of two Members (Rep.-Res.).	pp. 5–14
	Budget of the Parliament (Rep.-Res.).	14–18
	Activities of the ECSC (Rep.).	19–38
16 June	Activities of the ECSC (Rep.).	40–77

T

Date	Subject of Debate	*Official Report of Debates No.*
	ECSC: Budgetary and administrative questions (Rep.-Res.).	77–78
17 June	Transport of goods (Rep.).	83–100
	Activities of the ECSC (Rep.-Res.).	100–127 and 135–140
	Statement by the Commission on the activities of Euratom.	127–134
18 June	Statement by the Commission on the annual report on the activities of the EEC.	146–155
	Transport of goods (Rep.-Res.).	158–195
	Harmonisation of legislation on cocoa and chocolate (Rep.-Res.).	196–224
	AASM (Rep.-Res.).	225–226
	Health problems in the meat market (Rep.-Res.).	228–252
	Common organisation of the sugar markets (Rep.-Res.).	252–272
	Common agricultural policy (Rep.-Res.).	272–275
19 June	Professional activities in agriculture and horticulture (Rep.-Res.).	277–283
	Agricultural, horticultural and forest plants and seeds (Rep.-Res.).	284–318
	Plants and seeds (Rep.-Res.).	318
	Forest materials (Rep.-Res.).	318–319
		No. 73
22 September	Activities of Euratom (Rep.).	pp. 17–24
23 September	Statement by the Commission on economic matters.	26–36
	Association of the EEC and Greece (Rep.-Res.).	36–41
	Activities of Euratom (Rep.-Res.).	42–91
24 September	Energy policy and the merger of the Executives (Rep.-Res.).	94–100
	Draft budget of the European Parliament (Rep.-Res.).	101–103
	Budgetary problems and the merger of the Executives (Rep.-Res.).	103–107
	Milk products (Rep.-Res.).	108–109
		No. 74
19 October	World trade conference (Rep.-Res.).	pp. 4–15
	European Statute of Minors (Rep.-Res.).	16–21
20 October	Activities of the EEC (Rep.).	34–65

Date	Subject of Debate	*Official Report of Debates No.*
21 October	Activities of the EEC (Rep.).	68–109
	Debate on the democratisation of the European Community	109–134
	Debate on the mandate of the enlarged Bureau.	134–143
22 October	Activities of the EEC (Rep.-Res.).	147–186
	European Statute of Minors (Rep.-Res.).	188–199
	Colouring agents (Rep.-Res.).	199–200
	Sugar market (Rep.).	202–227
23 October	Remuneration of Community employees (Rep.-Res.).	231–242
	Administration accounts for 1962 (Rep.-Res.).	244–248
	Recruitment of officials of the nuclear research centre of Euratom (Rep.-Res.).	249–251
	Supplementary Budget of the EEC for 1964 (Rep.-Res.).	252–254
		No. 75
23 November	Bilateral relations of the EEC and AASM.	pp. 8–17
	European development fund (Rep.-Res.).	18–30
24 November	Budgets of the EEC and Euratom (Rep.-Res.).	34–68
25 November	Exchange of views between the Parliament, Councils and the Commissions of the Communities.	71–117
26 November	Relations of the Community and Latin America (Rep.-Res.).	120–123 and 148–155
	Debate on place of plenary meetings of the European Parliament.	123–147
	Debate on compensation to Luxembourg for the transfer of the ECSC.	155–161
27 November	Social situation in the Community (Rep.-Res.).	164–193
	Rules of competition in transport (Rep.-Res.).	195–199
	Census of pig livestock (Rep.-Res.).	199–201
		No. 76
18 January	Freedom of establishment—films (Rep.-Res.).	pp. 6–11
	Double taxation of road vehicles (Rep.-Res.).	11–18
	Harmonisation of legislation (Rep.-Res.).	18–28

Date	Subject of Debate	Official Report of Debates No.
19 January	Statement of the EEC Commission on the economic situation in the Community.	30–39
	European political unity (Rep.).	39–64
20 January	Participation of the Parliament in the procedure for the conclusion of commercial agreements (Rep.-Res.).	67–81
	Association of the EEC and the AASM (Rep.-Res.).	71–82
	Statement by the Commission on the agricultural policy.	83–92
	Amendment of Rule 36 of the Rules of Procedure of the Parliament (Rep.-Res.).	92–93
	Fruit and vegetables (Rep.-Res.).	93–118
	Sugar market (Rep.-Res.).	118–136
	Agricultural labour structure (Rep.-Res.).	137–160
	Agricultural regulations (Rep.-Res.).	160–166
	European political unity (Rep.-Res.).	167–176
21 January	Draft Budget for research and investment in Euratom in 1965 (Rep.-Res.).	177–186
	Research in Euratom (Rep.).	187–205
	Stocks of petrol products (Rep.-Res.).	205–212
22 January	Community policy on state aid to coalfields (Rep.-Res.).	213–227
	Agricultural products (Rep.-Res.).	227–239

SESSION 1965–1966

Date	Subject of Debate	No. 77
22 March	Collaboration with the Parliaments of the associated European States (Rep.-Res.).	pp. 12–21
	Change in the number of members of the Committee on research and culture (Res.).	22
23 March	Statement of the Commission of Euratom on the five year plan and Chapter VI of the Treaty.	26–34
	Economic Situation in the Community (Rep.-Res.).	41–70
	Contracts for public works (Rep.-Res.).	70–97
	Intervention of member states in favour of the coal industries (Rep.-Res.).	97–107

Date	Subject of Debate	Official Report of Debates No.
	Investment on transport infrastructure (Rep.-Res.).	108–115
	International carriage of passengers by road (Rep.-Res.).	115–124
24 March	Statement by the High Authority.	126–129
	Political Union of Europe and the Atlantic Alliance (Rep.-Res.).	129–188
	Financial plan of the EEC (Res.).	188–191
25 March	Statement on the activities of the Councils of the European Communities.	194–226
	Establishment of a joint parliamentary committee EEC—Greece (Res.).	226–227
	Relations between the Community and Israel (Rep.-Res.).	227–239 and 242–246
	Common commercial policy (Rep.).	239–242
26 March	Common commercial policy (Rep.-Res.).	250–267
	Housing of workers (Rep.-Res.).	267–273
	Compensatory agricultural taxes (Rep.-Res.).	273–275
	Accounts of the European Parliament (Rep.-Res.).	275–276
		No. 78
10 May	Commercial policy in the Community in relation to state-trading countries (Rep.-Res.).	pp. 4–14
	Organisation of the fruit and vegetable market (Rep.-Res.).	14–18
	Agricultural Regulations (Rep.-Res.).	48–81
11 May	Statement of High Authority and 13th General Report of ECSC.	53–57
	Amendment of Administrative Budget of ECSC for 1964–65 (Rep.-Res.).	57–58
	Financing of the agricultural policy; the financial resources and powers of the European Parliament (Rep.).	58–88
12 May	Financing of the agricultural policy; the financial resources and powers of the European Parliament (Rep.-Res.).	93–115
	Customs duties (Rep.-Res.).	115–123
	Market for certain agricultural products (Rep.-Res.).	123–125

Date	*Subject of Debate*	*Official Report of Debates No.*
	Potato market (Rep.-Res.).	125–127
	Abolition of checks on the movement of goods between member countries (Rep.-Res.).	127–131
	Pharmaceutical questions (Rep.-Res.).	131–147
	Freedom of establishment in certain trades (Rep.-Res.).	147–152
	Products originating from AASM (Rep.-Res.).	152–156
	Merger of the Executives and its effect on health and safety problems (Rep.-Res.).	156–166
13 May	Second programme of research of Euratom (Rep.).	173–182
	Social security of migrant workers (Rep.-Res.).	182–186
	Social aspects of the merger of the Executives (Rep.-Res.).	186–202
	Health protection against radiation (Rep.-Res.).	202–211
14 May	Integration of civil aviation in the Community (Rep.-Res.).	214–223
	Establishment of a joint parliamentary committee: EEC and Turkey (Res.).	223–226
	Freedom of establishment in certain trades (Rep.-Res.).	226–232
		No. 79
14 June	13th annual Report of the ECSC (Rep.-Res.).	pp. 9–47
	Compensatory tax on agricultural products (Rep.-Res.).	47–48
15 June	Statement of the Commission of Euratom on its annual report on the activities of Euratom.	51–54
	Provisional Estimates of the ECSC (Rep.-Res.).	54–61
	Amendment of the Euratom Treaty (Rep.-Res.).	61–90
	Supplementary budget for research and investment of Euratom (Rep.-Res.).	90–92
	Accounts of the European Parliament 1963 (Rep.-Res.).	92–96
	Estimates of income and expenditure of the European Parliament (Rep.-Res.).	96–100
16 June	Statements of the EEC Commission and the High Authority of the ECSC on competition within the Community.	102–119

Date	Subject of Debate	Official Report of Debates No.
	European Social Fund (Rep.-Res.).	119–138
	Social policy in the EEC (Rep.-Res.).	138–157
	The labour market and prospects for 1965 (Rep.-Res.).	157–160
	Specialisation of agricultural advisers (Rep.-Res.).	160–179
	Medical supervision of workers (Rep.-Res.).	179–183
	Primacy of community law (Rep.).	183–192
17 June	Statement of the EEC Commission on the annual general report of the EEC.	194–204
	Harmonisation of European legislation (Rep.-Res.).	204–208 and 242–243
	Primacy of Community law (Rep.).	218–242
18 June	Primacy of Community law (Res.).	246–247
	Agreement of the EEC with the Lebanon (Rep.-Res.).	247–249
	Organisation of the market in fats (Rep.-Res.).	249–274
	Products originating from the AASM (Rep.-Res.).	274–277
	Institution of a tax on fat products (Rep.-Res.).	277–288
	Indirect tax on the accumulation of capital (Rep.-Res.).	288–295
	Report to the Consultative Assembly of the Council of Europe (Rep.).	295
		No. 80
24 September	Current situation in the Community (Res.).	p. 9
		No. 81
18 October	Licensed workers in the sulphur mines of Italy (Rep.-Res.).	pp. 5–29
	Compensatory tax on agricultural products (Rep.-Res.).	31
19 October	Defence against dumping from outside the EEC (Rep.-Res.).	34–44
	Wines (Rep.-Res.).	44–56
20 October	Activities of the EEC (Rep.).	57–92
21 October	Freedom of establishment and free supply of services—the activities of the press (Res.).	118–120
	Activities of the EEC (Rep.-Res.).	120–133
	Activities of Euratom (Rep.-Res.).	133–163

Date	*Subject of Debate*	*Official Report of Debates No.*
22 October	Measures against vegetable pests (Rep.-Res.).	166–180
	Freedom of establishment and free supply of services—the retail trade (Rep.-Res.).	180–190
	Primacy of Community law (Rep.-Res.).	190–196
		No. 82
23 November	Association of EEC and Greece (Rep.-Res.).	pp. 4–13
	Importation of fat products from Greece (Rep.-Res.).	13–15
	Commercial relations between the EEC and India (Rep.-Res.).	16–23
	Increase of commercial contracts between the EEC and the AASM (Rep.-Res.).	23–26
24 November	Working conditions in the European Parliament (Rep.-Res.).	38–45
	Social situation in the Community in 1964 (Rep.-Res.).	46–73
	European Conference on social security (Rep.-Res.).	73–79
25 November	Statement of the Council of Ministers of 26 October 1965.	82–89
	Realisation of the aims of Article 39 of the EEC Treaty (Rep.).	89–90
	International market in ship-building—Community aid (Rep.-Res.).	90–120
26 November	Harmonisation of legislation on dangerous substances.	121–130
	Harmonisation of legislation on preservatives in human food (Rep.-Res.).	130–139
		No. 83
18 January	Protection of young people at work (Rep.-Res.).	pp. 13–26
	Food and drink industry (Rep.-Res.).	26–35
	The service industries (restaurants and hotels) (Rep.-Res.).	35–45
	Organisation of the transport market (Rep.).	45–48
19 January	Organisation of the transport market (Rep.-Res.).	50–71
	Market in oranges (Rep.-Res.).	72–90
	Indemnity for industrial diseases (Rep.-Res.).	90–98

Date	Subject of Debate	Official Report of Debates No.
20 January	Exchange of views between the Parliament, the Councils and the Executives of the Communities.	101–148
21 January	Supplementary Budgets of the EEC and Euratom for 1965 and for research and investment in Euratom for 1965 (Rep.-Res.).	150–154
	Agriculture (Rep.-Res.).	154–160

SESSION 1966–67

		No. 84
8 March	Harmonisation of turnover taxes (Rep.-Res.).	pp. 22–67
9 March	Budgets of the EEC and Euratom for 1966 (Rep.-Res.).	70–104
	Current situation in the Community (Rep.-Res.).	108–131
10 March	European schools (Rep.-Res.).	134–150
	European sports certificate (Rep.-Res.).	150–153
	Progress of the second and third stages of the transitional period (Res.).	153
	Economic situation in the Community (Rep.-Res.).	163–178
	Famine in India (Res.).	178–180
11 March	Parliamentary Conference of the Association with African states and Madagascar (Rep.-Res.).	182–189
	Vocational guidance (Rep.-Res.).	189–202
	Social services for migrant workers (Rep.-Res.).	202–206
		No. 85
9 May	Creation of a European Office for Youth (Rep.-Res.).	pp. 8–23
	Presentation of Fourteenth General Report of the High Authority of the ECSC.	26–30
	Company third-party insurance (Rep.).	41–46
11 May	Tax exemptions (Rep.-Res.).	51–53
	Company third-party insurance (Rep.-Res.).	56–73 and 84–101
	Forestry activities (Rep.-Res.).	73–82
	European Agricultural Fund (Rep.).	113–115
	Price-levels of certain agricultural products (Rep.).	115–126

Date	Subject of Debate	*Official Report of Debates No.*
12 May	Termination of mandates of Members of the European Parliament (Rep.).	128–133
	Price levels of certain agricultural products (Rep.-Res.).	142–181
	European Agricultural Fund (Rep.-Res.).	187
13 May	Certificates of origin of manufactures (Rep.-Res.).	190–204
	Procedure for administering quotas (Rep.-Res.).	204–209
	Licensed workers in sulphur mines (Rep.-Res.).	209–212
	Social security for migrant workers (Rep.-Res.).	212–216
		No. 86
27 June	Protection of mothers' health (Rep.-Res.).	pp. 8–21
	Termination of mandates of Members of the European Parliament (Res.).	21–23
	Regional policy (Rep.-Res.).	23–55
	Tariffs on goods transport (Rep.-Res.).	55–56
28 June	Colloquy between the Parliament, the Councils and the Executives of the Communities.	57–85
	World agreement on cereals (Rep.-Res.).	85–96
	Provisional accounts of the Parliament (Rep.-Res.).	96–103
29 June	Economic competition and concentration (Rep.).	112–116
	Equal pay (Rep.-Res.).	117–124
	Industrial medicine (Rep.-Res.).	125–132
	Social aspects of re-development (Rep.-Res.).	132–142
	Supplementary budget of the EEC for 1966 (Rep.-Res.).	142–144
	GATT negotiations (Rep.-Res.).	144–146
30 June	Future programme of Euratom (Rep.-Res.).	169–176
	Fourteenth Report of the High Authority of ECSC (Rep.).	179–212
	Budgetary and administrative problems concerning ECSC (Rep.-Res.).	212–219
1 July	Relations between ECSC and African states and Madagascar (Rep.-Res.).	223–226
	Fourteenth Report of the High Authority of the ECSC (Rep.-Res.).	226–240

Date	Subject of Debate	Official Report of Debates No.
	Stabilisation of world markets for primary products (Rep.-Res.).	243–253
	Cooperation between the EEC and the African states and Madagascar (Rep.-Res.).	253–256
	Aid from Euratom to developing states (Rep.-Res.).	256–260
	Agricultural aid (Rep.-Res.).	260–267
		No. 87
17 October	Food additives (Rep.-Res.).	pp. 9–10
18 October	Ninth General Report of the Euratom Commission (Rep.-Res.).	22–56
	Technical progress and scientific research. Science policy (Rep.-Res.).	57–84
	Supplementary budget for Euratom (Rep.-Res.).	85–86
	Accounts for 1964 of Euratom and EEC (Rep.-Res.).	87–91
19 October	Ninth General Report of the EEC Commission (Rep.-Res.).	93–135
20 October	Institutional development of the European Communities (Rep.-Res.).	138–160
	Petrol and natural gas (Rep.-Res.).	162–180
	Energy policy: coal industry (Rep.-Res.).	180–191
21 October	Draft budgets of EEC and Euratom and supplementary estimates relating to the European Parliament (Rep.-Res.).	194–198
	Freedom of establishment and of provision of services (Rep.-Res.).	198–200
	Agricultural cooperatives (Rep.-Res.).	200–202
	Agricultural credits (Rep.-Res.).	202–206
	Freedom of establishment: transitional provisions (Rep.-Res.).	206–214
		No. 88
28 November	Colloquy between the Parliament and the Councils and Executives of the European Communities.	pp. 8–46
29 November	Budgets of the EEC, Euratom, and the European Parliament for 1967, and supplementary budgets for 1966 (Rep.-Res.).	62–97
	Association between Nigeria and the EEC (Rep.)	98–107

Date	Subject of Debate	*Official Report of Debates No.*
30 November	Medium-term economic policy (Rep.-Res.).	110–158
	Association between Nigeria and the EEC (Rep.-Res.).	161–164
	Monetary policy (Rep.-Res.).	164–175
1 December	Aid for flooded areas of Italy (Rep.-Res.).	178–184
	Work market for agricultural products (Rep.-Res.).	184–206
	Social situation in the EEC (Rep.-Res.).	206–227
2 December	Regulations concerning the agricultural fund (Rep.-Res.).	230–233
	Powdered milk and eggs (Rep.-Res.).	233–235
	Preservatives (Rep.-Res.).	235–237
	Recommendations of the joint parliamentary committee between Greece and the EEC (Rep.-Res.).	237–243
	Establishment of a veterinary board (Rep.-Res.).	243–267
		No. 89
30 January	Supplementary budget of Euratom for 1966 (Rep.-Res.).	pp. 7–12
31 January	General objectives for the steel industry (Rep.-Res.).	14–76
1 February	European social policy (Rep.-Res.).	78–111
	Prevention of industrial accidents (Rep.-Res.).	111–115
2 February	World sugar market (Rep.-Res.).	129–138 and 153–155
	Agricultural regulations (Rep.-Res.).	138–150
	Agricultural inquiries in France and Italy (Rep.-Res.).	150–153
3 February	Sugar market (Res.).	158–163
	Vehicle regulations (Rep.-Res.).	163–188

SESSION 1967–68

Date	Subject of Debate	*No. 90*
13 March	Colouring in pharmaceutical products and foodstuffs (Rep.-Res.).	pp. 9–15
	Right of establishment in ancillary medical professions (Rep.-Res.).	15–18
14 March	Disposal of iron (Rep.-Res.).	22–29
	Colour television (Rep.-Res.).	29–34

Date	Subject of Debate	Official Report of Debates No.
	Activities of the Councils of Ministers	34–54
15 March	Parliamentary conference of the Association with Madagascar and the African states (Rep.-Res.).	64–79
	Economic situation in the European Economic Community (Rep.-Res.).	79–98
16 March	World markets for beef products (Rep.-Res.).	114–127
	Accounts of the Parliament for 1966 (Rep.-Res.).	127
	Measuring instruments (Rep.-Res.).	128–136
	Activity of Euratom within the single executive (Rep.).	154–169
	Recommendations of the joint parliamentary committee of the EEC and Turkey (Rep.-Res.).	169–173
	The forthcoming conference of the Six (Rep.-Res.).	173–182
	Preserves (Rep.-Res.).	182–184
	Preservatives for fruit (Rep.-Res.).	184–198
	Reduction of customs duties in the third phase (Rep.-Res.).	198–200
	Road and river transport (Rep.-Res.).	202–225
	Agricultural regulations (Rep.-Res.).	225–230
		No. 91
9 May	Community relations with other countries and international organizations (Rep.).	pp. 21–47
10 May	Community relations with other countries and international organisations (Res.).	65–67
	Monetary exchanges between member states and other countries (Res.).	78–81
	Request from the United Kingdom for accession to the three Communities (Rep.-Res.).	83–85
	Aid to transport undertakings (Rep.-Res.).	85–92
	Application of Community law (Rep.-Res.).	92–110
11 May	Association with Greece (Res.).	114–117
	Agricultural regulation (Rep.-Res.).	123–215
		No. 92
19 June	Provisional estimates of the European Parliament for 1968 (Rep.-Res.).	pp. 7–9

Date	*Subject of Debate*	*Official Report of Debates No.*
	Monetary exchanges between member states (Rep.-Res.).	21–23
20 June	Tenth General Report of the Commission of Euratom.	26–35
	Fifteenth General Report of the High Authority of the Coal and Steel Community (Rep.-Res.).	35–83
	Financial and budgetary problems of the ECSC (Rep.-Res.).	83–85
21 June	Tenth General Report of the EEC Commission.	88–102
	Kennedy Round (Rep.-Res.).	103–118
	Results of the Rome Conference of the Six (Rep.-Res.).	118–130
	Common agricultural policy (Rep.).	130–138
22 June	Situation in the Middle East (Rep.-Res.).	143–162
	Common transport policy (Res.).	163
	Agricultural regulations (Rep.-Res.).	164–183
		No. 93
19 July	Measures concerning the establishment and revision of prices for certain agricultural products (Rep.-Res.).	pp. 9–45
	Regulations concerning the agricultural fund (Rep.-Res.).	45–49
	Fruit and vegetable products (Rep.-Res.).	50
		No. 94
20 September	Statement by the President of the European Commission.	pp. 9–38
	Amendment of Rules of Procedure of the European Parliament (Res.).	15
	Draft Budget of Euratom for 1967 (Rep.-Res.).	38–45
		No. 95
16 October	Directive on freedom of establishment in the field of petrol and natural gas discovery (Rep.-Res.).	pp. 8–9
	Management accounts of the EEC and Euratom for 1965 (Rep.-Res.).	9–15
17 October	Legal problems concerning the consultation of the European Parliament by other Community institutions (Rep.-Res.).	19–35
	Regulation and directive on the free movement of labour within the Community (Rep.-Res.).	35–51

Date	Subject of Debate	Official Report of Debates No.
18 October	Tenth General Report of the Euratom Commission (Rep.-Res.).	64–90
19 October	Amendment of the Rules of Procedure of the European Parliament (Rep.-Res.).	92–95
	Directive on the control of animal foodstuffs and Decision on the establishment of a permanent committee on animal foodstuffs (Rep.-Res.).	95–102
	Movement of fruit and vegetable products (Rep.-Res.).	102–103
		No. 96
27 November	Recommendations of the joint parliamentary committee of the Association between the EEC and Turkey (Rep.-Res.).	pp. 12–20
	Scientific and technical research policy (Rep.-Res.).	21–46
28 November	Exchange of views between the European Parliament, and the Council and Commission of the European Communities.	65–104
	Situation in Cyprus (emergency resolution).	105–106
29 November	Common ports policy (Rep.-Res.).	108–111
	Agricultural regulations.	128–135
30 November	Fourth General Report of the EEC Commission (Rep.-Res.).	138–183
1 December	Social situation in the Communities (Rep.-Res.).	187–196
	Directive on freedom of establishment in film distribution (Rep.-Res.).	197
	Transport by road, rail and navigable waterways (Rep.-Res.).	197
	Tax rebates for cereal and sugar exported (Rep.-Res.).	197–198
	Guideline for the work of the European Commission in the field of social affairs (Rep.-Res.).	198–207
		No. 97
8 January	Research and investment budget of Euratom for 1968 (Rep.-Res.).	pp. 6–26
	Supplementary budget of the Communities for 1967 (Rep.-Res.).	26–27

Date	Subject of Debate	Official Report of Debates No.
		No. 98
22 January	Directive concerning exchange rates (Rep.-Res.).	pp. 12–14
	Parliamentary Conference of AASM (Rep.-Res.).	14–32
	Organisation of pork market (Rep.-Res.).	32–33
23 January	Application by the United Kingdom and other countries for accession to the European Communities (Rep.-Res.).	36–57, 68–81 and 92–105
	Economic situation in the Community.	57–68
24 January	Discrimination in transport (Rep.-Res.).	109–110
	Increase of Turkish exports to the Communities (Rep.-Res.).	110–115
	Coal situation in the Community (Rep.-Res.).	115–136
	Current situation and future prospects in Euratom (Rep.-Res.).	141–158
	Results of the Kennedy Round (Rep.-Res.).	158–164
	Second session of UNCTAD (Rep.-Res.).	164–171
25 January	Social security for salaried employees and their families (Rep.-Res.).	175–188
	Community definition of 'invalidity' (Rep.-Res.).	189–198
	Statute of Personnel of the European Communities (Rep.-Res.).	199–208
	Draft budget of the Communities for 1968 (relating to the European Parliament) (Rep.-Res.).	208–211
	Common fisheries policy (Rep.-Res.).	211–223
	Agricultural producer groups (Rep.-Res.).	223–243
26 January	Regulations on the policy section of the agricultural fund (Rep.-Res.).	246–268
	Reparation of damage caused by African pig disease in Italy (Rep.-Res.).	268–269
		No. 99
21 February	Regulation concerning the common organisation of the market in milk and milk products (Rep.).	pp. 8–45
22 February	Regulations concerning the common organisation of the market in milk and milk products (Rep.-Res.).	48–53 and 68–75
	Regulation concerning the common organisation of the beef market (Rep.-Res.).	53–68

Date	Subject of Debate	Official Report of Debates No.
11 March	Directives concerning direct insurance other than life insurance (Rep.).	No. 100 pp. 5–17

SESSION 1968–69

Date	Subject of Debate	Official Report of Debates No.
12 March	Statement on the first General Report of the Commission of the European Communities by the President of the Commission.	No. 101 pp. 8–17
	Commercial relations between the Community and East European state trading countries (Rep.-Res.).	26–44
	The regulation of importation of certain products from other countries (Rep.-Res.).	44–47
13 March	Directives concerning direct insurance other than life insurance (Rep.-Res.).	49–52
	Statement on the social situation in the Community in 1967.	61–68
	Economic situation of the Community in 1967 and the prospects for 1968 (Rep.).	68–89
14 March	The public service concept of transport in member countries (Rep.-Res.).	93–96
	Application of the Yaoundé Convention *re* sugar products by the AASM (Res.).	96
	Economic situation of the Community in 1967 and prospects for 1968 (Rep.-Res.).	96–107
	Accounts of the European Parliament for 1967 (Rep.-Res.).	107
	The production of oil from grape pips (Rep.-Res.).	107
	Budget of the European Communities for 1968 (Rep.-Res.).	107–122
15 March	The community programmes of the Agricultural Fund (Rep.-Res.).	138–156
	Directive on the general agricultural census recommended by the FAO (Rep.-Res.).	156
21 March	Structural equilibrium of the milk market (Rep.).	No. 102 pp. 2–37

U

Date	*Subject of Debate*	*Official Report of Debates No.*
22 March	Structural equilibrium of the milk market (Rep.-Res.).	39–77
	Financing of a census of pig livestock (Rep.-Res.).	77
		No. 103
13 May	Activities of the Standing Organisation for Safety in the Coal Mines (Rep.-Res.).	pp. 12–18
	Equal pay for male and female workers (Rep.-Res.).	23–31
14 May	Nuclear non-proliferation Treaty (Rep.-Res.).	34–62
	Debate on the activities of the Council of Ministers.	62–86
15 May	Commitments of the EEC concerning food aid in the context of the Kennedy Round (Rep.-Res.).	103–115
	Statement by the President of the Commission on the prospects for economic union.	119–130
	The Merger Treaty (Rep.-Res.).	130–144
	Directive on different forms of aid to farmers (Rep.-Res.).	144–146
16 May	Agricultural regulations (Rep.-Res.).	149–161
17 May	Customs legislation (Rep.-Res.).	162–172
		No. 104
18 June	Regulations concerning products from the AASM and overseas countries and territories (Rep.-Res.).	pp. 8–10
	Agricultural regulations (Rep.-Res.).	10–15 and 28–40
	Trade problems (Rep.-Res.).	15–27
19 June	Trade regulations (Rep.-Res.).	44–51
	Agricultural regulations (Rep.-Res.).	51–71
		No. 105
1 July	Directives on the activities of architects (Rep.-Res.).	pp. 9–24
2 July	Directive on the activities of the press (Rep.-Res.).	27–29
	Iron industry problems in the Community (Rep.-Res.).	29–49

Date	Subject of Debate	Official Report of Debates No.
	Provision Estimates for the European Parliament for 1969 (Res.).	50
	Conventions on social affairs made in the framework of other international organisations (Rep.-Res.).	50–55
	Financial and technical co-operation of the EEC and AASM (Rep.-Res.).	57–69
	Recommendation of the joint parliamentary committee: EEC—Turkey (Rep.-Res.).	69–74
	Directives on pharmaceutical problems (Rep.-Res.).	74–85
3 July	General Report on the Activities of the Communities (Rep.-Res.).	103–139
	Social Situation in the Community in 1967 (Rep.-Res.).	139–157
	Directive on Community trade in fresh jointed meat (Res.).	157–158
4 July	Budgetary and financial affairs in the ECSC (Rep.-Res.).	171–174
	Second UNCTAD Conference (Rep.-Res.).	175–191
	Transport of goods by road (Rep.-Res.).	191–204
	Producing and marketing butter (Rep.-Res.).	204
5 July	Accounts of the Agricultural Fund (Rep.-Res.).	206–207
	Draft annual report to the Consultative Assembly of the Council of Europe (Res.).	207–208
	Fruit and vegetable regulations (Rep.-Res.).	208
	Supplementary budget of the Communities for 1968 (Rep.-Res.).	208
		No. 106
30 September	Administration Accounts of the EEC and Euratom for 1966 (Rep.-Res.).	pp. 7–9
	Harmonisation of turnover taxes (Rep.-Res.).	9–22
	Water transport (Rep.-Res.).	22–35
1 October	Political consequences of the events in Czechoslovakia (Rep.-Res.).	37–61
	European policy for research and technology (Rep.-Res.).	61–87
	Supplementary research and investment budget of the ECSC (Rep.-Res.).	87–94

Date	*Subject of Debate*	*Official Report of Debates No.*
	Agreement of Association with East Africa (Rep.-Res.).	94–106
2 October	Renewal of the Yaoundé Convention (Rep.-Res.).	111–135
	Fisheries (Rep.).	152–156
	Agricultural Directives (Rep.-Res.).	156–157
3 October	Directive on the harmonisation of legislation on crystal glass (Rep.-Res.).	160–161
	Implementation of Community law (Rep.-Res.).	161–175
	Programme for the removal of technical obstacles to free exchange (Rep.-Res.).	175–183
	Agricultural regulations (Res.).	183–184
	Preliminary Draft Budget of the European Parliament for 1969 (Rep.-Res.).	184
		No. 107
24 October	Fishing regulations (Rep.-Res.).	pp. 4–35
25 October	Basic price and quality of slaughtered pork (Rep.-Res.).	39–45
	Price of olive oil (Rep.-Res.).	45–49
	Agricultural Fund (Rep.-Res.).	49–61
		No. 108
25 November	Social security of migrant workers (Rep.-Res.).	pp. 5–12
26 November	Exchange of views between the European Parliament, the Council and the Commission.	15–58
27 November	Research and investment in Euratom (Rep.-Res.).	60–67
	Budget of the European Communities for 1969 (Rep.).	67–82
	Second medium term economic programme (Rep.).	82–87 and 103–115
28 November	Budget of the European Communities for 1969 (Rep.-Res.).	121–122
	Second medium term economic programme (Rep.-Res.).	122–131
	Agricultural regulations (Rep.-Res.).	131–132 and 148–153
	Recommendations of the joint commitee: EEC – Turkey (Rep.-Res.).	153–159
	Directives on dangerous substances and materials (Rep.-Res.).	159–161

Date	Subject of Debate	Official Report of Debates No.
29 November	The application of the Protocol of Privileges and Immunities (Rep.-Res.).	164
	Transport regulations (Rep.-Res.).	164–173
		No. 109
13 December	Current problems of the ECSC (Res.).	pp. 4–29
	Price of butter (Res.).	29
		No. 110
21 January	The position of the consumer in the Common Market (Rep.-Res.).	4–23
	Transport of passengers by road (Rep.-Res.).	23–27
22 January	Statement by the Commission on the economic situation of the Community.	29–36
	Statement by the Commission on the agricultural policy.	42–56
	Legal and political implications of Article 8 of the EEC Treaty (Rep.-Res.).	56–68
23 January	Statement by the Commission on the current situation of Euratom.	71–76
	Petition No. 1/68 on the evolution of European policy – draft budget of research and investment of Euratom for 1969 (Rep.-Res.).	76–84
	Operational budget of the ECSC (Rep.-Res.).	85–91
	Agricultural regulations (Rep.-Res.).	91–99
24 January	Agricultural regulations (Rep.-Res.).	101–104
	Safety in the construction of pipelines (Rep.-Res.).	104–111
		No. 111
20 February	Agricultural prices (Rep.).	pp. 4–32
21 February	Agricultural prices (Rep.-Res.).	36–54
	Community policy for the Mediterranean basin (Rep.-Res.).	54–62
		No. 112
10 March	Regulation of the Accounts of the European Parliament for 1968 (Rep.-Res.).	pp 4–5
	Delegation of the Parliament to the East African Community (Rep.-Res.).	5–9
	Fifth Meeting of the Parliamentary Conference EEC–AASM (Rep.-Res.).	9–18
	Costs of transport infrastructure (Rep.-Res.).	18–20

Date	Subject of Debate	*Official Report of Debates No.*

SESSION 1969–1970

		No. 113
11 March	Amendment of the Rules of Procedure of the European Parliament (Res.).	pp. 8–9
12 March	Statement on the social situation in the Communities in 1968.	15–20
	Second General Report on the activities of the Communities in 1968.	20–41
	The direct election of Members of the European Parliament (Rep.–Res.).	43–61
	Agricultural prices (Rep.).	61–93
13 March	Composition of committees of the Parliament (Res.).	104
	Research and investment budget of Euratom for 1969 (Rep.-Res.).	104–118
	Agricultural prices (Rep.-Res.).	118–156
14 March	Agricultural regulations and directives.	158–161
		No. 114
5 May	Activities of the standing organisation for security in coal mines.	pp. 7–18
	Report of the European Commission on the relationship between the social policy and other policies of the Community.	18
6 May	Statement on regional policy in the Community.	21–29
	The economic situation and the state of the capital market (Rep.-Res.).	29–67
7 May	Directive on taxes for utility vehicles (Rep.-Res.).	70–76
	Exchange of views between the Council and the European Parliament.	76–84, 94–100 and 128–134
	Effect of the political situation in Greece on the Association of Greece and the EEC (Rep.-Res.).	110–128
8 May	Collective actions of the member states and of the Council of Ministers not envisaged under the Treaties (Rep.-Res.).	139–154
	Directive on food pastes (Rep.).	168–177
	Directives on the distribution and use of toxic products (Rep.-Res.).	178–179

Date	Subject of Debate	Official Report of Debates No.
	Directive on the measurement of the weight of cereals by hectolitres (Rep.-Res.).	180
9 May	Agricultural regulations (Rep.-Res.).	182–190
3 June	Association agreements with Tunisia and Morocco; importation of citrus fruits from Turkey, Israel and Spain (Rep.).	*No. 115* pp. 25–55
4 June	Supplementary budget No. 1 of the European Communities and supplementary budget of Euratom for 1969 (Rep.-Res.).	57–59
	Association agreements with Tunisia and Morocco; importation of citrus fruits from Turkey, Israel and Spain (Rep.-Res.).	59–70
	Rice and cereal products from A A S M and from the overseas territories (Rep.-Res.).	70–75
30 June	Provisional estimates for the European Parliament for 1970 (Rep.-Res.).	*No. 116* pp. 7–13
	Statute of Personnel (Rep.-Res.).	13–28
	Transportation of produce by road between member states (Rep.-Res.).	29–33
	Organisation of the market in fruit and vegetables (Rep.-Res.).	24–38
1 July	Statement on collaboration between the Parliament and the Council of Ministers.	40–41
	Reorganisation of Euratom and of the common research centre (Rep.-Res.).	41–71
	Report of the European Commission on the relationship between the social policy and other policies of the Community (Rep.-Res.).	71–88
	Social situation in the Community in 1968 (Rep.-Res.).	88–102
	Pesticide residues on and in fruit and vegetables (Rep.-Res.).	102–107
	Directive on pharmaceutical special products (Res.).	107
2 July	Real resources of the Communities; the powers of the European Parliament (Res.).	109–130
	Second General Report on the activities of the Communities in 1968 (Rep.-Res.).	130–171

Date	Subject of Debate	Official Report of Debates No.
3 July	Regulations on the organisation of the tobacco market (Rep.-Res.).	175–248
	Agricultural prices for 1970–1971 (Rep.-Res.).	249–270
	System of importing fruit and vegetables into member countries from non-member countries (Rep.-Res.).	273
	Measures to safeguard certain agricultural sectors (Res.).	273
	Buttermilk and powdered buttermilk (Rep.-Res.).	273–274
	Organisation of the milk market (Rep.-Res.).	274
4 July	Manufacture and sale of margarine (Rep.-Res.).	277–291
	Organisation of the sugar market (Rep.-Res.).	292
	Organisation of the cereal market (Rep.-Res.).	292–294
	Forestry materials (Rep.-Res.).	292
	Agricultural fund (Res.).	294
	Import and export certificates (Res.).	295
	Draft report to the Consultative Assembly of the Council of Europe (Res.).	295
		No. 117
6 October	Administrative accounts of the European Communities for 1967 (Rep.-Res.).	pp. 9–21
	Accounts of the Coal and Steel Community July–December 1967 (Rep.-Res.).	21–23
	Indemnity for the fall in value of olive oil in stock in Italy (Rep.-Res.).	23–26
7 October	Extension of the powers of the European Parliament (Rep.-Res.).	37–61
	Europeanisation of universities and mutual recognition of diplomas (Rep.-Res.).	61–85
8 October	Application of Article 177 of the EEC Treaty of 1957 (Rep.-Res.).	99–115
	Automated control of road transport (Rep.-Res.).	115–124
9 October	Organisation of the common market in wine (Rep.-Res.).	128–146
	Directive on turnover taxes (Rep.-Res.).	146–156 and 158–175
	Draft budget for 1970 (Rep.-Res.).	156–158

Date	Subject of Debate	Official Report of Debates No.
	Establishment of a European capital market (Rep.-Res.).	193–206
10 October	Directive on dietary foodstuffs (Rep.-Res.).	207–209
	Directive on emulsifying agents, gelatines, etc. (Rep.-Res.).	209–212
	Products originating in countries of AASM and in the overseas territories (Rep.-Res.).	212–215
		No. 118
3 November	Position of the European Parliament with regard to fundamental problems of European and Community policies (Rep.-Res.).	pp. 4–35
		No. 119
24 November	Tariffs applicable to road transportation (Rep.-Res.).	pp. 5–9
	Directives on certain characteristics of motor vehicles (Rep.-Res.).	9–17
25 November	Trade in products derived from agricultural produce (Rep.-Res.).	19–20
	Relations between the Communities and Latin America (Rep.-Res.).	21–35
	Decision on the trade relations of member states with non-member countries and the negotiation of Community accords (Rep.-Res.).	36–58
26 November	Statement on the Yaoundé Convention and the Association with Tanzania, Uganda and Kenya.	62–67
	Budget of the European Communities for 1970 (Rep.-Res.).	67–76 and 99–112
	Directives on agricultural tractors (Rep.-Res.).	135–138
27 November	Harmonisation of laws in the Community (Res.).	147–160
	Judicial uniformity in the field of customs and commercial law (Rep.-Res.).	160–163
	Consequences for agriculture of the revaluation of the Deutschmark (Rep.-Res.).	163–174
	Activities of the standing organisation for safety in the mines (Rep.-Res.).	174–185
	Training of qualified workers in machine tools (Rep.-Res.).	185–190

Date	Subject of Debate	Official Report of Debates No.
	Fruit juices and similar products (Rep.).	190–199
	Transport of fresh meat and of cattle and pigs (Rep.-Res.).	197–198
28 November	Agricultural regulations (Rep.-Res.).	201–226
	Import and export certificates (Res.).	226
		No. 120
9 December	Yaoundé Convention (Rep.-Res.).	pp. 7–30
	Association agreement with Tanzania, Uganda and Kenya Rep.-Res.).	30–42
	Reform of the European Social Fund (Rep.-Res.).	42–62
10 December	Self-financing of the Communities and the increase in the budgetary powers of the European Parliament (Rep.-Res.).	65–123
	Regulations concerning the financing of the common agricultural policy (Rep.-Res.).	124–151
	Regulation on the procedure of management committees (Rep.-Res.).	151–158
11 December	Exchange of views between the European Parliament, and the Council and Commission of the Communities after the Hague Conference.	159–215
12 December	Decision extending the minimum-price system (Rep.-Res.).	217
	Regulation on the common market in milk and milk products (Rep.-Res.).	218
	Regulation on the market in products derived from fruit and vegetables (Rep.-Res.).	218
	Directive on textiles (Rep.-Res.).	218–226
		No. 121
2 February	Manufacture and sale of fruit juices (Rep.-Res.).	pp. 8–12
	Directive on edible pastes (Rep.-Res.).	12–28
	Decision on the protection of livestock from foot and mouth disease (Rep.-Res.).	28–32
	Trade relations between the Six and Japan (Rep.-Res.).	32–39
	Tariffs applicable to road transportation (Rep.-Res.).	39–44
	Bus services between member countries (Rep.-Res.).	44–48

Date	Subject of Debate	*Official Report of Debates No.*
3 February	Internal financing of the Communities (Rep.-Res.).	62–101 and 116–118
	Research and investment budget for Euratom in 1970 (Rep.-Res.).	102–116
	Direct election of Members of the European Parliament (Rep.-Res.).	118–122
	Revision of Article 206 of the EEC Treaty of 1957 (Rep.-Res.).	122
4 February	Aid to Nigeria (Res.).	141–143
	Regulation concerning the market in wine (Rep.-Res.).	143–180
	Equilibrium of the agricultural markets (Rep.-Res.).	181–228
5 February	Textile fibres (Rep.-Res.).	231–240
	European patents laws (Rep.).	240–274
	National tobacco monopolies (Rep.).	275–280
6 February	National tobacco monopolies (Rep.-Res.).	282–284
	Operational budget of the Coal and Steel Community for 1970 (Rep.-Res.).	284–286
	Directive on liquid measures for liquids other than water (Rep.-Res.).	286–289
	Directive on non-automatic weighing machines (Rep.-Res.).	289–290
	Rebates on the export of eggs (Res.).	290
		No. 122
9 March	Premiums on the slaughter of cows and on the non-marketing of milk and milk products (Rep.-Res.).	pp. 4–9
	Regulation concerning agriculture in Luxembourg (Rep.-Res.).	9–13
	Draft Accounts of the European Parliament for 1969 (Rep.-Res.).	13
	Directive on intra-Community trade in animals (Rep.-Res.).	14

SESSION 1970–71

Date	Subject of Debate	*Official Report of Debates No.*
		No. 123
10 March	Statement of the third report of the activities of the Communities.	pp. 7–12
	Agricultural regulations (Rep.-Res.).	13–26
	Rules of competition (Rep.).	26–39
11 March	Statement of the Commission on the social situation of the Community in 1969.	42–46

Date	Subject of Debate	Official Report of Debates No.
	Resources of the Communities and budgetary powers of the European Parliament (Rep.-Res.).	46–68
	Common energy policy (Rep.-Res.).	80–103
12 March	Statement of the Council on transport policy (Res.).	105–127
	Directives on motor vehicles (Rep.-Res.).	127–128
	Import of citrus fruits from Spain and Israel (Rep.-Res.).	129–133
	Association of overseas countries and territories to the EEC (Rep.-Res.).	133–135
	Results of the 16th meeting of the Parliamentary Conference of the Association of the EEC and AASM (Rep.-Res.).	135–148
		No. 124
9 April	Directive on taxation matters (Rep.-Res.).	pp. 7–29
	Milk producing centres in Italy (Rep.-Res.).	30–34
	Technical education of engineers (Rep.-Res.).	34–39
10 April	Economic situation of the Community in 1969 (Rep.-Res.).	41–54
		No. 125
11 May	Regulation on the administration of quotas (Rep.-Res.).	pp. 5–9
	Directive on the production of films (Rep.-Res.).	10
	Directive on hospital attendants (Rep.-Res.).	10–12
12 May	Death benefits of migrant workers (Rep.-Res.).	15–23
	Regional policy (Rep.-Res.).	23–58
	Gas meters (Rep.-Res.).	58
13 May	Provisions regarding the Community's own resources and amendments to the budgetary provisions of the treaties (Rep.-Res.).	68–99
	Letter of the Council on the budget of the Communities for 1970 and for research and investment in Euratom in 1970 (Rep.-Res.).	100–105
14 May	Milk regulations (Rep.-Res.).	115–120
	Directives on food additives (Rep.-Res.).	135–137
	Common commercial policy (Rep.-Res.).	147–150
	Price of table wines (Rep.-Res.).	151–160
	Organisation of the market in fish products (Rep.-Res.).	160–162

Date	Subject of Debate	*Official Report of Debates No.*
15 May	Reform of the European Social Fund (Rep.-Res.).	164–165
	EEC and Austria (Res.).	165–168
	Ratification of the new Yaoundé Convention (Res.).	168–174
	Recommendation of the joint parliamentary committee of the EEC and Turkey (Rep.-Res.).	175–178
		No. 126
15 June	Programme of importation of hydrocarbons and investment in the energy field (Rep.-Res.).	pp. 6–20
	Statement on the current transport policy by the President of the Council.	20–31
16 June	Activities of the Communities and the social situation in 1969 (Rep.-Res.).	33–90
17 June	Agricultural regulations (Rep.-Res.).	95–96
	Food aid from the Community (Rep.).	96–106
	Aid to victims of the Peruvian earthquake and the Rumanian floods (Rep.-Res.).	106–108
18 June	Results of the meeting of the Council of Labour and Social Affairs Ministers in May 1970 (Res.).	110–113
	Commercial agreement with Yugoslavia (Rep.-Res.).	114–120
	Food aid of the Community (Res.).	121
		No. 127
8 July	Estimates of the Parliament for 1971 (Rep.-Res.).	pp. 7–21
	Legal Directives (Rep.-Res.).	27–35
	Recommendation of the joint parliamentary committee of the EEC and Turkey (Rep.-Res.).	35–38
9 July	Agriculture regulations (Rep.-Res.).	40–67
10 July	Economic situation in the Community (Rep.-Res.).	69–86
		No. 128
15 September	Debate on Community policy for youth.	pp. 8–35
	Statement by the Commission and debate thereon.	36–62

Date	*Subject of Debate*	*Official Report of Debates No.*
16 September	Debate on the statement of the President of the Council.	65–111
	Supplementary budget No. 1 of the Communities for 1970 (Rep.-Res.).	111–112
	Amendment of the Association Agreement of the EEC and Tunisia (Rep.-Res.).	112–113
	Amendment of the Statutes of the European Investment Bank (Rep.-Res.).	113
		No. 129
5 October	Imports from AASM and Tanzania, Uganda and Kenya (Rep.-Res.).	pp. 5–14
6 October	Correlation of social and other community policies (Rep.-Res.).	16–38
	Generalised tariff preferences for finished and semi-finished goods from under-developed countries (Rep.-Res.).	38–60
7 October	Political future of the Communities (Rep.-Res.).	64–78 and 80–100
	Accountants report on the ECSC Accounts for 1968 (Rep.-Res.).	79–80
	Agricultural regulations (Rep.-Res.).	80–108
8 October	Recommendations of the joint parliamentary committee of the EEC and Turkey (Rep.-Res.).	112–113
	Reform of the European Social Fund (Rep.-Res.).	113–114
	Own resources for the Community (Rep-Res.).	114–119
	Agricultural imports regulations (Rep.-Res.).	119–124
		No. 130
16 November	Commercial Agreement of the EEC and Spain (Rep.-Res.).	pp. 15–22
	Commercial Agreement of the EEC and Israel (Rep.-Res.).	22–29
17 November	Budget of the Communities for 1971.	32–41
	Aid to victims of the tragedy in East Pakistan (Res.).	53
	Prospects for Euratom (Res.).	53–64
	Administration accounts of the Communities for 1968 (Rep.-Res.).	64–69
	Agricultural Fund (Rep.-Res.).	69–83

Date	Subject of Debate	Official Report of Debates No.
	Directive on certain activities of the barrister (Rep.).	84–96
18 November	Exchange of views between the Parliament, the Council and the Commission of the Communities.	99–144
	Supplementary Budget No. 2 of the Communities for 1970 (Rep.-Res.).	145–147
	Pharmaceutical problems (Rep.-Res.).	147–152
19 November	Struggle against river pollution (Rep.-Res.).	154–166
	Agricultural and food regulations (Rep.-Res.).	166–176
		No. 131
2 December	Transport regulation (Rep.-Res.).	pp. 7–8
	Agricultural regulations (Rep.-Res.).	8–36
3 December	Stages of economic and monetary union of the Community (Rep.-Res.).	39–66
	Third medium-term economic programme (Rep.-Res.).	66–87
	Supplementary Budget No. 3 of the Communities for 1970 (Rep.-Res.).	87–88
	Community Budget for 1971 and research and investment Budget of Euratom for 1971 (Rep.).	91–109
4 December	Community Budget for 1971 (Rep.-Res.).	111–123
	Decision on mid-term financial competition (Rep.-Res.).	124–137
		No. 132
19 January	Commercial relations with the United States and Japan (Res.).	pp. 12–38
	Operational Budget of the ECSC for 1971 (Rep.-Res.).	38–42
	Financing of the Common Agricultural Policy (Rep.-Res.).	42–44
	Revision and consideration of financial regulations (Rep.-Res.).	44–48
	Activities of the standing organisation on safety in the coal mines (Rep.-Res.).	48–54
	Draft Treaty for the amendment of Article 194 of the EEC Treaty and Article 166 of the Euratom Treaty (Rep.-Res.).	54–55
20 January	Agricultural Regulations (Rep.-Res.).	57–62
	Mayonnaise and other sauces (Rep.-Res.).	62–66

Date	Subject of Debate	*Official Report of Debates No.*
		No. 133
8 February	Motor insurance (Rep.-Res.).	pp. 6–10
	Agricultural Regulation (Rep.-Res.).	10–11
	Association of the EEC and Turkey (Rep.-Res.).	11–18
	Turkish fishing products (Rep.-Res.).	18–19
9 February	Association Agreement between the EEC and Malta (Rep.-Res.).	22–27
	Commercial policy of the Community in the Mediterranean basin (Rep.-Res.).	28–53
	Uniformity of commercial agreements with other countries (Rep.-Res.).	53–62
	Import of citrus fruits from Turkey.	62–63
	Memorandum on the industrial policy of the Community (Rep.).	63–94
10 February	Memorandum on the industrial policy of the Community (Res.).	96–102
	Statement by the Commission on the future activities of the Community.	102–111
	Directives and regulations concerning the reform of agriculture (Rep.).	111–169
11 February	Directives and regulations concerning the reform of agriculture (Res.).	172–182
	Corrected Budget of the Communities for 1971 (Rep.-Res.).	183–189
	Debate on the statement of the President of the Commission on economic and monetary union.	212–233
12 February	Freedom of establishment and free supply of services (Rep.-Res.).	234–238
	Agricultural and food regulations (Rep.-Res.).	238–240
		No. 134
8 March	Draft rules of the Accounts of the European Parliament for 1970 (Rep.-Res.).	pp. 3–5

SESSION 1971–72

		No. 135
10 March	Economic situation in the Community (Statements).	pp. 18–26
	Movement of fresh meat within the Community (Rep.-Res.).	26–28

Date	Subject of Debate	*Official Report of Debates No.*
		No. 136
18 March	Special measures to be taken in consequence of health difficulties in certain agricultural sectors (Rep.-Res.).	pp. 3–4
	Regulations concerning the fixing of prices for certain agricultural products (Rep.).	4–21
19 March	Regulations concerning the fixing of prices for certain agricultural products (Rep.-Res.).	23–47
		No. 137
19 April	Directive on natural mineral waters (Rep.-Res.).	pp. 5–10
	First report on the general commission for industrial safety in the iron industry (Rep.-Res.).	10–15
20 April	Application of the principle of equal pay for men and women (Rep.-Res.).	17–36
	Directives on certain non-salaried occupations and on freedom of establishment for opticians and in the transport industry (Rep.-Res.).	36–50
	Buenos Aires meeting of the special committee on Latin-American co-operation (Rep.-Res.).	50–65
21 April	Economic situation in the Community in 1970 and prospects for 1971 (Rep.-Res.).	67–98
	Re-organisation of the common Centre for Scientific and Technical Research (Rep.-Res.).	104–116
	Current state of Community energy policy (Rep.-Res.).	117–142
22 April	Agricultural prices (Rep.-Res.).	144–165
	Agricultural regulations (Rep.-Res.).	165–168
23 April	Common definition of the origin of goods (Rep.-Res.).	170–171
	Transit of goods (Rep.-Res.).	171
		No. 138
17 May	Visit to the Netherlands Antilles and Surinam (Rep.-Res.).	pp. 4–13
	Seventh annual meeting of the parliamentary conference of AASM (Rep.-Res.).	13–20

Date	Subject of Debate	Official Report of Debates No.
	Amendment of Rules of Procedure of the European Parliament (Budgetary procedures) (Rep.-Res.).	21
18 May	Question on monetary problems.	28–68
	Question on delays in the development of a common transport policy.	69–83
19 May	Directive on taxes on hydrocarbon fuels (Rep.-Res.).	88–100
	Accounts of the Coal and Steel Community for 1969 (Rep.-Res.).	100–102
		No. 139
7 June	Recommendations of the joint parliamentary committee of the Association with Turkey (Rep.-Res.).	pp. 7–15
	Directive on customs-free zones (Rep.-Res.).	15–16
	Report of the EEC Committee on economic relations between Greece and the Community (Rep.-Res.).	16–18
	Rules of competition and the position of European companies (Rep.-Res.).	18–39
9 June	General tariff preferences for developing countries (Rep.-Res.).	44–78
	Catastrophe in East Pakistan (Res.).	78
	Regulation on the reform of the European Social Fund (Rep.-Res.).	78–107
	Monetary problems (Rep.-Res.).	107–109
	Agricultural regulations (Rep.-Res.).	109–122
10 June	Provisional estimates of the European Parliament for 1972 (Rep.-Res.).	124–128
	Management accounts of the Communities for 1969 (Rep.-Res.).	128–135
	New budgetary terminology (Rep.-Res.).	135–140
	Social problems relating to road transport (Rep.-Res.).	148–151
	Progress towards political unification (Rep.-Res.)	162–172
11 June	Statement by the President of the Council of Ministers.	174–194
		No. 140
5 July	Egg products in the world food programme (Rep.-Res.).	pp. 8–14
	Import of peaches from Morocco and Tunisia (Rep.-Res.).	14–15

Date	Subject of Debate	Official Report of Debates No.
	Directive on exchange controls (Rep.-Res.).	15–20
	Directives on the non-salaried activities of insurance agents and brokers (Rep.-Res.).	20–23
6 July	Directives on the non-salaried activities of opticians (Rep.-Res.).	26–34
	The energy situation in the Community (Rep.-Res.).	34–52
	Credits for research and investment (Rep.-Res.).	52–58
	Removal of restrictions on intra-Community travellers (Rep.-Res.).	58–63
7 July	Statements on negotiations for British entry into the EEC.	69–78
	Fourth General Report of the European Commission (Rep.-Res.).	78–115
	Social situation in the Community in 1971 (Rep.-Res.).	117–135
	Regulations on agricultural prices (Rep.).	135–163
9 July	Agricultural regulations (Rep.-Res.).	194–203
	Harmonisation of legislation on dietary foods (Rep.-Res.).	203
		No. 141
21 September	Directive on liquid measures (Rep.-Res.).	pp. 6–7
	Petition on the plight of Italian migrants in the Community (Rep.-Res.).	7–15
22 September	Monetary situation (Res.).	18–73
23 September	Regulations on the Statute of Personnel (Rep.).	73–85
		No. 142
18 October	Regulation on the reform of the European Social Fund (Rep.-Res.).	pp. 8–17
	Second Convention on Food Aid (Rep.-Res.).	17–25
	Agricultural regulations (Rep.-Res.).	23–29
19 October	Annual report on the economic situation in the Community (Rep.-Res.).	32–70
	Directive on limited companies (Rep.-Res.).	70–80
	Agricultural regulations (Rep.-Res.).	80–87
20 October	Co-ordination of foreign policies (Rep.-Res.).	89–106
	Community budgets for 1972 (Rep.-Res.).	106–128
	Agricultural regulations (Rep.-Res.).	128–146

x*

Date	*Subject of Debate*	*Official Report of Debates No.*
21 October	Directive on beer (Rep.-Res.).	148–161
	Meat products (Rep.-Res.).	162–164
22 October	Supplementary budgets of the Communities (Rep.-Res.).	166–167
	European Social Fund (Rep.-Res.).	167–168
	Regulation on the Statute of Personnel (Rep.-Res.).	169–170
		No. 143
15 November	Amendment of the Rules of Procedure of the European Parliament (Rep.).	pp. 5–15
	Directive on crude oil stocks (Rep.-Res.).	16–25
	Amendment of Chapter VI of the Euratom Treaty (Rep.-Res.).	25–33
16 November	Provisional estimates of the European Parliament for 1972 (Rep.).	36–38
	General Budget of the European Communities for 1972 (Rep.).	38–55 and 59–65
	Amendment of the Rules of Procedure of the European Parliament (Rep.).	55–56
	Agricultural regulations (Rep.-Res.).	56–59
	Directives and regulation on the reform of agriculture (Rep.).	66–113
17 November	Exchange of views between the European Parliament, and the Council and the Commission of the European Communities.	115–161
18 November	Directives and regulation on the reform of agriculture (Res.).	170–173
	Provisional estimates of the European Parliament for 1972 (Res.).	173–174
	General Budget of the European Communities for 1972 (Res.).	174–181
	Directive on weights and dimensions of commercial road vehicles (Rep.-Res.).	184–194
	Social problems in road transport (Rep.-Res.).	194–197
19 November	Operational Budget of the Coal and Steel Community for 1972 (Rep.-Res.).	199–202
	Application of social security to migrant workers and their families (Rep.-Res.).	202–205
	Recommendations of the joint parliamentary committee of the Association with Turkey (Rep.-Res.).	205–210

Date	Subject of Debate	Official Report of Debates No.
		No. 144
15 December	Decision extending the system of minimum prices (Rep.-Res.).	pp. 7–9
	Agricultural regulations (Rep.-Res.).	9–11
	Directive on harmonisation of turnover taxes (Rep.).	11–13
16 December	Directive on tobacco taxes (Rep.-Res.).	16–28
	European Social Fund (Rep.-Res.).	29–31
	Directive on the movement and residence of foreigners (Rep-Res.).	31–33
	Activities of the permanent organisations for safety in the coalmines and in iron-works (Rep.-Res.).	33–34
	Progress towards harmonisation of statistics (Rep.-Res.).	54
	Research programmes of Euratom and the EEC (Rep.-Res.).	58–64
	Directive on standard measures of length (Res.).	64
17 December	Accession of Mauritius to AASM (Rep.-Res.).	78–80
	Agricultural activities (Rep.-Res.).	84–89
		No. 145
17 January	Directive on company mergers (Rep.).	pp. 10–12
	Financing of nuclear power stations (Rep.-Res.).	14–22
	Campaign against drug-taking (Rep.-Res.).	22–44
18 January	Directive on ice-cream (Rep.-Res.).	55–56 and 73–77
	Directive on confectionery products (Rep-Res.).	57–62
	Directive on detergents (Rep-.Res.).	77–80
19 January	Agricultural regulations and directives (Rep.-Res.).	81–82
		No. 146
7 February	Directive on the removal of restrictions on residence and movement (Rep.-Res.).	pp. 7–9
	Taxes and charges on international travel (Rep.-Res.).	9–16
	Directives on veterinary activities (Rep.-Res.).	17–21
	Regulations on food aid (Rep.-Res.).	21–33

Date	*Subject of Debate*	*Official Report of Debates No.*
8 February	Statement on the Fifth General Report of the European Commission.	35–43
	Community youth and education policy (Rep.-Res.).	43–74
9 February	Statement on the social situation in the Community in 1971.	76–81
	Economic situation in the Community at the beginning of 1972 (Rep.-Res.).	99–132
	Commercial agreement between the EEC and Argentina (Rep.-Res.).	140–142
10 February	Plan of action of the European Commission for 1972.	144–175
	Campaign against air pollution (Rep.-Res.).	175–191
	Community information policy (Rep.-Res.).	191–214
11 February	Agricultural regulations (Rep.-Res.).	215–216
		No. 147
13 March	Modernisation of agriculture (Rep.-Res.).	pp. 16–61
	Agricultural regulations (Rep.-Res.).	62–65

Appendix D

Presidents of the Parliament

PRESIDENTS OF THE PARLIAMENT

Presidents

1958–60	M. Robert Schuman	France
1960–62	Professor Furler	Federal Republic of Germany
1962–64	Dr. Gaetano Martino	Italy
1964–65	M. Jean Duvieusart	Belgium
1965–66	M. Victor Leemans	Belgium
1966–69	M. Alain Poher	France
1969–71	Sr. Mario Scelba	Italy
1971–	Herr Walter Behrendt	Federal Republic of Germany

Secretaries-General of the European Parliament

1958–60	Mr. M.F.F.A. de Neree tot Babberich	Netherlands
1961–	Mr. Hans Nord	Netherlands

Abbreviations

AASM   Association of African States and Madagascar

ECA   Economic Commission for Africa

ECAFE   Economic Commission for Asia and the Far East

ECE   Economic Commission for Europe

ECLA   Economic Commission for Latin America

EEC   European Economic Community

ECOSOC   Economic and Social Council

ECSC   European Coal and Steel Community

EFTA   European Free Trade Association

EMA   European Monetary Agreement

ENEA   European Nuclear Energy Agency

EURATOM   European Atomic Energy Community

FAO   Food and Agriculture Organisation

GATT   General Agreement on Tariffs and Trade

IAEA   International Atomic Energy Agency

ILO   International Labour Organisation

IMCO	International Maritime Consultative Organisation
INIS	International Nuclear Information System
NATO	North Atlantic Treaty Organisation
OECD	Organisation for Economic Co-operation and Development
OEEC	Organisation for European Economic Co-operation
u.a.	Unit of account, equivalent to one U.S. dollar
UN	United Nations
UNCITRAL	United Nations Commission on International Trade Law
UNCTAD	United Nations Conference on Trade and Development
UNESCO	United Nations Educational, Scientific and Cultural Organisation
UNHCR	United Nations High Commissioner for Refugees
UNIDO	United Nations Industrial Development Organisation
UNOIL	United Nations Organisation for International Law
VAT	Value-added Tax
WEU	Western European Union
WHO	World Health Organisation
WMO	World Meteorological Organisation

Index

Y

Nigeria, agreement with, 43

Nord, Mr., Hans, Secretary-General of Parliament, 140, 317

North Atlantic Assembly: 70, 74–75
committees, 70–71
membership, 70
relations with the Parliament, 75
structure, 70

Norway:
application for membership of EEC (1961), 5–6
second application (1967), 5
application approved (1971), 6
decision not to accede (1972), 6, 150
member of Council of Europe, 62
member of EFTA, 53

Nuclear non-proliferation Treaty, 61

Observers at committee meetings, 124

Official Journal:
details of political groups published in, 82
legislation published in, 12–14, 30
Minutes of proceedings published in, 146
Official Report of Debates annexed to, 146
Questions and answers published in, 135, 136, 137

Official Report of Debates, 136, 141, 146–7

Opinion, committee asked for, 121, 122, 127–28

Opinions of the Economic and Social Committee, 13

Order, maintenance of, 101

Order, in committees, 126

Orders of the Day: *see* Agenda

Organisation for Economic Co-operation and Development (O E C D): 48–50
aims, 49
Board of Management, 50
committees, 50
Conventions, 49, 50
Council, 49
Executive Committee, 50

Organisation for European Economic Co-operation (O E E C):
collapse of negotiations with, 37, 38
relations with Communities, 46
replaced by OECD (1961), 49

Paris, Treaty of (1951): *see* Treaty of Paris

Parliament: *see* European Parliament

Parliamentary committees on associations:
with African states and Madagascar, 38, 42, 116, 120, 125
with Greece, 38, 39, 116, 120
with Malta, 36, 45
with Turkey, 38, 41, 116, 120
to study problems of association, 37

Parliamentary Conference of the A A S M, 38, 43, 120

Parliamentary Questions: *see* Questions, parliamentary

Parliaments, national: *see* National parliaments

Personal statements, 100

Petitions: 138–139
inadmissibility of, 139
preservation of texts of, 139
reference to committees, 123, 138
register of, 138
transmission to Commission or Council, 138

Place of meeting of the Parliament, 93–94, 98, 104

Secretariat: *cont.*

General Directorate of Administration, 141–42

General Directorate of Committees and Parliamentary Studies, 141

General Directorate of General Affairs, 141

General Directorate of Parliamentary Documentation, 141

General Directorate of Research and Documentation, 141n

Library, 141, 148

number of employees, 140

Secretary-General of the Parliament: 140, 317

appointed by Bureau, 90, 140

assists the Parliament, 90

issues admission cards for Gallery, 101

makes report for provisional estimates, 90, 143

signs Minutes of proceedings, 146

solemn undertaking given by, 90

Session:

alteration of breaks in, 91, 93

date and duration of, 84, 93

extraordinary, 94

opening, 93, 131–32

Sittings:

bells rung before opening, suspension and close, 95

days and hours of sitting, 94

meetings before and after luncheon, 95

meetings of committees and political groups during, 94, 123

register of attendance at, 95

Soames, Rt. Hon. Sir Christopher, 11n

Social Affairs and Public Health, parliamentary committee on, 116, 119–20, 121

Socialist Group, 82, 118

Soviet Union, 58

Spain:

application for associate membership of EEC (1967), 5

examination of agreement with EEC by GATT, 52

member of OECD, 49

special agreement with Communities, 35

Special Committee on Preferences (of UNCTAD), 59

Specialised Agencies of the United Nations, 55–61

Speeches:

giving way, to allow questions, 100

limitation of number, 99

no interruptions except on point of order, 100

on amendments, 113

on procedural motions, 102

passages deleted from Official Report, 101

priority of Commissioners and members of the Council, 99

reading of, discouraged, 100

relevance, 101

sanctions against disorderly speeches, 101

scope, 101

speakers' book, 99

Statutory Instruments (U.K.), 30–31

Statute of Personnel, 90, 140

Strasbourg, 94, 98, 104

Subsistence allowances, 142–3

Substitutes in committees, 83, 118

Summary report of debates, 126, 146

Surinam, 36

Sweden:

application for membership of Communities, 5

member of Council of Europe, 62

member of EFTA, 53

member of OECD, 49

talks with Commission, 53

Printed in England for Her Majesty's Stationery Office by Staples Printers Limited at The Priory Press, St Albans
Dd500198 K14 12/72